Discovering the Character of God

GEORGE MACDONALD

Discovering the Character of God

Compiled, Arranged, and Edited by
Michael R. Phillips

BETHANY HOUSE PUBLISHERS
MINNEAPOLIS, MINNESOTA 55438

Published by Bethany House Publishers
A Ministry of Bethany Fellowship International
11400 Hampshire Avenue South
Minneapolis, Minnesota 55438
www.bethanyhouse.com

Printed in the United States of America by
Bethany Press International, Minneapolis, Minnesota 55438

ISBN 0-7642-2311-9 (Trade Paper)
ISBN 1-55661-068-8 (Hardcover)

Library of Congress Cataloging-in-Publication Data

MacDonald, George, 1824–1905.
  Discovering the character of God / George MacDonald ; compiled, arranged, and edited by Michael R. Phillips.
      p.   cm.
  Includes bibliographical references.

  1. God—Literary collections. I. Phillips, Michael R., 1946–
II. Title.
PR4966.P48   1989
823'.8—dc20   89-39037
ISBN 1-55661-068-8   CIP

No teacher should strive to make others think as he thinks, but to lead them to the living Truth, to the Master himself, of whom alone they can learn anything, who will make them in themselves know what is true by the very seeing of it.

George MacDonald
Unspoken Sermons, Third Series

PREFACE

Nineteenth-century Scotsman George MacDonald, principally known for his fantasy and fiction, was also a theologian of considerable repute in Victorian Britain. Raised in a strict Calvinist setting, his later writing and preaching attempted to present a more complete and biblically rounded view of God's character than he had known in his youth. His discoveries were unsettling in certain ecclesiastical circles in his own day and often challenged concepts long taken for granted even in this present age.

This compilation of selections, primarily from MacDonald's sermons but also drawing from his poetry and fictional writings, brings into focus his convictions about God's character. Unlike MacDonald's stories, these nonfictional selections may prove occasionally difficult to grasp, even for the serious devotee of MacDonald. The reader will find he must pause and ponder every few lines, rereading here and there, in order to lay hold of the author's progression of thought and the bold new concepts he is attempting to convey. Though the material has been edited—sermons of over fifty pages broken into more manageable portions; five-page paragraphs divided; sentences of up to 200 words and multiple semi-colons, colons, and dashes restructured—MacDonald's Victorian expression and syntax can still sound a somewhat unfamiliar note to our modern ears. His original audience was accustomed to a different style than we are today. A second or third reading, possibly with a dictionary in hand and perhaps aloud, can help to clarify troublesome passages. MacDonald was a *thinker*, and neither his logic nor his ideas can be considered light reading to be quickly skimmed and assimilated. This is certainly no book to master in one sitting!

The persistent reader, however—whether housewife, pastor, businessperson, student, missionary, laborer, or professional—will discover much to suscitate, enrich, and deepen an understanding of the character of God and His relation to the men and women He has made. Even at those points where a reader may take exception to MacDonald, the stimulation of thought is invigorating and valuable. For he never sought total harmony of viewpoint. He hoped to encourage Christians to think and reason, rather than allowing themselves to be spoonfed spiritual teaching without due consideration for themselves.

It was because of such depth and variety and even the disconcerting nature of some of his thought that several noted Christians of the twentieth century point to MacDonald's writings as among the profound influences in their lives—Oswald Chambers, C. S. Lewis, G. K. Chesterton, Madeleine L'Engle. And this is the reason many others were known to read him avidly—J.R.R. Tolkien, Charles Spurgeon, Phillips Brooks, Mark Twain, Queen Victoria, Lewis Carroll, Lucy Montgomery, Elizabeth Yates, Oliver Wendell Holmes, John Whittier, Ralph Waldo Emerson, and Florence Nightingale.

It is our sincere prayer that serious seekers after truth will be challenged by MacDonald into deeper regions of faith in their own walks with God. After all the underlining, note-taking, discussion with others, rereading, agreeing and disagreeing and arguing mentally with MacDonald, hopefully you will come away having inwardly digested these truths, and thus be stronger of mind and more intimately related in heart with God the Father, to whom MacDonald would ever have us go in our quest for truth.

CONTENTS

INTRODUCTION

I n a life of eighty years and a literary career spanning nearly five decades, Scotsman George MacDonald (1824–1905) produced some fifty-three books of tremendous diversity. These may roughly be categorized as novels, short stories, fantasies, poems, sermons, and essays.

Out of this vast literary productivity, it is principally as a writer of fiction that George MacDonald has been recognized. Though he was said to have considered himself a poet first, a preacher second, and a novelist third, almost three-quarters of his published work was fiction. In the nineteenth century his reputation was based on Victorian novels similar to those of his contemporary, Charles Dickens. In the twentieth it has been founded primarily on fantasies and children's stories. Thus, though he studied for the pulpit and lost few opportunities to preach throughout his long life, it remains as a spinner of yarns that Mac-Donald is most widely known.

An unfortunate result of this reputation, however, is that Mac-Donald's contribution to nineteenth and twentieth-century religious thought is often overlooked. George MacDonald himself would have found the term "theologian" odious if applied to him. I cannot, therefore, use it with clear conscience except by attempting to throw light sideways onto the image of the man as I think we ought to view him.

Whether or not he was a theologian in the strict sense of the term I leave to others to determine. The fact is, George MacDonald was certainly a spiritual philosopher, a seeker after truth, and a communicator of that truth as he perceived he had discovered it—a profound and original thinker whose driving vision was to share his quest with others. Discovery and growth were the very foundation stones of George MacDonald's being. Of neither could he ever have enough.

As a boy growing up in northeast rural Scotland, from a very early age, George MacDonald began to pose questions to himself about the character of God. Raised in a family of strict Calvinist convictions, he found it difficult to accept within his own heart the "harsh taskmaster" view of the Almighty, which seemed the prevalent notion in the teaching he received. His search to discover what God was *really* like took him down many unexpected theological and doctrinal roads and often landed him squarely in the middle of controversy. But it was a search born out of an honest and humble desire to know God in intimate and personal friendship and to obey Him in every aspect of life. It was an inner pilgrimage of the heart, which lasted throughout every day of MacDonald's life.

At the end of that life, with the earthly portion of his quest to know God nearly done, MacDonald wrote—and these are among the last pieces of recorded letters left us before his death: "To be rid of self is to have the heart bare to God. . . . My God, art thou not as good as we are capable of imagining thee? Shall we dream a better goodness than thou has ever thought of? Be thyself, and all is well."

Even then, MacDonald was continuing to search to discover yet more of God's nature, still asking God for deeper revelation concerning himself. Later MacDonald wrote a friend, "Would that my being were consciously filled with the gladness of his obedience! Nothing less can content me."

What began in boyhood continued until death—a hunger to know and obey the nature, personality, and essential character of God. What you will read in the pages which follow offer significant glimpses into the mind and heart of MacDonald as he progressed along his personal spiritual journey.

George MacDonald's ideas of religion, nature, and man's relationship to the universe and its Creator were rooted in a portrait of God unique in his own day and perhaps still largely uncomprehended in our own. Many who study MacDonald's works are convinced that the greater passage of time will reveal more and more that George MacDonald stands out in the annals of Christian thought as a humble sage casting a giant shadow spreading across the wide reaches of Christendom. (It is fruitless here to attempt a classification of MacDonald in the broad spectrum from liberal to conservative, from Calvinist to High Anglican, from fundamental to modern, because his views span the entire scope of religious ideas and doctrines. Christians of every persuasion will find much in MacDonald to embrace, and no doubt much to dispute as well. He is stubbornly unclassifiable.)

Once his ideas have been more carefully examined, MacDonald may be read with the enthusiasm today associated with his protege C. S. Lewis and others who point reverently back to MacDonald as the foundation of much in their own spiritual development. Lewis himself credits MacDonald for beginning him on the road out of atheism toward being a Christian, and later expressed frustration that no one seemed to pay any attention to the high regard in which he held MacDonald. As his own fame grew, Lewis felt everyone ought to be showing more interest in MacDonald as the man most responsible for his own conversion and subsequent growth as a Christian. Finally Lewis went public, published an anthology of small quotes from MacDonald, and issued the following statement to get people to stand up and take notice of MacDonald: "In making this collection I was discharging a debt of justice. I have never concealed the fact that I regarded him as my master; indeed I fancy I have never written a book in which I did not quote from him. But it has not seemed to me that those who have received my books kindly take even now sufficient notice of the affiliation. Honesty drives me to emphasize it."

Even though Lewis wrote those words almost fifty years ago, it has been only in the last ten or fifteen years that they have begun to be heeded. When MacDonald's conception of the magnificently huge possibilities inherent in God's wondrously loving character is truly seen for what it is, his work may be considered one of the great turning points in how we view God in his interaction with human beings. It will no doubt astound scholars of the twenty-first century to learn that MacDonald's writings were nearly lost sight of for more than five decades after his death. They will find it incredible that thinkers and readers of the mid-twentieth century could have so utterly overlooked this man, especially in light of the comments on his profound influence upon their thought and spiritual journeys, and the esteem in which he was held by renowned twentieth-century writers such as J. R. R. Tolkien ("stories of power and beauty"), W. H. Auden ("one of the most remarkable writers of the nineteenth century"), G. K. Chesterton ("one of the three or four greatest men of the nineteenth century . . . made a difference to my whole existence"), and of course Lewis, who, after he read MacDonald's *Phantastes*, said, "I knew that I had crossed a great frontier."

Why, then, *did* MacDonald's reputation nearly vanish for such a long period of time?

I think it is precisely because of his reputation as a storyteller. Most men and women have the inborn tendency to categorize and pigeonhole people they meet into prescribed slots. Because most of his writing was fictional and because George MacDonald made no attempt to systematize his ideas, he has become known as a storyteller who also "happened" to be a preacher, and a novelist who also wrote poetry.

Yet such an analysis misses the mark. For it is as a thinker, not a storyteller, as an elucidator of God's truths, as an illuminator of God's character, as a man upon whom God bestowed wisdom and insight that George MacDonald will be known to posterity. His stories, fairy tales, poems, fantasies, and symbolic myths were but the vehicles that enabled him to carry forward his unexpected and progressive view of true spirituality. As great a novelist and poet as many consider him, as acclaimed as his imaginative and allegorical works are, it is nevertheless *not* as a novelist, poet, mythmaker, or symbolic muse that his mark will most dynamically be felt in the decades ahead. For in themselves such literary accolades are empty praise in light of eternity. The greatest novelist, the best poet, the most imaginative spinner of fantasies will yet stand before God, as will all people, with nothing in their hands—no books, no poems, no praising reviews. We will each take with us through death nothing but our inner selves, our souls—the essential character that is the *real* me, the real you, which we have used the opportunities of this life to become.

It is *there*—in the life of the soul, the essential inner heart and will, that core of spiritual being—toward which George MacDonald focused the light of his intellect and imagination. The forces of life on a deeper spiritual plane were the realities that drove MacDonald to communicate, through whatever medium presented itself—be it the Victorian novel, the poem, the fairytale, or the pulpit—his view of God's being. I think he himself would be astonished (perhaps *is* astonished) at how assiduously his various works are discussed and analyzed on the intellectual and literary level, while all the time the critics and scholars miss the deepest import of what MacDonald himself intended—that his writings point toward the inner life of the journey of the soul toward eternity, that life hid with God in the human heart.

In his own lifetime MacDonald's first choice of career was as a preacher. God ultimately had other designs on his life, and MacDonald held only two brief pastorates. He did, however, continue to preach in guest pulpits throughout his life; his pulpit reputation was great, and he remained in high demand both in Britain and the United States. By his own admission, although he turned his hand to the penning of stories, his remained primarily a pulpit ministry rather than an artistic or literary one. His message weighed more heavily on his heart than the characters and fantasies and myths he employed to convey it. His imagination and the stories it spun out were but means to an end. The most clearly crystallized legacy George MacDonald has left the world is a spiritual vision of life with a knowledge of God's character at its core. He was no *mere* storyteller, but a preacher who had been endowed with artistic sensibilities and authorial gifts and whose platform therefore took on literary forms.

In recent years new generations of readers the world over are rediscovering the works of George MacDonald in new editions of his works in nearly all genres. There yet remains, however, a need for a concentrated presentation of the shining light of George MacDonald's *thought*—his ideas, spiritual perspectives, beliefs, and—if you will—his theology, drawn from different sources.

During his lifetime George MacDonald preached hundreds of spoken sermons which were never recorded or written down, and which are therefore lost to us. There remain, however, several volumes of published sermons, which, along with selections from some of his stories and other nonfiction material, provide the foundation for this present work. In speaking of MacDonald's volumes of sermons, C. S. Lewis said, "My own debt to [them] is almost as great as one man can owe to another; and nearly all serious inquirers to whom I have introduced [them] acknowledge that [they have] given them great help."

In the chapters that follow, from MacDonald's pen but newly arranged and in places edited for clarity, the perceptive reader will recognize, occasionally in strikingly parallel language, certain passages that ring a familiar note, and will find himself wondering if MacDonald gleaned some of his ideas from Lewis. In fact, just the opposite is the case. As you read, you will slowly discover just why throughout most of his adult life Lewis steadfastly referred to MacDonald as his master. When Lewis said he had probably never written anything in which he did not quote from him, he was alluding to MacDonald's ideas.

For MacDonald, all knowledge, all wisdom, all practicality of faith, indeed all relationship that can exist in the universe is rooted in the view one has of the character of God. *Who is God?* and *What is God like?* were to him the most vital questions of life. Only by coming to grips with who God truly is can one begin to know God intimately. These were the fundamental issues that plagued George MacDonald during the early years of his life. What is God's nature, his personality? What are his designs upon his creatures? Do we have a clear picture of him from the theologies out of which we have been taught? Or is God's character in truth something more, something greater?

Such was the path of discovery upon which George MacDonald marked out his own footprints for others to follow. In an understanding

of God's character, the path toward true spirituality begins.
The course of his own quest lies before you. Perhaps when you
have read his words, and I confess that for myself they often take two
or three times through, you will understand why Madeleine L'Engle
called him "the grandfather of us all—all of us who struggle to come
to terms with truth through imagination."

Michael Phillips
Eureka, California

The Hills

Behind my father's cottage lies
　A gentle grassy height
Up which I often ran—to gaze
　Back with a wondering sight,
For then the chimneys I thought high
　Were down below me quite!

All round, where'er I turned mine eyes
　Huge hills closed up the view;
The town 'mid their converging roots
　Was clasped by rivers two;
From one range to another sprang
　The sky's great vault of blue.

It was a joy to climb their sides,
　And in the heather lie!
A joy to look at vantage down
　On the castle grim and high!
Blue streams below, white clouds above,
　In silent earth and sky!

And now, where'er my feet may roam,
　At sight of stranger hill
A new sense of the old delight
　Springs in my bosom still,
And longings for the high unknown
　Their ancient channels fill.

For I am always climbing hills,
　From the known to the unknown—
Surely, at last, on some high peak,
　To find my Father's throne,
Though hitherto I have only found
　His footsteps in the stone!

And in my wanderings I did meet
　Another searching too:
The dawning hope, the shared quest
　Our thoughts together drew;
Fearless she laid her hand in mine
　Because her heart was true.

She was not born among the hills,
　Yet on each mountain face
A something known her inward eye
　By inborn light can trace;
For up the hills must homeward be,
　Though no one knows the place.

Clasp my hand close, my child, in thine—
　A long way we have come!
Clasp my hand closer yet, my child,
　Farther we yet must roam—
Climbing and climbing till we reach
　Our heavenly Father's home.

1

GOD THE SOURCE OF LIFE

In the beginning God . . .
Genesis 1:1

What Kind of God Do You Believe In?

E verything depends on the kind of God one believes in. This is the starting point toward discovering who God truly is.

How many ideas of God might there be? Everyone who believes in him must have a different idea. Some of them must be nearer right than others.

Instead of automatically blaming the person who does not believe in a God, we should ask first if his notion of God is a god that ought to be believed in. Perhaps the one to be blamed is he who, by inattention to the duties given him, has become less able to believe in God than he once was. Because he did not obey the true voice when it came, God may have to let him taste what it would be to have no God.

A man may have been born of so many generations of unbelief that now, at this moment, he cannot believe; that now, at this moment, he has no notion of a God at all and cannot care in the least whether there be a God or not. But he can still be true to what he knows. And everything hinges upon whether he does or not. That alone can clear the moral atmosphere and make it possible for the true idea of God to be born in him.

How Does a Right Belief Begin?

We have all felt our hearts drawn at times—in strange, tender fashion, perhaps previously unknown to us—to the blue of the sky, or to the first sweetness of a summer morning. Our souls now and then go out of us, in a passion of embrace, to the simplest flower. We spread out our arms to the wind, now when it meets us in its strength, now when it kisses the face. In our weaker moments of belief we never admit to ourselves that it is one force in all the forms that draws us—that perhaps it is the very God, the All in all about us. But we fully recognize the fact that nature is more alive than she has ever been to us. And all the time a divine power of truth and beauty has laid hold upon us and is working in us as only the powers of God can work in a man or woman.

We have not the slightest idea that we are beginning to entertain the notion of a real God. We have not yet come to consider the fact that the *very best* of men said he knew God, that God was like himself, only greater, that whoever would do what he told him should know God and know that he spoke the truth about God, that he had come from God to tell the world that God was truth and love.

No man is a believer, no matter what else he may do, except he give his will, his life to the Master. No man is a believer who does not obey God. Thousands talk about God for every one who believes in him in this sense. Thousands will do what the priests and scribes—their parsons and pastors—say, for every one who searches to find what God says and to obey it—who takes his orders from the Lord himself, and not from other men. A man must come to the Master, listen to his Word, and do what he says. Then he will come to know God, and know that he knows him.[1]

God Gives the Highest Life

The life the Lord came to give us is a life exceeding that of the highest mere human being, by far more than the life of that man exceeds the life of the least animal. More and more of that divine life awaits each who will receive it, and to eternity.

The Father has given to the Son to have life in himself, and that life of the Son is *our* light. We know life only as light; it is the life in us that makes us see. All the growth of the Christian is the more and more life he is receiving.

At first a man's religion may hardly be distinguishable from the mere prudent desire to save his soul. But at last he loses that very soul in the glory of love, and so saves it. Self becomes but the cloud on which the white light of God divides into harmonies unspeakable.

Life is the law, the food, the necessity of life.

Life is everything!

Many doubtless mistake the joy of life for life itself. Longing after the joy, they eventually languish with a thirst at once poor and inextinguishable. But even that thirst points to the one spring.

Those who mistake the joy of life for life, love self, not life. And self is but the shadow of life. When it is taken for life, and set as the man's center, it becomes a live death in the man, a devil he worships as his god.

The soul in harmony with his Maker has more life, a larger being, than the soul consumed with cares. The sage has a larger life than the clown. The poet is more alive than the man whose life flows out that money may come in. The man who loves his fellow is infinitely more alive than he whose endeavor is to exalt himself above his neighbor. The man who strives to be better in his being is more alive than he who longs for the praise of many.

But the man to whom God is all in all, who feels his life roots hid with Christ in God, who knows himself the inheritor of all wealth and worlds and ages, yes, of power essential and in itself, that man has begun to be alive indeed.

What We Need Is More Life

Let us in all the troubles of life remember that our one lack is life—that what we need is more *life*—more of the life-making presence in us making us more, and more largely, *alive*. When most oppressed, when most weary of "life," as our unbelief would phrase it, let us remember that it is, in truth, the inroad and presence of death we are weary of. When most inclined to sleep, let us rouse ourselves to *live*.

Of all things, let us avoid the false refuge of a weary collapse, a hopeless yielding to things as they are. It is the life in us that is discontented. We need more of what is discontented, not more of the cause of its discontent. Discontentment, I repeat, is the life in us that has not enough of itself, is not enough to itself, so calls for more. He has the victory who, in the midst of pain and weakness, cries out, not for death, not for the repose of forgetfulness, but for strength to fight, for more power, more consciousness of being, more God in him.

The true man trusts in a strength which is not his, which he does not feel, does not even always desire. He believes in a power that seems far from him, that is yet at the root of his fatigue itself and his need of rest—rest as far from death as is labor.

To trust in the strength of God in our weakness; to say, "I am weak; so let me be. God is strong"; to seek from him who is our life, as the natural, simple cure of all that is amiss with us, power to do and be and live, even when we are weary—*this* is the victory that overcomes the world.

To believe in God our strength in the face of all seeming denial; to believe in him out of the heart of weakness and unbelief, in spite of numbness and weariness and lethargy; to believe in the wide-awake reality of his being, through all the stupefying, enervating, distorting dream; to will to wake, when the very being seems athirst for a godless repose—these are the broken steps up to the high fields where repose is but a form of strength, strength but a form of joy, joy but a form of love.

"I am weak," says the true soul, "but not so weak that I would not be strong, not so sleepy that I would not see the sun rise, not so lame but that I would walk! Thanks be to him who perfects strength in weakness and gives to his beloved of his very life even while they sleep!"

What Life Might Be!

If we will but let our God and Father work his will with us, there can be no limit to his enlargement of our existence, to the flood of life with which he will overflow our consciousness. We have no conception of what life might be, of how vast the consciousness of which we could be made capable.

If every sunlit, sail-crowded sea under blue heaven flecked with wind-chased white filled your soul, as with a new gift of life, think what sense of existence must be yours if he, whose thought has but fringed its garment with the gladness of such a show, were to make his abode with you, and while thinking of the gladness of God inside your being, let you know and feel that he is carrying you as a Father in his bosom!

Life Is Active, Creative Be-ing

It is easy to mistake life and the consciousness *of that life* as one. But the consciousness of life is not life. It is only the outcome of life. The real life is that which *is* of and by itself—is life because it wills itself—which is, in the active, not the passive sense.

This can only be God.

But in us there ought to be a life correspondent to the life that is God's. In us must also be possible the life that wills itself into existence—a life so far resembling the self-existent Life and partaking of its image, that it has a share in its own being. There is an original act possible to man, which must initiate the reality of his existence.

He must live in and by willing to live.

A tree lives. I hardly doubt it has some vague consciousness, known not to itself but only to God who made it. I trust that life in its lowest forms is on the way to thought and blessedness, is in the process of that separation, so to speak, from God, in which consists the creation of living souls. But the life of these lower forms is not life in the high sense—in the sense in which the word is used in the Bible. True life knows and rules itself. The eternal life is life come awake.

No Mere Elongation of Consciousness

The condition of most men and women seems to me a life in death, an unreal dream existence, a pre-waking, empty, mere going-on. That they do not feel it so does not mean such is not the case. The sow wallowing in the mire may assert it her way of being clean. But this is not the life of the God-born. The day must come when such who have not awakened themselves to life as they were created to live it will hide their faces with shame.

There is nothing for man worthy to be called life, but the life eternal—God's life, that is.

God intends for man to partake of this life of the Most High, to be alive as he is alive. Of this life, the outcome and the light is righteousness, love, grace, and truth.

But the life itself is a thing that will not be defined, even as God will not be defined. It is a power, the formless cause of form. It has no limits whereby to be defined. It shows itself to the soul that is hungering and thirsting after righteousness. But that soul cannot show it to another, except in the shining of its own light.

The ignorant soul understands by this life eternal only an endless elongation of consciousness. But duration is not true *life*.

Partaking in God's Essential Life

What God means by life eternal is giving a being life like his own, beyond the attack of decay or death. Such a being is so essential that it has no relation whatever to nothingness; a something which is, and can never go to that which is not, for with that it never had to do, but came out of the heart of Life, the heart of God, the fountain of being.

Life eternal is an existence partaking of the divine nature and having nothing in common, any more than the Eternal himself, with what can pass or cease. God owes his being to no one, and his child has no lord but his Father.

This life, this eternal life, consists for man in absolute oneness with God and all divine modes of being, oneness with every phrase of right and harmony. It consists in a love as deep as it is universal, as conscious as it is unspeakable, a love that can no more be reasoned about than life itself, a love whose presence is its all-sufficing proof and justification.

He who has it not cannot believe in it. How should death believe in life, though all the birds of God are singing jubilant over the empty tomb!

The delight of such a being, the splendor of a consciousness rushing from the wide open doors of the fountain of existence, the ecstasy of the spiritual sense into which the surge of life essential, immortal, increate, flows in silent fullness from the heart of hearts—what may it, what must it not be, in the great day of God and the individual soul![2]

UNAWARE OF THE WELLSPRINGS OF LIFE

(A Fictional Selection from *The Curate's Awakening*)

The morning which had given birth to this stormy afternoon had been a fine one, and the curate had gone out for a walk. Not that he was a great walker; his strolls were leisurely and comprised of many stops. He was not in bad health and was not lazy. Yet he had little impulse for much activity of any sort. The springs in his well of life did not seem to flow quite fast enough.

He sauntered through Osterfield Park and down the descent to the river. There he seated himself upon a large stone on the bank. He knew that he was there and that he answered to "Thomas Wingfold"; but *why* he was there, and why he was not called to something else, he did not know. On each side of the stream rose a steeply sloping bank on which grew many fern bushes, now half-withered. The sunlight upon them this November morning seemed as cold as the wind that blew about their golden and green fronds.

Thomas felt rather cold, but the cold was of the sort that comes from the look rather than the feel of things. With his stick he kept knocking pebbles into the water and listlessly watching them splash. The wind blew, the sun shone, the water ran, the ferns waved, the clouds went drifting over his head—but he never looked up or took any notice of the doings of Mother Nature busy with her housework.

His life had not been particularly interesting. He had known from the first that he was intended for the church, and had not objected but accepted it as his destiny. Yet he had taken no great interest in the matter.

The church was to him an ancient institution of approved respectability. He had entered her service, and in return for the narrow shelter, humble fare, and not quite shabby garments she allotted him, he would perform her observances.

Thomas did not philosophize much about life, nor his position in it. Instead, he took everything with an unemotional kind of acceptance and laid no claim to courage or devotion. He had a certain dull prejudice in favor of not telling a lie, and yet was completely uninstructed in the things that constitute practical honesty. He liked reading the prayers in church, for he had a somewhat musical voice. He visited the sick—with some repugnance, it is true, but without delay—and spoke to them such religious commonplaces as occurred to him.

He did not read much, browsing over his newspaper at breakfast with a polite curiosity sufficient to season the loneliness of his slice of fried bacon, taking more interest in some of the naval intelligence than in anything else. Indeed, it would have been difficult to say in what he did take much interest.

Could he in all honesty have said he believed there was a God? Or was this not all he really knew—that there was a Church of England which paid him for reading public prayers to a God in whom the congregation was assumed to believe?

It was not a question Wingfold had yet considered.[3]

I Would I Were A Child

I would I were a child,
That I might look, and laugh, and say, My Father!
And follow thee with running feet, or rather
 Be led through dark and wild!

How I would hold thy hand,
My glad eyes often to thy glory lifting!
Should darkness 'twixt thy face and mine come
 drifting,
 My heart would but expand.

If an ill thing came near,
I would but creep within thy mantle's folding,
Shut my eyes close, thy hand yet faster holding,
 And soon forget my fear.

O soul, O soul, rejoice!
Thou art God's child indeed, for all thy sinning;
A poor weak child, yet his, and worth the winning
 With saviour eyes and voice.

Who spake the words? Didst Thou?
They are too good, even for such a giver:
Such water drinking once, I should feel ever
 As I had drunk but now.

Yet sure the Word said so,
Teaching our lips to cry with his, Our Father!
Telling the tale of him who once did gather
 His goods to him, and go!

Ah, thou dost lead me, God!
But it is dark and starless, the way dreary;
Almost I sleep, I am so very weary
 Upon this rough hill-road.

Almost! Nay, I do sleep;
There is no darkness save in this my dreaming;
Thy fatherhood above, around, is beaming;
 Thy hand my hand doth keep.

With sighs my soul doth teem;
I have no knowledge but that I am sleeping;
Haunted with lies, my life will fail in weeping:
 Wake me from this my dream.

How long shall heavy night
Deny the day? How long shall this dull sorrow
Say in my heart that never any morrow
 Will bring the friendly light?

Lord, art thou in the room?
Come near my bed; oh, draw aside the curtain!
A child's heart would say Father, were it certain
 That it would not presume.

But if this dreary sleep
May not be broken, help thy helpless sleeper
To rest in thee; so shall his sleep grow deeper—
 For evil dreams too deep.

Father! I dare at length;
My childhood sure will hold me free from blaming;
Sinful yet hoping, I to thee come, claiming
 Thy tenderness, my strength.

2

GOD OUR TENDER LOVING FATHER

And because you are sons, God hath sent forth the Spirit of his Son into your hearts, crying, Abba, Father.

Galatians 4:6

God's Essential Being

What is the deepest in God?

His power? No, for power could not make him what we mean when we say *God*. A being whose essence was only power would be such a negation of the divine that no righteous worship could be offered him; his service would be only fear.

The God himself whom we love could not be righteous were he not something deeper and better still than we generally mean by the word *righteous*—but, alas, how little can language truly say!

In one word, God is love.

Love is the deepest depth, the essence of his nature, at the root of all his being. Love is the heart and hand of his creation. It is his right to create, and his power to create. But it is out of his love that he *does* create.

His perfection is his love. All his divine rights, his power, his justice, his righteousness, his mercy, his fatherhood—every divine attribute we think to ascribe to him—rests upon his love. God's love is what he *is*.

Ah, he is not only the great monarch, the Almighty, the powerful, the ruler of heaven and earth. He is all that, of course—and more! And the more is the essence of his being, the foundation out of which flows everything else.

The simplest peasant loving his cow is more divine than any monarch whose monarchy is his glory.[1]

Truly God is love, and love is that which is, and was, and shall be for evermore—boundless, unconditional, self-existent, creative! God is all in all! In him love evermore breaks forth anew into fresh personality—in every new consciousness, in every new child of the one creating Father. In every burning heart, in everything that hopes and fears and is, love is the creative presence, the center, the source of life—yea, life itself; yea, God himself![2]

Human Fatherhood Reflects the Divine

The truth and faith which the great Father has put in the heart of the child make him the nurturer of the fatherhood in his own father. Thus in part it is that the children of men will come at last to know the great Father. The family, with all its powers for the development of society, is a family because it is born and rooted in and grows out of the very heart of God.[3]

Nobody knows what the relation of father and son may yet come to. Those who accept the Christian revelation are bound to recognize that there must be in it depths infinite, ages removed from being fathomed. For is it not a reproduction in small of the loftiest mystery in human ken—that of the infinite Father and infinite Son? If man be made in the image of God, then human fatherhood and sonship is the image of the eternal relation between God and Jesus.[4]

There is a live heart at the center of the lovely order of the universe—a heart to which all the rest is but a clothing form—a heart that bears every truthful thought, every help-needing cry of each of its children, and must deliver them.

All my life, I can nearly say, I have been trying to find that one Being and to know him consciously present. Hope grows and grows with the years that lead me nearer to the end of my earthly life, and in my best moods it seems ever that the only thing worth desiring is that his will be done, that there lies before me a fullness of life, sufficient to content the giving of a perfect Father, and that the part of his child is to yield all and see that he does not himself stand in the way of the mighty design.[5]

God Is Our Friend!

Our Lord was, is, and ever shall be divinely childlike. Childhood belongs to the divine nature.

Obedience is as divine as will; *service*, as divine as rule.

How? Because they are one in their nature. They are both a doing of the truth. The love in them is the same.

The Fatherhood and the Sonship are one, except that the Fatherhood looks down lovingly, and the Sonship looks up lovingly. Love is all. And God is all in all. He is ever seeking to get down to us—to be the divine man to us. And yet we are ever saying, "That be far from thee, Lord!"

In our unbelief we are careful over the divine dignity, of which he is too grand to think. Better pleasing to God is the audacity of Job, who, rushing into God's presence and flinging the door of his presence-chamber to the wall, like a troubled—or it may be even angry, yet faithful—child, cries out to him whose perfect Fatherhood Job is in the process of learning.

The devotion of God to his creatures is perfect. He does not think about himself but about them. He wants nothing for himself, but finds his blessedness in the outgoing of blessedness.

Ah! It is a terrible glory! Shall it also be a lonely one? We will draw near with our human response, our abandonment of self in the faith of Jesus. He gives himself to us—shall we not give ourselves to him? Shall we not give ourselves to each other whom he loves?

For when is the child the ideal child in our eyes and to our hearts? Is it not when with gentle hands he takes his father by the hand or even the beard, and turns that father's face up to his brothers and sisters to kiss? When even the lovely selfishness of love-seeking has vanished and the heart is absorbed in loving?

In this, then, is God like the child: that he is simply and altogether our friend, our father—our more than friend, father, and mother—our infinite love-perfect God. Grand and strong beyond all that human imagination can conceive of poet-thinking and kingly action, he is delicate beyond all that a human tenderness can conceive of husband or wife, homey beyond all that human heart can conceive of father or mother.

He does not think of us in two separate ways. With him all is simplicity of purpose and meaning and effort and end—namely, that we should be as he is, think the same thoughts, mean the same things, possess the same blessedness. It is so plain that anyone may see it, everyone ought to see it, everyone shall see it. It must be so. God is utterly true and good to us, and nothing shall withstand his will.

Our Father Wants to Be Near Us

How terribly have the theologians misrepresented God's character. They represent him as a great king on a huge throne, thinking how grand he is, and making it the business of his being and the end of his universe to keep up his glory, wielding the bolts of a Jupiter against them that take his name in vain. They would not admit to such of course, but follow out what they say and it amounts to the same thing.

But how contrary this is to what the Gospel accounts plainly tell us. Brothers, sisters, have you found our King? There he is, kissing little children and saying they are like God. There he is at the table with the head of a fisherman lying on his chest, and somewhat heavy at heart that even he, the beloved disciple, cannot yet understand him well. The simplest peasant who loves his children and his sheep would be the true type of our God beside that monstrosity of a monarch.

The God who is ever uttering himself in the changeful profusions of nature; who takes millions of years to form a soul that shall understand him and be blessed; who never needs to be, and never is, in haste; who welcomes the simplest thought of truth or beauty as the return for seed he has sown upon the old fallows of eternity; who rejoices in the response of a faltering moment to the age-long cry of his wisdom in the streets; the God of music, of painting, of building, the Lord of Hosts, the God of mountains and oceans; the God of history working in time unto Christianity—this God is the God of little children, and he alone can be perfectly, abandonedly simple and devoted.

The deepest, purest love of a woman has its wellspring in him. Our longing desires can no more exhaust the fullness of the treasure of the Godhead, than our imagination can touch their measure. Of him not a thought, not a joy, not a hope of one of his creatures can pass unseen. And while one of them remains unsatisfied, he is not Lord over all.

Therefore, with angels and with archangels, with the spirits of the just made perfect, with the little children of the kingdom, yea, with the Lord himself, and for all them that do not yet know him, we praise and magnify and laud his name in itself, saying *Our Father.*

We do not draw back from him because we are unworthy, nor even because we are hardhearted and do not care for the good as we should. For it is his childlikeness that makes him our God and Father. The perfection of his relation to us swallows up all our imperfections, all our defects, all our evils. For our childhood is born of his fatherhood. That man is perfect in faith who can come to God in the utter emptiness of his feelings and his desires, without a glow or an aspiration, with the weight of low thoughts, failures, neglects, and wandering forgetfulness, and say to him, "Thou art my refuge, because thou art my home."[6]

EARTHLY FATHERHOOD AND SONSHIP

(A Fictional Selection from *The Laird's Inheritance*)

osmo stood and looked into his father's eyes—the eyes of
the two of them were of the same color, that bright, sweet,
soft Norwegian blue—his right hand still clasped in his father's
left, and his left hand leaning gently on his father's knee. A
silent man ordinarily, Cosmo's father suffered from no lack of
the power of speech, for he had a Celtic gift of simple eloquence.

"This is your birthday, my son," he began.

"Yes, Papa."

"You are now fourteen."

"Yes, Papa."

"You are growing into quite a man."

"I don't know, Papa."

"So much of a man, at least, my Cosmo, that I am going to
treat you like a man on this day and tell you some things that I
have never talked about to anyone since your mother's death.
You remember your mother, Cosmo?"

"Yes, Papa, I do."

"Tell me what you remember about her," said the old man.
"What color were her eyes, Cosmo?"

"I don't know. I never saw the color of them. But I remember
they looked at me as if I could run right into them."

"We must be very good that we may see her again someday,
my boy."

"I will try. I do try, Papa."

"When a woman like that is taken from us, Cosmo, the least
we can do is to give her the same love after she is gone as when
she was with us. It may be that God lets her look down and
watch us—who can tell? She can't be very anxious about me
now, for I am getting old, and my warfare is nearly over. I have
been trying to keep the straight path, as far as I could see it,
though sometimes the grass and heather has got the better of
it, so that it was hard to find. But you must remember, Cosmo,
that it is not enough to be a good boy, as I shall tell her you have

always been: you've got to be a good man, and that is a different and sometimes a harder thing. For as soon as a man has to do with other men, he finds they expect him to do things they ought to be ashamed of, and then he has to stand on his own honest legs, and not move an inch for all their pushing and pulling. And when a man loves his fellow man and tries to do good for him and be on good terms with him, that is not easy. The thing is just this, Cosmo: when you are a full-grown man, you must still be a boy. That's the difficulty. For a man to be a boy, and still a good boy, he must be a thorough man. And you can't keep true to your mother, or be a thorough man, except you remember him who is father and mother both to all of us.

"I have tried to teach you, Cosmo, to do as I have done when I was in any trouble, just to go into my closet, and shut the door, and pray to my Father who is in secret. But I am getting old and tired, and shall soon go where I hope to learn faster. Oh, my boy, listen to your father who loves you! Never do anything you would be ashamed for your mother or me to know. Remember, nothing drops out; everything hid shall be revealed. But of all things, if ever you should fail or fall, don't lie still because you are down. Get up again—for God's sake, for your mother's sake, for my sake—get up and try again.

"And now it is time you should know a little about the family of which you come. I don't doubt there have been some in it who would consider me a foolish man for bringing you up as I have done, but those of them who are up there with your mother don't. They see that the business of life is not to get as much as you can, but to do justly, and to love mercy, and walk humbly with your God. They may say I have made a poor thing of it, but I shall not hang my head before the public of that country because I've let the land slip from me. Some would tell me I ought to shudder at the thought of leaving you to such poverty, but I am too concerned about you yourself, my boy, to think about the hardships that may be awaiting you. The inheritance of your earthly father may be this land about us here, an inheritance that is dwindling, and which we may lose someday. But the inheritance of your Father in heaven, a Father who owns the cattle on a thousand hills, and all the hills of the earth, is an inheritance no one can take from you. And that is the legacy I want to leave you, my son, a heritage of righteousness, of truth, of love for God, and of service to your kind. That is a more lasting inheritance than any earthly fortune that I could pass on to you.

"So, Cosmo, I do not care what people may think. I should be far more afraid about you if I were leaving you rich. I have seen rich people do things I never knew a poor man to do. I don't mean to say anything against the rich—there's good and bad of all sorts. But I just can't be so very sorry that I am leaving you to poverty, though if I might have had my way; it wouldn't have been so bad. But he knows best who loves best. I have struggled hard to keep the old place for you, but there's hardly an acre outside the garden and close by that wasn't mortgaged before I even came into the property. I've been all my life trying to pay it off but have made little progress. The house is free, however, and the garden. And don't you part with the old place, my boy, except you see that you genuinely ought to and that God is leading you to. But rather than anything not out-and-out honest, anything the least doubtful, sell every stone. Let it all go rather than sacrificing an inch of honesty, even if it means you should have to beg your way home to us. Stay clean, my son, as the day you were born."[7]

Love Is Strength

Love alone is great in might,
Makes the heavy burden light,
Smoothes rough ways to weary feet,
Makes the bitter morsel sweet:
  Love alone is strength!

Might that is not born of Love
Is not Might born from above,
Has its birthplace down below
Where they neither reap nor sow:
  Love alone is strength!

Love is stronger than all force,
Is its own eternal source;
Might is always in decay,
Love grows fresher every day:
  Love alone is strength!

Little ones, no ill can chance;
Fear ye not, but sing and dance;
Though the high-heaved heaven should fall
God is plenty for us all:
  God is Love and Strength!

3

JESUS OUR SAVIOR

*Thou shalt call his name Jesus: for he shall save his people
from their sins.*

Matthew 1:21

The Only Cure

The cause of every man's discomfort is evil, moral evil. First of all evil in himself, his own sin, his own wrongness, his own unrightness. Then secondly, evil in those he loves. With this latter, the only way to get rid of it is for the man to get rid of his *own* sin.

Foolish is the man, and there are many such men, who would rid himself or his fellows of discomfort by setting the world right, by waging war on the evils around him, while he neglects that integral part of the world where lies his business, his first business—namely, his own character and conduct. Even if it were possible—an absurd supposition—that the world should thus be righted from the outside, it would still be impossible for such a man, remaining what he was, to enjoy the perfection of the result, for he would yet be out of tune with the organ he had tuned.

No evil can be cured in mankind except by its being cured in individual men and women. Rightness alone is cure. The return of the organism of man to its true self is its only possible ease from discomfort. To free a man or woman from suffering—whether it be physical, mental, spiritual, or emotional—he or she must be set right, put in health.

And the health at the root of man's being, his rightness, is to be free from sin.

I do not mean set free from the sins he has done; that will follow. I mean the sin in his being, which spoils his nature—the wrongness in him, the sin he *is*, which makes him do the sins he does.

To save a man from both his sin and his sins is to say to him, in a perfect and eternal sense, "Rise up and walk. Be at liberty in your essential being." To do this for us, Jesus was born, and remains born to all the ages.

When misery drives a man to call out to the source of his life, the promised deliverance will in all probability not be what the man desired. He will want only to be rid of his suffering. But that he cannot have except in being delivered from its essential root, a thing infinitely worse than any suffering it can produce. If he will not have that complete root-deliverance, he must keep his suffering. There can be no deliverance but to come out of his evil dream into the glory of God.[1]

The World Needs a Savior

What a breeding nest of cares and pains is the human heart! Surely it needs some refuge! How the world needs a Savior to whom anyone might go, at any moment, without a journey, without letters or commendations or credentials.

Surely such a God as would send his own Son into the world, would have him appear among us, clothed in the garb of humanity, to take all the consequences of being the Son of obedience among the children of disobedience, engulfing their wrongs in his infinite forgiveness, and winning them back, by slow, unpromising, and tedious renewal, to the heart of his Father—surely such a God would not have created men knowing that some of them would commit such horrible sins from which he could not redeem them.

The words rise to mind, *"Come unto me, all that labor and are heavy laden, and I will give you rest."*

Ah, the heart fills! Did ever a man really say such words? Such words they are! If a man did utter them, either he was the most presumptuous of mortals, or he could do what he said.

In God's eyes all sin is equally abhorrent—killing, plagiarizing, faulty business practices, or a hateful unforgiveness. All sin, whatever the degree, is equal in its capacity to separate us from God's heart of love. Therefore, it all equally needs to be repented of and forgiven by him whose heart is forgiveness.

"Come unto me, all ye that labor and are heavy laden, and I will give you rest."

It is rest we want. *Rest*—such peace of mind as we had when we were children. Do not waste time asking yourself how he can give it. That is for him to understand, not you—until it is done. Ask him to forgive you and make you clean and set things right for you. If he will not do it, then he is not the Savior of men, and was wrongly named Jesus.

Come then at the call of the Maker, the Healer, the Giver of repentance and light, the Friend of sinners, all you on whom lies the weight of a sin or the gathered heap of a thousand crimes. He came to call such as you that he might make you clean. He cannot bear that you should live in such misery, such blackness of darkness. He wants to give you your life again, the bliss of your being. He will not speak to you one word of reproach, unless you should try to justify yourself by accusing your neighbor. He will leave it to those who cherish the same sins in their hearts to cast stones at you; he who has not sin casts no stones. Heartily he loves you; heartily he hates the evil in you. The rest of you, keep aloof, if you will, until you shall have done some deed that compels you to cry out for deliverance. But you that already know yourselves to be sinners, come to him that he may work in you his perfect work, for he came not to call the righteous, but sinners— us, you and me—to repentance.[2]

✝ ⸙ ✝ *True Deliverance*

It is true that Jesus came, in delivering us from our sins, to deliver us also from the painful consequences of our sins. But these consequences exist by the one law of the universe, the true will of God. When that will is broken, suffering is inevitable.

But in the perfection of God's creation, the result of that suffering is curative. The pain works toward the healing of the breach.

The Lord never came to deliver men from the consequences of their sins while those sins yet remained. That would be to cast out the window the medicine of cure while still the man lay sick. Yet, feeling nothing of the dread hatefulness of their *sin*, men have constantly taken this word that the Lord came to deliver us from our *sins* to mean that he came to save them from the *punishment* of their sins.

This idea has terribly corrupted the preaching of the Gospel. The message of the Good News has not been truly communicated. Unable to believe in the forgiveness of their Father in heaven, imagining him not at liberty to forgive, or incapable of forgiving forthright; not really believing him God who is fully our *Savior*, but a God bound—either in his own nature or by a law above him and compulsory upon him— to exact some recompense or satisfaction for sin, a multitude of religious teachers have taught their fellow men that Jesus came to bear our punishment and save us from hell. But in that they have misrepresented his true mission.

The mission of Jesus was from the same source and with the same object as the punishment of our *sins*. He came to do more than take the punishment for our sins. He came as well to set us free from our *sin*.

No man is safe from hell until he is free from his sin. But a man to whom his sins are a burden, while he may indeed sometimes feel as if he were in hell, will soon have forgotten that he ever had any other hell to think of than that of his sinful condition. For to him his sin is hell. He would go to the other hell to be free of it. Free of his sin, hell itself would be endurable to him.

For hell is God's and not the Devil's. Hell is on the side of God and man, to free the child of God from the corruption of death. Not one soul will ever be redeemed from hell but by being saved from his sin, from the evil in him. If hell be needful to save him, hell will blaze, and the worm will writhe and bite, until he takes refuge in the will of the Father. "Salvation from hell" is salvation as conceived by such to whom hell, and not the evil of the sin, is the terror.[3]

God takes our sins on himself, and while he drives them out of us with a whip of scorpions, he will yet make them work for his good ends. He defeats our sins, makes them prisoners, forces them into the service of good, and chains them like galley slaves to the rowing benches of the gospel ship. He makes them work toward salvation for us.[4]

✝ *Putting to Death the Sin Nature*

There is an important misapprehension in the words of the messengers of the Gospel in the New Testament. It is wrongly thought that they threaten us with punishment because of sins we have committed, whereas in reality their message is of forgiveness, not of vengeance—of deliverance, not of evil to come.

No man shall be condemned for any or all of his sins that are past. He needs not dread remaining unforgiven even for the worst of them. The sin he *dwells* in, the sin he will not come out of—that is the sole ruin of a man. His present, his live, sins—those pervading his thoughts and ruling his conduct, the sins he keeps doing and will not give up, the sins he is called to abandon and clings to—these are they for which he is even at this moment condemned. "This is the condemnation, that light is come into the world, and men loved darkness rather than light, because their deeds were evil."

It is the indwelling badness, ready to produce bad actions—the indwelling *sin* which leads to *sins*—that we need to be delivered from.

Against this sin, if a man will not strive, he is left to commit evil and reap the consequences. To be saved from these consequences would be no deliverance; it would be an immediate, ever deepening damnation. Jesus came to *deliver* us, not rescue us from needful consequences. It is the sin in our being—no essential part of it, thank God!—the miserable fact that we as a very child of God do not care for our Father and will not obey him, causing us to desire wrongly and act wrongly—*this* is what he came to deliver us from, not the things we have done, but the possibility of doing such things any more.

The bad that lives in us, our evil judgments, our unjust desires, our hate and pride and envy and greed and self-satisfaction, these are the souls of our sins, our live *sin nature*, more terrible than the bodies of our sins (namely, the deeds we do). This, the sin that dwells and works in us, is the sin from which Jesus came to deliver us. When we turn against it and refuse to obey it, it rises in fierce insistence, but at the same moment begins to die. We are then on the Lord's side, as he has always been on ours, and he begins to deliver us from it and from the sinful deeds that result.

The Redemptive Flowering of the Universe

As the love of him who is love transcends ours as the heavens are higher than the earth, so must God desire in his child infinitely more than the most conscientious and loving of mothers can desire in hers.

He would have his child rid of all discontentment, all fear, all grudging, all bitterness in word or thought, all measuring of his own with a different gauge than he would apply to another's. He will have no curling of the lip, no indifference toward any person, no desire to excel over another. He will not have him receive the smallest service without gratitude, would not hear from him a tone to jar the heart of another, a word to make it ache.

From such, as from all other sins, Jesus was born to deliver us— not primarily, or by itself, from the punishment of any of them. When all are gone, when the sin nature which causes them has been put to death and his Spirit substituted inside the part of our hearts that rules our deeds, then the holy punishment will have departed also.

He came to make us good, and therein blessed children.

One master sin is at the root of all the rest. It is no individual action or deed toward another. It is the nonrecognition by man and woman of the highest of all relations, the relation which is the root and first essential condition of every other true relation of or in the human soul. It is the absence in the man of harmony with the Being whose thought is the man's existence, whose word is the man's power of thought.

The highest creation of God in man is his will, and until the highest in man meets the highest in God, their true relation is not yet a spiritual fact. The flower lies in the root, but the root is not the flower. The relation exists, but while one of the parties neither knows, loves, nor acts upon it, the relation is, as it were, yet unborn. The highest in man is neither his intellect nor his imagination nor his reason. All are inferior to his will, and indeed, in a grand way, dependent upon it; his will must meet God's—a will *distinct* from God's—otherwise no harmony would be possible between them.

God creates in man the power to will His will. It may cost God suffering that man can never know to bring the man to the point at which he wills His will. But when he is brought to that point, and declares it for the truth—that is, for the will of God—the man becomes one with God, and the end for which Jesus was born and died is gained. The man is saved from both his sin and his sins, and the universe flowers yet again in his redemption.

But I would not be supposed, from what I have said, to imagine the Lord without sympathy for the sorrows and pains which reveal what sin is. With everything human he sympathizes. Evil is not human; it is the defect and opposite of the human. But the suffering that follows it is human, belonging of necessity to the human who has sinned. Although it is caused by sin, suffering is *for* the sinner, that he may be delivered from his sin.

Jesus is in himself aware of every human pain. He feels it also. In him too is pain. With the energy of tenderest love he wills his brothers and sisters free, that he may fill them to overflowing with that essential thing, joy. For that they were indeed created. But the moment they exist, truth becomes the first thing, not happiness; and he must make them true. Were it possible, however, for pain to continue after evil was gone, he would never rest while one ache was yet in the world.

The man may recognize the evil in him only as pain; he may know little and care nothing about his sin. Yet is the Lord sorry for his pain. He cries aloud, "Come unto me, all ye that labor and are heavy laden, and I will give you rest." He does not say, "Come unto me, all ye that feel the burden of your sins." He opens his arms to all weary enough to come to him in the poorest hope of rest. Right gladly would he free them from their misery, but he knows only one way: he will teach them to be like himself, meek and lowly, bearing with gladness the yoke of his Father's will. This is the one, the only right, the only possible way of freeing them from their sin, the cause of their unrest.

With us the weariness comes first; with him the sin. There is but one cure for both—the will of the Father. That which is his joy will be their deliverance!

Mental Understanding Will Never Bring Salvation

Even the disobedient and selfish would like to possess the liberty and gladness that belong to purity and love.

But they cannot have them. They are weary and heavy laden, both with what they are, and because of what they were made for but are not. The Lord knows what they need; they know only what they want. They want happiness without the cost. They want the joy of life without the *life* in them.

They want ease. He knows they need purity.

It may be my reader will desire me to say *how* the Lord will save him from his sin. That is like the lawyer's "Who is my neighbor?" The spirit of such a mode of receiving the offer of the Lord's salvation is the root of all the horrors of a corrupt theology. Such questions spring from the passion for the fruit of the tree of knowledge, not the fruit of the tree of life.

Men would *understand*; they do not care to *obey*. They try to understand where it is impossible they should understand except by obeying. They would search into the work of the Lord instead of doing their part in it—thus making it impossible for the Lord to go on with his work, and for themselves to become capable of seeing and understanding what he does. Instead of immediately obeying the Lord of life, the one condition upon which he can help them, and in itself the beginning of their deliverance, they set themselves to question their unenlightened intellects as to his plans for their deliverance. Incapable of understanding the first motions of freedom in themselves, they proceed to interpret the riches of his divine soul in terms of their own beggarly notions, and then, in the growing presumption of imagined success, to insist upon their neighbors' acceptance of their distorted shadows of "the plan of salvation" as the truth of him in whom is no darkness and the one condition of their acceptance with him. They delay setting their foot on the stair that alone can lead them to the house of wisdom, until they shall have determined the material and mode of its construction. For the sake of knowing, they postpone that which alone can enable them to know, and substitute for the true understanding which lies beyond, a false persuasion that they already understand. They will not accept—that is, act upon—their highest privilege, that of obeying the Son of God. It is on them that *do* his will that the day dawns. To them the day star arises in their hearts. Obedience is the soul of knowledge.

By obedience, I intend no kind of obedience to man, or submission to authority claimed by man or community of men. I mean obedience to the will of the Father, however revealed in our conscience.

God forbid I should seem to despise understanding. The New Testament is full of urgings to understand. Our whole life, to be life at all, must be a growth in understanding. What I cry out upon is the misunderstanding that comes of man's endeavor to understand while not obeying. Upon obedience must our energy be spent; understanding will follow. Not anxious to know our duty, or knowing it and not doing it, how shall we understand that which only a true heart and a clean soul can ever understand? The power in us that would understand if it were free lies in the bonds of imperfection and impurity and is therefore incapable of judging the divine. It cannot see the truth. If it could see it, it would not know it, and would not have it. Until a man begins to obey, the light that is in him is darkness.

Any honest soul may understand this much, however—that the Lord cannot save a man from his sins while the man holds to his sins. Even God in his omnipotence cannot do and not do the same thing at the same moment. The very thought is self-contradictory.

But the Lord is not unreasonable; he requires no perfection of motives where such could not yet exist. He does not say, "You must be sorry for your sins, or you need not come to me." To be truly sorry for his sins a man must love God and man, and yet love is the very thing that has to be developed in him. It is but common sense that if a man would be delivered from the suffering upon him or the evil within him, he must himself begin to cast it out. Equally it is common sense that a man should look for and expect the help of his Father in the endeavor. Alone he might labor to all eternity and not succeed. He who has not made himself cannot set himself right without him who made him. But his Maker is in him, and is his strength.

The man, however, who, instead of doing what he is told, speculates on the metaphysics of him who calls him to his work, stands leaning against the door by which the Lord would enter to help him! The moment he sets about putting straight the thing that is crooked— I mean doing right where he has been doing wrong—he withdraws from the entrance and gives way for the Master to come in. He cannot make himself pure, but he can leave that which is impure. He can spread out the "defiled, discolored web" of his life before the bleaching Sun of Righteousness. He cannot save himself, but he can let the Lord save him. The struggle of his weakness is as essential to the coming victory as the strength of Christ, who resisted unto death, striving against sin.

The sum of the whole matter is this: the Son has come from the Father to set the children free from their sins and the sin that is in them. He is their Savior. He is our Savior! He is my Savior! The children must hear and obey him, that he may send forth judgment unto victory.

Son of our Father, help us to do what you say, and so with you die unto sin, that we may rise to the sonship for which we were created. Help us to repent even to the sending away of our sins.[5]

THE TRUE GLORY OF GOD

(A Fictional Selection from *The Musician's Quest*)

Do you know, Grannie, what's at the heart of my hopes in the misery and degradation I see from morning to night in the great city?"

"I trust it's the glory o' God, laddie."

"I hope that's not lacking either. For I love God with all my heart. But it's oftener the saving of my earthly father than the glory of my heavenly one that I'm thinking about."

Mrs. Falconer heaved a deep sigh.

"God grant ye success, Robert," she said. "But that can't be right."

"What can't be right?"

"Not t' put the glory o' God first an' foremost."

"But you know there's no glory to God like the repenting of a sinner. What greater glory can God have than that?"

"It's true, what ye say. But still, if God cares for that same glory, ye ought t' think o' that first, even before the salvation o' yer father."

"Maybe you're right, Grannie. And if it be as you say—he's promised to lead us into all truth, and he'll lead me into that truth. But I'm thinking it's more for our sakes than his own that he cares about his glory. I don't believe that he thinks about his glory except for the sake of truth and men's hearts dying for the lack of it."

Mrs. Falconer thought for a moment. "It may be that ye're

right, laddie, but ye hae a way o' saying things that is some fearsome."

"God's not like a proud man to take offense, Grannie. There's nothing that pleases him like the truth, and there's nothing that displeases him like lying, particularly when it's pretended praise. He wants no false praising. Now, you say things about him sometimes that sound fearsome to me."

"What kind o' things, laddie?" asked the old lady, with offense glooming in the background.

"Like when you speak of him as if he were a poor, proud man, full of his own importance and ready to be down on anybody that didn't call him by the name of his office—always thinking about his own glory, instead of the quiet, mighty, grand, self-forgetting, all-creating, loving being that he is. Eh, Grannie! Think of the face of that Man of Sorrows, that never said a hard word to a sinful woman or a despised publican. Was he thinking about his own glory, do you think? And whatever isn't like Christ isn't like God."

"But laddie, he came t' satisfy God's justice by sufferin' the punishment due t' our sins, t' turn aside his wrath an' curse. So Jesus couldn't be altogether God."

"Oh, but he is, Grannie. He came to satisfy God's justice by giving him back his children, by making them see that God was just, by sending them back home to fall at his feet. He came to lift the weight of the sins off the shoulders of them that did them by making them turn against the sin and toward God. And there isn't a word of reconciling God to us in the New Testament, for there was no need of that; it was *us* that needed to be reconciled to him. And so he bore our sins and carried our sorrows, for those sins caused him no end of grief of mind and pain in his body. It wasn't his own sins or God's wrath that caused him suffering, but our own sins. And he took them away. He took our sins upon him, for he came into the middle of them and took them up—by no sleight of hand, by no quibbling of the preachers about imputing his righteousness to us and such like. But he took them and took them away, and here am I, Grannie, growing out of my sins in consequence, and there are you, growing out of yours in consequences, too."

"I wish that may be true, laddie. But I don't care how ye put it," returned his grandmother, bewildered no doubt, "just so long as ye put him first an' say wi' all yer heart, 'His will be done!' "

"His will be done, Grannie," responded Robert readily.[6]

Mary

She sitteth at the Master's feet
  In motionless employ;
Her ears, her heart, her soul complete
  Drinks in the tide of joy.

She is the Earth, and He the Sun;
  He shineth forth her leaves;
She, in new life from darkness won,
  Gives back what she receives.

Ah! who but she the glory knows
  Of life, pure, high, intense;
Whose holy calm breeds awful shows,
  Transfiguring the sense!

The life in voice she drinks like wine;
  The Word and echo found;
Her ear the world, where Thought divine
  Incarnate was in sound.

Her holy eyes, brimful of light,
  Shine all unseen and low;
As if the radiant words all night
  Forth at those orbs would go.

The opening door reveals a face
  Of anxious household state:
"Car'st thou not, Master, for my case,
  "That I alone should wait?"

Heavy with light, she lifts those eyes
  To Him who calmly heard;
Ready that moment to arise,
  And go, before the word.

Her fear is banished by His voice,
  Her fluttering hope set free:
"The needful thing is Mary's choice,
  "She shall remain with Me."

Oh, joy to every doubting heart,
  Doing the thing it would,
If He, the Holy, take its part,
  And call its choice the good!

Not now as then His words are poured
  Into her lonely ears;
But many guests are at the board,
  And many tongues she hears.

With sacred foot she cometh slow,
  With daring, trembling tread;
With shadowing worship bendeth low
  Above the godlike head.

The sacred chrism in snowy stone
  A gracious odor sends.
Her little hoard, so slowly grown,
  In one full act she spends.

She breaks the box, the honoured thing!
  The ointment pours amain;
Her priestly hands anoint her King,
  And He shall live and reign.

They called it waste. Ah, easy well!
  Their love they could endure;
For her, her heart did ache and swell,
  That she forgot the poor.

She meant it for the coming crown;
  He took it for the doom;
And his obedience laid Him down,
  Crowned in the quiet tomb.

4

JESUS THE KING

Thou are the Son of God; thou art the King of Israel.

John 1:49

King by His Essential Being

Consider John 18:36–37: "My kingdom is not of this world. . . . Pilate therefore said unto him, Art thou a king then? Jesus answered, Thou sayest that I am a king. To this end was I born, and for this came I into the world, that I should bear witness unto the truth. Every one that is of the truth heareth my voice."

Pilate asks Jesus if he is a king. The question is called forth by what the Lord had just said concerning his kingdom, closing with the statement that it was not of this world. He now answers Pilate that he is a king indeed, but shows him that his kingdom is of a very different kind from what is called kingdom in this world.

The rank and rule of this world are uninteresting to him.

He might have had them. With his disciples to follow him and twelve legions of angels to help them, he might soon have driven the Romans into the abyss. What would have been easier for him than to have thus cleared the way and then reigned over the world as the just monarch that was the dream of the Jews? He might from Jerusalem have ruled the world, not merely dispensing what men call justice, but compelling atonement.

But he did not care for government. No such kingdom would serve the ends of his Father in heaven, or comfort his own soul.

What was the perfect empire to the Son of God, when he might teach one human being to love his neighbor and be good like his Father! To be a love-helper to one heart, for its joy, and the glory of his Father, was the beginning of true kingship! The Lord would rather wash the feet of his weary brothers than be the one only perfect monarch that ever ruled the world.

It was empire he rejected when he ordered Satan behind him like a dog to his heel. Government, I repeat, was to him flat, stale, unprofitable.

What then is the kingdom over which the Lord cares to reign, for he says he came into the world to be a king? I answer, a kingdom of kings, and no other. Where every man is a king, there and there only does the Lord care to reign, in the name of his Father. The Lord cares for no kingdom over anything this world calls a nation. A king must rule over his own kind. Jesus is a king in virtue of no conquest, inheritance, or election, but in right of his essential being. His subjects must be of his own kind, in their very nature and essence kings.

The Lord's is a kingdom in which no man seeks to be above another: ambition is of the dirt of this world's kingdoms. He says, "I am a king, for I was born for the purpose of bearing witness to the truth." Thereupon Pilate—as would most Christians nowadays—instead of setting about being true, requests a definition of truth, a presentation to his intellect in set terms of what the word "true" means.

Whatever interpretations we put on Pilate's action, he must be far less to be blamed than those "Christians" who, instead of setting themselves to be pure "even as he is pure," to be their brother and sister's keeper, and to serve God by being honorable in shop and office and labor market, proceed to "serve" him, as they would call it, by going to church, some by condemning the opinions of their neighbors, and some by teaching others what they do not themselves heed. Neither Pilate nor they ask the one true question, *How am I to be a true man? How am I to become a man or woman worth bearing the name?*

The Lord is a king because his life, the life of his thoughts, of his imagination, of his will, of every smallest action, is true—true first to God in that he is altogether his, true to himself in that he forgets himself altogether, and true to his fellows in that he will endure anything they do to him without ceasing to declare himself the Son and messenger and likeness of God.

They will kill him, but it matters not: the truth *is* as he says!

Bearing Witness to the Truth

Jesus is a king because his business is to bear witness to the truth: all truth; all verity of relation throughout the universe—first of all, that his Father is good, perfectly good, and that the crown and joy of life is to desire and do the will of the eternal source of will and of all life.

He deals thus the death blow to the power of hell. For the one principle of hell is, "I am my own. I am my own king and my own subject. *I* am the center from which go out my thoughts. *I* am the object and end of my thoughts. My own glory is my chief care; my ambition to gather the regards of men to myself. My pleasure is *my* pleasure. My right is what I desire. I will be free with the freedom that consists in doing whatever I am inclined to do. To do my own will, so long as I feel anything to be my will, is to be free, is to live."

To all these principles of hell, or of this world—they are the same thing, and it matters not whether they are actually said or defended so long as they are acted upon—the lord, the king, gives the direct lie. It is as if he said: "My perfect freedom, my pure individuality, rests on the fact that I have no other will than my Father's. My will is all for his will, for his will is right. He is righteousness itself. His very being is love and equity and self-devotion, and he will have his children such as himself—creatures of love, of fairness, of self-devotion to him and their fellows. I was born to bear witness to the truth—in my own person to be the truth visible, the very likeness and manifestation of the God who is true. My very being is his witness. Every fact of me witnesses him. He is the truth, and I am the truth."

Remember, friends, I said, "It is as if he said." I am daring to present a shadow of the Lord's witnessing. If I mistake, he will forgive me. I do not fear him; I fear only lest, able to see and write these things, I should fail of witnessing to them, and be, after all, no king but a talker, no disciple of Jesus, ready to go with him to the death, but an arguer about the truth, and not a doer of the Word.

We see, then, that the Lord bore his witness to the Truth, to the one God, by standing as just what he was before the eyes and lies of men. The true king is the man who stands up as a true man and speaks the truth, and will die but not lie. The robes of such a king may be rags or purple; it matters neither way. The rags are the more likely, but neither better nor worse than the robes. Of the men who before Christ bore witness to the truth, some were sawn asunder, some subdued kingdoms. It matters nothing which; they witnessed.

The truth is *God*; the witness to the truth is Jesus. The kingdom of the truth is the hearts of men. The bliss of men is the true God. The thought of God is the truth of everything. All well-being lies in true relation to God. The man who responds to this with his whole being is of the truth. The man who knows these things, but merely knows them in his head; the man who sees them to be true, and does not order life and action, judgment and love by them, is of the worst of lying.

Little thought the sons of Zebedee and their ambitious mother what the earthly throne of Christ's glory was which they and she begged they might share. For the king witnessed to the height of his uttermost argument when he hung upon the cross. Infinitely more than had he sat on the throne of the whole earth, did Jesus witness to the truth when Pilate brought him out for the last time, saying, "Behold your king!" Just because of the those robes and that crown, that scepter and that throne of ridicule, he was the only real king that ever sat on any throne.

Is every Christian expected to bear witness? A man content to bear no witness to the truth is not in the kingdom of heaven: One who believes must bear witness. One who sees the truth must live witnessing to it. Is our life, then, a witnessing to the truth? Do we carry ourselves in bank, on farm, in house or store, in study or room or workshop as the Lord would, or as the Lord would not?

Are we true? Do we try to live to the height of our ideas? Or are we self-serving? When contempt is cast on the truth, what is our reaction? When the truth is wronged in our presence, do we make no sign that we hold by it?

I do not say we are called upon to dispute and defend the truth with logic and argument, but we are called upon to show by our lives that we stand on the side of truth. But when I say *truth*, I do not mean *opinion*. To treat opinion as if that were truth is grievously to wrong the truth. The soul that loves the truth and tries to be true will know when to speak and when to be silent. Jesus defended his kingship, not with argument, logic, or opinion, but rather by the laying down of his earthly life. He bore witness to the truth, not by words, but by the essence of his very being. Thus he *is* king, today, as he was when he spoke the words to Pilate. And his kingdom is still not of this world.[1]

WHO IS CHRIST? WHAT AM I DOING AS A RESULT?

(A Fictional Selection from *The Curate's Awakening*)

There are those who in their very first seeking of it are nearer to the kingdom of heaven than many who have for years believed themselves in it. In the former there is more of the mind of Jesus, and when he calls them, they recognize him at once and go after him. The others examine him from head to foot, and finding him not sufficiently like the Jesus of their conception, turn their backs, and go to church to kneel before a vague form mingled of tradition and imagination.

Wingfold soon found that his nature was being stirred to depths unsuspected before. His first sermon showed that he had begun to have thoughts of his own. The news of that strange outpouring of honesty had of course spread through the town, and the people came to church the next Sunday in crowds—twice as many as the usual number—some who went seldom, some who went nowhere, some who belonged to other congregations. Mostly they were bent on witnessing whatever eccentricity the very peculiar young man might be guilty of next.

His second sermon was like the first. Proposing no text, he spoke the following:

"This church stands here in the name of Christianity. But what is Christianity? I know but one definition. Christianity does not mean what you think or what I think concerning Christ, but who *Christ is*. Last Sunday I showed you our Lord's very words—that anyone is his disciple who does what he commands. I said, therefore, that I dared not call myself a disciple, a Christian. Yet it is in the name of Christianity that I stand here. I have signed my name as a believer to the articles of the Church of England, with no better reason than that I had no particular dissent with any of the points of it at the time. Thus, knowing no better, I was ordained as one of her ministers. So it remains my business, as an honest man in the employment of the church, to do my best to set forth the claims of Jesus Christ, upon whom the church is founded and in whose name she exists. As one standing on the outskirts of a listening Galilean crowd, a word comes now and then to my hungry ears and hungrier heart. I turn and tell it again to you—not that you have not heard it also. If anything, I certainly am behind you rather than ahead of you in the hearing of these things. I tell you what I have learned only that I may stir you up to ask yourselves, as I ask myself, 'Do I then obey this word? Have I ever, have I once, sought to obey it? Am I a pupil of Jesus? Am I a Christian?' Hear then his words. For me, they fill my heart with doubt and dismay.

"The Lord says, *'Love your enemies.'* Do you say, *'It is impossible'*? Do you say, *'Alas, I cannot'*? But have you tried to see whether he who made you will not increase your strength when you step out to obey him?

"The Lord says, *'Be perfect.'* Do you then aim for perfection, or do you excuse your shortcomings and say, *'To err is human'*? If so, then you must ask yourself what part you have in him.

"The Lord says, *'Lay not up for yourselves treasures on earth.'* My part is not now to preach against the love of money, but to ask you, *'Are you laying up for yourselves treasures on earth'*? As to what the command means, the honest heart and the dishonest must each settle it in his own way. No doubt you can point to other men who are no better than you, and of whom yet no one would dare question the validity of their Christianity. But all that matters not a hair. All that does is confirm that you may all be pagans together. Do not mistake me. I am not judging you. For my finger points at myself along with you. But I ask you simply to judge yourselves by the words of Jesus.

"The Lord says, *'Take no thought for your life. Take no thought for tomorrow.'* Explain it as you may, but ask yourselves, *'Do I take no thought for my life? Do I take no thought for tomorrow?'*

"The Lord says, *'Judge not.'* Did you judge your neighbor yesterday? Will you judge him again tomorrow? Are you judging him now in the very heart that sits hearing the words, *'Judge not'*? Or do you sidestep the command by asking, 'Who is my neighbor?' Does not your own profession of Christianity counsel you to fall upon your face, and cry to him, 'I am a sinful man, O Lord'?

"The Lord said, *'All things you would that men should do to you, do also to them.'* You that buy and sell, do you obey this law? Examine yourselves and see. You would want men to deal fairly to you: do you deal just as fairly to them as you would count fairness in them toward you? If conscience makes you hang your head inwardly, however you sit with it erect in the pew, can you dare to add to your crime against the law and the prophets the insult to Christ of calling yourselves his disciples?

" 'Not every one that says unto me, "Lord, Lord," shall enter into the kingdom of heaven, but he that does the will of my Father who is in heaven.' "[2]

Three Sonnets

If Thou hadst been a painter, what fresh looks,
What shining of pent glories, what new grace
Had burst upon us from the great Earth's face!
How had we read, as in new-languaged books,
Clear love of God in lone retreating nooks!
A lily, as thy hand its form would trace,
Were plainly seen God's child, of lower race;
And, O my heart, blue hills! and grassy brooks!
Thy soul lay to all undulations bare,
Answering in waves. Each morn the sun did rise,
And God's world woke beneath life-giving skies,
Thou sawest clear thy Father's meanings there;
'Mid Earth's Ideal, and expressions rare,
The ideal Man, with the eternal eyes.

But I have looked on pictures made by man,
Wherein, at first, appeared but chaos wild:
So high the art transcended, it beguiled
The eye as formless, and without a plan;
Until the spirit, brooding o'er, began
To see a purpose rise, like mountains piled,
When God said: Let the dry earth, undefiled,
Rise from the waves: it rose in twilight wan.
And so I fear thy pictures were too strange
For us to pierce beyond their outmost look;
A vapour and a darkness; a sealed book;
An atmosphere too high for wings to range:
At God's designs our spirits pale and change,
Trembling as at a void, thought cannot brook.

And is not Earth thy living picture, where
Thou utterest beauty, simple and profound,
In the same form by wondrous union bound;
Where one may see the first step of the stair,
And not the next, for brooding vapours there?
And God is well content the starry round
Should wake the infant's inarticulate sound,
Or lofty song from bursting heart of prayer.
And so all men of low or lofty mind,
Who in their hearts hear thy unspoken word,
Have lessons low or lofty, to their kind,
In these thy living shows of beauty, Lord;
While the child's heart that simply childlike is,
Knows that the Father's face looks full in his.

5

GOD THE CREATOR OF TRUTH

The heavens declare the glory of God; and the firmament
sheweth his handywork.

Psalm 19:1

Fact and Truth

If the story of Jesus Christ is true, there must be a Father to be loved. The poorest glimmer of Christ's loveliness gives a dawn to our belief in God, and even a small amount of genuine knowledge of him will neutralize the most confident declaration against him.

Nothing can be known except what is true. A negative may be a *fact*, but it cannot be *known* except by the knowledge of its opposite. Nothing can really be *believed*, except it be true. But people think they believe many things they do not and *cannot*, in the real sense, believe.[1]

If the Lord calls himself the truth, it must be well for us to know what he means by the word with which he identifies himself. Let us therefore try to arrive at his meaning by a gently ascending stair.

If a thing is so, the word that declares it is the truth.

But the fact may or may not be of value in itself. Of most facts it may be said that the truth concerning them is of no consequence.

For instance, it cannot be in itself important whether on a certain morning I took one side of the street or the other. It may be of importance to someone to know which I took. But *in itself* it is of none.

It would therefore be improper for me to say, "It is *a truth* that I walked on the sunny side." The correct word would be *a fact*, not *a truth*.

If a question arose whether a statement concerning the thing were correct, we should still be in the region of fact. But when we come to ask whether the statement was true or false, then we are concerned with the matter as the assertion of a human being and ascend to another plane of things. It may be of no consequence which side I was on, or it may be of some consequence to someone else to know which side I was on. But it is of vital importance to the witness who takes it upon himself to declare which side I was on, whether or not he believes the statement he makes—whether the man himself is true or false.

Concerning the thing itself, it can be a question of *fact*. It remains a question of fact even whether the man has or has not spoken the truth. But concerning the man himself it is a question of truth: he is either a pure soul as far as his witness of this particular thing is concerned, or he is a false soul, capable and guilty of a lie.

There are both *truths* as well as *facts*. And there can be lies against truths as well as facts. Mistaking which side of the street I walked on is a misrepresentation of a fact. When the Pharisees said *Corban*, they lied against the truth that a man must honor his father and mother.

Law

Let us go up now from the region of facts that seem casual, to those facts that are invariable, by us unchangeable, which therefore involve what we call law.

It will be seen at once that the *fact* here is of more dignity, and the truth or falsehood of a statement in this region of more consequence in itself. It is a small matter whether the water in my jug was frozen on a certain morning. But it is a fact of great importance that at thirty-two degrees Fahrenheit water always freezes. We rise a step here in the nature of facts.

The question may then be asked: have we come therefore into the region of truths? Is it a truth that water freezes at thirty-two degrees?

I think not. There is no principle, open to us, involved in the changeless fact. The principle that lies at the root of it in the mind of God must be a truth, but to the human mind the fact is as yet only a fact.

The word *truth* ought to be kept for higher things.

There are those who think such facts the highest that can be known. Therefore they put the highest word they know to the highest thing they know, and call the facts of nature truths. But it seems to me that however high you come in your generalization, however wide you make your law—including, for instance, all solidity under the law of freezing—even to the point of embodying all the laws of physics related to the workings of matter, you have still not risen higher than the statement that such and such is an invariable fact.

If it always is so, call it a law, if you will—a law of nature, if you choose—but not a truth. It cannot be to us a truth until we discover the reason of its existence, its relation to mind and intent, yes, to self-existence. Tell us why it *must* be so, and you state a truth.

When Fact and Law Become Truth

When we come to see that a law is such because it is the embodiment of a certain eternal thought, beheld by us in it, a fact of the being of God, the facts of which alone are truths, then indeed it will be to us, not a law merely, but an embodied truth.

A law of God's nature is a way he would have us think of him; it is a necessary truth of all being.

When a law of nature makes us see this; when we say, "I understand that law; I see why it ought to be; it is just like God," then it rises, not to the dignity of a truth in itself, but to the truth of its own nature—namely, a revelation of character, nature, and will in God. It is a picture of something in God, a word that tells a fact about God. It is therefore far nearer being called a truth than anything below it.

I believe that every fact in nature is a revelation of God, is there such as it is because God is such as he is. And I suspect that all its facts impress us so that we learn of God unconsciously. True, we cannot think of any one fact thus, except as we find the soul of it—its fact of God. But from the moment when first we come into contact with the world, it is to us a revelation of God, his things seen, by which we come to know the things unseen.

How should we imagine what we may of God, without the firmament over our heads, a visible sphere, yet a formless infinitude! The truth of the sky is what it makes us feel of the God that sent it out to our eyes. If you say the sky could not but be such and so, I grant it—with God at the root of it. In its discovered laws, light seems to me to be such because God is such. Its so-called laws are the waving of his garments, waving so because he is thinking and loving and walking inside them.

God's Idea of the Flower

We have now come into a region far above that commonly claimed for science, open only to the heart of the child and the childlike man and woman—a region in which the poet is among his own things, and to which he has often to go to fetch them.

For things as they truly exist are the revelation of God to his children. There is no fact of science not yet incorporated in a law, no law of science that has got beyond the hypothetical and tentative, that has not in it the will of God, and therefore may not reveal God. But neither fact nor law is there for the sake of fact or law. Each is but a means to an end; in the perfected end we find the intent, and there God—not in the laws themselves, except as his means of revealing himself.

For that same reason, human science cannot discover God. For human science is but the backward undoing of the tapestry-web of God's science, it works with its back to him, and is always leaving him—his intent, that is, his perfected work—behind it, always going farther and farther away from the point where his work culminates in revelation. Doubtless it thus makes some small intellectual approach to him, but at best it can only come to his back. Science will never find the face of God; while those who would reach his heart will find also the springhead of his science.

Analysis is good, as death is good. But neither is life. Mere science, in and of itself, is a following back of God's footsteps, too often without appreciation of the result for which the feet took those steps. If a man could find out why God worked in such and such a way, he would be discovering God. But even then he would not be discovering the best and the deepest of God; for God's means cannot be so great as his ends.

Ask a man of mere science what is the truth of the flower. He will pull it to pieces, show you its parts, explain how they operate, how they each minister to the life of the flower. He will tell you what changes are wrought in it by scientific cultivation; where it lived originally, where it can live, the effects upon it of another climate, what part the insects bear in its varieties—and no doubt many more facts about it.

Ask the poet what is the truth of the flower, and he will answer: "Why the flower itself, the perfect flower, and what it cannot help saying to him who has ears to hear it."

The truth of the flower is not the facts about it, however completely correct they may be. Rather the truth of the flower is the shining, glowing, gladdening, patient thing throned on its stalk—the compeller of smile and tear from child and prophet.

The man whose brain is filled with facts, but whose heart is yet unopen to truths, laughs at this because he does not know what it means. But the poet and the child care as little for his laughter as the birds of God care for his treatises. The children of God must always be mocked by the children of the world—children with sharp ears and eyes, but dull hearts.

God's science in the flower exists for the existence of the flower in its relation to his children. If we understand, if we are at one with, if we love the flower, we have that for which the science is there, that which alone can equip us for the true search into the means and ways by which the divine idea of the flower was made to be presented to us.

The idea of God *is* the flower. His idea is not the botany of the flower. Its botany is but a thing of ways and means—of canvas and color and brush in relation to the picture in the painter's brain. The mere intellect can never find out that which owes its being to the heart.

The idea of God, I repeat, is the flower. He thought it, invented its means, sent it, a gift of himself, to the eyes and hearts of his children. When we see how they are loved by the ignorant and poor, we may well believe the flowers have a place in the history of the world, as written for the archives of heaven, that we are yet a long way from understanding.

Watch that child kneeling in the grass! He has found one of his silent and motionless brothers, with God's clothing upon it, God's thought in its face. Watch his mother when he takes it home to her! It is no old memory that brings those tears to her eyes, powerful in that way as are flowers. Rather it is God's thought, unrecognized as such, holding communion with her. She weeps with a delight inexplicable. It may be only a daisy, only a primrose, only a narcissus, only a lily of the field, only a snowdrop, only a sweetpea, only a brave yellow crocus! But here to her is no mere fact. Here is no law of nature. Here is a *truth* of nature, the truth of a flower—a perfect thought from the heart of God—a truth of God! Not an intellectual truth, but a divine fact, a dim revelation, a movement of the creative soul! Who but a Father could think up, call into being, such creations as the flowers for his little ones?

Now at last we are near the region in which the Lord's word is at home—"I am the truth."[2]

HOW RICH GOD IS

(A Fictional Selection from *The Laird's Inheritance*)

The wind kept him company as he walked, flitting softly about him, like an attendant that needed more motion than the young man's pace would afford. The breeze seemed so full of thought and love that he found himself wondering if all things having to do with the earth might not—in the true eternal reality—be in fact spirit rather than what we call *matter*. Then came the thought of the infinitude of our moods, of the hues and shades and endless kinds and varieties of feeling, especially in our dreams. And he said to himself how rich God must be, since from him we become capable of such differences and depths of conscious life.

How poor and helpless, he said to himself; *what a mere pilgrim and stranger in this world must he be who does not have God one with him! Without God life cannot be free. In no other way can we move in harmony with the will and life of all that is about us!*

As he walked up the hill thinking, the stream was by his side, tumbling out its music as it ran to find its eternity. And the wind blew on from the moist west, where the gold and purple had fallen together in a ruined heap over the tomb of the sun. And the stars came thinking out of the heavens, and the things of the earth withdrew into the great nest of the dark.[3]

From:

Somnium Mystici

Lord, I have spoken a poor parable,
    In which I would have said thy name alone
    Is the one secret lying in Truth's well,
Thy voice the hidden charm in every tone,
    Thy face the heart of every flower on earth,
    Its vision the one hope; for every moan
Thy love the cure! O sharer of the birth
    Of little children seated on thy knee!
    O human God! I laugh with sacred mirth
To think how all the laden shall go free;
    For, though the vision tarry, in healing ruth
    One morn the eyes that shone in Galilee
Will dawn upon them, full of grace and truth,
    And thy own love—the vivifying core
    Of every love in heart of age or youth,
Of every hope that sank 'neath burden sore!

6

JESUS THE TRUTH

I am . . . the truth.

John 14:6

Truth, the Blossom

To love the truth is a far greater thing than to know it, for it is itself truth in the inward parts—*act-truth*, as distinguished from *fact-truth*. In the highest truth the knowledge and love of it are one, or, if not identical, then coincident. The very sight of the truth is the loving of it.[1]

What is the truth of water?

Is it that it is formed of hydrogen and oxygen? Is it for the sake of the fact that hydrogen and oxygen combined form water that the precious thing exists? Or has God put the two together only that man might separate and find them out? He allows his child to pull his toys to pieces, but was that the purpose for which they were made? A schoolteacher might see therein the best use of a toy, but not a father!

Find what in the constitution of the two gases makes them fit and capable to be thus honored in forming the lovely thing and you will give us a revelation about more than water, namely about the God who made oxygen and hydrogen. There is no water in oxygen, no water in hydrogen. It comes bubbling fresh from the imagination of the living God, rushing from under the great white throne of the glacier.

The very thought of it makes one gasp with an elemental joy no metaphysician can analyze. The water itself, that dances, and sings, and slakes the wonderful thirst—symbol and picture of that draught for which the woman of Samaria made her prayer to Jesus—this lovely thing itself, whose very wetness is a delight to every inch of the human body in its embrace, this live thing, which, if I could, I would have babbling through my room, this water is its own self, its own truth and is therein a truth of God.

Let him who would know the love of the Maker become sorely athirst and drink of the brook beside his path—then lift up his heart to the inventor and mediator of thirst and water, that man might foresee a little of what his soul may find in God. If he become not then as a hart panting for the water-brooks, let him go back to his science and its husks; for they will in the end make him thirsty.

Let a man go to the hillside and let the brook sing to him until he loves it, and he will find himself far nearer the fountain of truth than any triumphal chemist at the moment of a great discovery. He will draw from the brook the water of joyous tears, "and worship him that made heaven, and earth, and the sea, and the fountain of waters."

The truth of a thing, then, is the blossom of it, the thing it is made for, the topmost stone set on with rejoicing. Truth in a man's imagination is the power to recognize this truth of a thing. And wherever, in anything that God has made, in the glory of it, be it sky or flower or human face, we see the glory of God, there a true imagination is beholding a truth of God.

Moral Facts—The Doing of Truth

The moment that whatever goes by the name of truth comes into connection with man, the moment that, instead of merely mirroring itself in his intellect as a thing outside of him, it comes into contact with him as a being of action, the moment the knowledge of it affects or ought to affect his sense of duty, it becomes a thing of far nobler import.

The question of truth then enters upon a higher plane, looks out of a loftier window.

A fact, which in itself is of no value, becomes at once a matter of moral life and death when a man has the imperative choice of being true or false concerning it. When the truth, the heart, the summit, the crown of a thing is perceived by a man, he approaches the fountain of truth whence the thing came, and perceiving God by understanding what it is, becomes more of a man, more of the being he was meant to be. In virtue of this perceived truth, he has relations with the universe until then undeveloped in him. But far higher will the doing of the least, the most insignificant duty raise him.

There, in the obedience of his *actions*, he begins to be a true man.

A man may delight in the vision and glory of a truth, and not himself be true. The man whose vision is weak, but who—as far as he sees, and wanting to see farther—does the thing he sees, is a true man. The man who recognizes the truth of any human relation and neglects the duty involved is not a true man. The man who knows the laws of nature and does not heed them, the more he teaches them to others, the less he is a true man. The man who takes good care of himself and none of his brother and sister is false. A man may be a poet or preacher, student or teacher, aware of the highest truths of many things, aware of that beauty which is the final cause of existence; he may be a man who would not tell a lie, or steal, or slander; and yet he may not be a true man, inasmuch as the essentials of manhood are not his aim: he has not come into the flower of his own being.

There are relations closer than those of the facts around him that he is failing to see, or seeing, fails to acknowledge, or acknowledging, fails to fulfill. Man is man only in the doing of truth; perfect man, only in the doing of the highest truth, which is the fulfilling of his relations to his origin. Fulfilling them, he is himself a *truth*, a living truth. The man is a true man who chooses duty; he is a perfect man who at length never thinks of duty. Relations, truths, duties are shown to the man away beyond him, that he may choose them, and be a child of God, choosing righteousness like him.

The man who regards duties only as facts, or even the man who regards them as essential truths, but goes no farther, is a man of untruth. He is a man indeed, but not a true man. He is a man in possibility, but not yet in reality. The recognition of these things is the imperative obligation to fulfill them. Not fulfilling these relations, these duties, a man is undoing the right of his own existence, destroying his raison d'être.

When the soul, or heart, or spirit, or whatever you please to call that which is the man himself and not his body, sooner or later becomes aware that he needs someone above him, whom to obey, in whom to rest, from whom to seek deliverance from what in himself is despicable, disappointing, and unworthy, then indeed is that man in the region of truth, and beginning to come true in himself. When a man bows down before a power that can account for him, a power that knows whence he came and whither he is going, who knows everything about him and can set him right, longs indeed to set him right, making of him a creature confident as a child whom his father is leading by the hand to the heights of happy-making truth—then is that man bursting into his flower. Then the truth of his being, his real nature—born in God at first, and responsive to the truth, the being of God, his origin— begins to show itself. Then is his nature coming into harmony with itself.

In obeying the will that is the cause of his being, he begins to stand on the apex of his being. He begins to feel himself free. The truth—not as known to his intellect, but as revealed in his own sense of being true—has made him free.

No abstract truth held by purest insight can make a man free. But the truth done, the truth loved, the truth lived by the man, the truth *of* and not merely *in* the man himself—that is the truth that makes him free.

Jesus, the Live Truth

The one originating, living, visible truth, embracing all truths in all relations, is Jesus Christ.

He is true. He is *the* live truth. His truth, chosen and willed by him, the ripeness of his being, the flower of his sonship, which is his nature, the crown of his one topmost perfect relation acknowledged and gloried in, is his absolute obedience to his Father.

The obedient Jesus is Jesus, the Truth.

He is true and the root of all truth and development of truth in men. Their very being, however far from the true human, is the undeveloped Christ in them, and his likeness to Christ is the truth of a man, even as the perfect meaning of a flower is the truth of a flower.

The Blossom of Every Man and Woman

When an individual is, with his whole nature, loving and willing the truth, he or she is then a live truth. This he has not originated in himself. He has seen it and striven for it, but not originated it.

The truth of every man, I say, is the perfected Christ in him. As Christ is the blossom of humanity, so the blossom of every man is the Christ perfected in him. The vital force of humanity working in him is Christ; He is his root—the generator and perfector of his individuality. The stronger the pure will of the man to be true, the freer and more active his choice, the more definite his individuality, ever the more is the man and all that is his, Christ's. Without him he could not have been; being, he could not have become capable of truth; capable of truth, he could never have loved it; loving and desiring it, he could not have attained to it.

God gives us the will wherewith to will, and the power to use it. But we ourselves must will the truth, and for that the Lord is waiting. The work is his, but we must take our willing share.

When the blossom breaks forth in us, the more it is ours, the more it is his. For the highest creation of the Father is the being that can, like the Father and Son, of his own self will what is right. The groaning and travailing, the blossom and the joy, are the Father's and the Son's and ours. The will, the power of willing, may be created, but the willing is begotten. Because God wills first, man wills also.

When my being is consciously and willingly in the hands of him who called it to live and think and suffer and be glad—given back to him by a perfect obedience—I thenceforward breathe the breath, share the life of God himself. Then I am free, and in that I am true—which means one with the Father. And freedom knows itself to be freedom.

When a man is true, if he were in hell, he could not be miserable. He is right with himself, because right with him from whom he came. To be right with God is to be right with the universe; one with the power, the love, the will of the mighty Father, the cherisher of joy, the Lord of laughter, whose are all glories, all hopes, who loves everything, and hates nothing but selfishness, which he will not have in his kingdom.

Christ then is the Lord of life. His life is the light of men. The light mirrored in them changes them into the image of him, the Truth.

And thus the Truth, who is the Son, makes them free.[2]

The True

I envy the tree-tops that shake so high
  In winds that fill them full of heavenly airs;
I envy every little cloud that shares
With unseen angels evening in the sky;
I envy most the youngest stars that lie
  Sky-nested, and the loving heaven that bears,
    And night that makes strong worlds of them unawares;
And all God's other beautiful and nigh!

Nay, nay, I envy not! And these are dreams,
  Fancies and images of real heaven!
  My longings, all my longing prayers are given
For that which is, and not for that which seems.
  Draw me, O Lord, to thy true heaven above,
  The Heaven of thy Thought, thy Rest, thy Love.

LEARNING FROM THE BODIES OF THINGS

(A Fictional Selection from *The Seaboard Parish*)

Everything has a soul and a body, or something like them. By the body we know the soul. But we are always ready to love the body instead of the soul. Therefore, God makes the body die continually, that we may learn to love the soul indeed. The world is full of beautiful things, but God has saved many men from loving the mere bodies of them by making them poor. Alas for some Christians!—Bibles even, shall vanish away. I say *alas* only from their point of view, not from mine. I mean such as are always talking and arguing from the Bible, and never giving themselves any trouble to do what it tells them. They insist on the anise and cummin, and forget the judgment, mercy, and faith. They worship the body of truth and forget the soul of it.

If the flowers were not perishable, we should cease to contemplate their beauty, either blinded by the passion for hoarding the bodies of them, or dulled by the commonplaceness that the constant presence of them would occasion.

To compare great things with small, the flowers wither, the bubbles break, the clouds and sunsets pass, for the very same holy reason, in the degree of its application to them, for which the Lord withdrew from his disciples and ascended again to his Father—that the Comforter, the Spirit of Truth, the Soul of things, might come to them and abide with them, and so, the Son return, and the Father be revealed.

The flower is not its loveliness. And it is its *loveliness* we must love, else we shall treat them only as flower-greedy children, who gather and gather and fill hands and baskets from a mere desire of acquisition.

Therefore God, that we may always have them, and ever learn to love their beauty, and yet more truth, sends the beneficent winter that we may think about what we have lost, and welcome them when they come again with greater tenderness and love, and with clearer eyes to see, and purer hearts to understand, the spirit that dwells in them.[3]

Rondel

I do not know thy final will,
  It is too good for me to know:
  Thou willest that I mercy show,
That I take heed and do no ill,
That I the needy warm and fill,
  Nor stones at any sinner throw;
But I know not thy final will—
  It is too good for me to know.

I know thy love unspeakable—
  For love's sake able to send woe!
  To find thine own thou lost didst go,
And wouldst for men thy blood yet spill!—
How should I know thy final will,
  Godwise too good for me to know!

7

ℐESUS, TEACHER OF MEN

*I have yet many things to say unto you, but ye cannot bear them now.
Howbeit when he, the Spirit of truth, is come, he will guide
you into all truth.*

John 16:12–13

God Has Not Revealed Everything

The aspiring child, or new learner in the things of faith, is often checked by the dull teacher who has learned his lessons so imperfectly that he has never got beyond his schoolbooks. Full of fragmentary rules, he has perceived the principle of none of them. The child draws near to him with some outburst of unusual feeling, some scintillation of a lively hope, some wide-reaching imagination that draws the world of nature and the yet wider world of humanity into the circle of religious theory, with his heart full, only to be told by his dull teacher, "God has said nothing about that in his Word; therefore we have no right to speculate on such matters."

For such a teacher is incapable of suspecting that what has remained hidden from him may have been revealed to the babe. He believes in no revelation but the Bible, and in the Word of that alone. For him all revelation has ceased with and been buried in the Bible, to be with difficulty exhumed, and, with much questioning of the decayed form, reunited into a rigid skeleton of metaphysical and legal contrivance for letting the love of God have its way unchecked.

But to the man who would live throughout the whole divine form of God's being, not confining himself to one broken corner of his kingdom, and leaving the rest to the demons that haunt such deserts, a thousand questions will arise to which the Bible does not even allude.

Has man nothing to do with such? Do they lie beyond the sphere of his responsibility?

No. Questions imply answers. If God has put the questions in my heart, then he must hold the answers in his. I will seek them from him. I will wait, but not until I have knocked. I will be patient, but not until I have asked. I will seek until I find. He has something for me. My prayer shall go up unto the God of my life.

Sad indeed would the whole matter be if the Bible told us *everything* God meant us to believe. But herein is the Bible itself greatly wronged. It nowhere lays claim to be regarded as *the* Word, *the* Way, *the* Truth. The Bible leads us to Jesus, the inexhaustible, the ever-unfolding Revelation of God. It is Christ "in whom are hid all the treasures of wisdom and knowledge," not the Bible, except as leading to him.

Jesus Will Reveal Truth

And why are we told that these treasures are hid in him who is the *Revelation* of God? So that we should *not* seek the Revelation?

Surely not. Are they not hid in him that they may be revealed to us in due time—that is, when we are in need of them? Is not their hiding in him the mediatorial step toward their unfolding in us? Is he not the Truth—the Truth to men? Is he not the High Priest of his brethren, to answer all the troubled questionings that arise in their dim humanity?

Certainly there may be things which the mere passing into another stage of existence will illuminate. But the questions that come here must be inquired into here. There is more hid in Christ than we shall ever learn, here or there either; but they that begin first to inquire will soonest be gladdened with revelation; and with them he will be best pleased, for the slowness of his disciples troubled him of old. To say that we must wait for the other world, to know the mind of him who came to this world to give himself to us, seems to me the foolishness of a worldly and lazy spirit.

The Son of God *is* the Teacher of men, giving to them of his Spirit— that Spirit which manifests the deep things of God, being to a man the mind of Christ.

The great heresy of the church in the present day is unbelief in this Spirit. The mass of the church does not believe that the Spirit has a revelation for every man individually. If we were once filled with the mind of Christ, we would know that the Bible had done its work and was fulfilled, that thereby the Word of our God might abide forever. The one use of the Bible is to make us look at Jesus, that through him we might know his Father and our Father, his God and our God. Till we thus know God, let us hold the Bible dear as the moon of our darkness, by which we travel toward the east; not dear as the sun whence her light comes, and toward which we haste, that, walking in the Sun himself, we may no more need the mirror that reflected his absent brightness.

It Pleases God for Us to Seek Truth

I think that a man will please God by believing some things that are not told him, not confining his faith only to those things that are expressly said—said to arouse in us the truth-seeing faculty, the spiritual desire, the prayer for the good things that God will give to them that ask him.

"But this is dangerous doctrine. Will not a man thus come to believe the things he likes best, forming his beliefs according to his own opinion rather than by the truth of God's Word?"

There is of course this possibility, to the degree that the man is not completely humble and honest in his quest for truth. If the man is of the Lord's company, he is safer with the Lord than with those who would secure their safety by hanging on the outskirts and daring nothing. If he is not taught of God on some particular question, God will let him know it. If it be possible he can pray to God for anything not good, the answer will come in the flames of that consuming fire. These will soon bring him to some of his spiritual senses. But it will be far better for him to be thus sharply tutored, than to go on at a snail's pace in the journey of the spiritual life.

And to whom shall a man, whom the blessed God has made, look for what he likes best, but to that blessed God? If we have been indeed enabled to see that God is our Father, as the Lord taught us, let us advance from that truth to understand that he is far more than Father— that his nearness to us is beyond the embodiment of the highest idea of father; that the fatherhood of God is but a step toward the Godhood for them that can receive it. What a man likes best may be God's will. And if, as I have said, it be not so—there is the consuming fire.

The danger lies not in asking from God what is not good, but in not asking him at all, in not having him of our council.

Let Us Dare Think High of God

But it is about hopes rather than prayers that I wish to write. What should I think of my child if I found that he limited his faith in me and hope from me to the few promises he had heard me utter? The faith that limits itself to the promises of God seems to me of the same paltry character as that of my child—good enough for pagan, but for a Christian, a miserable faith indeed. Those who rest in such a faith try to believe in the truth of God's Word, but the truth of his *being*, they understand not. They persuade themselves that they have confidence in his promises, as pledges of his honor; in *himself*, his being, the outcome of his character, they do not believe, for they know him not.

Brother, sister, if such is your faith, you must come out of this bondage of the law to which you give the name of grace, for there is little that is gracious in you. You will yet know the dignity of your high calling and the love of God that passeth knowledge. He is not afraid of your presumptuous approach to him. It is you who are afraid to come near him. He is not watching over his dignity. It is you who fear to be sent away as the disciples would have sent away the little children. It is you who think so much about your souls and are so afraid of losing your life, that you dare not draw near to the Life of life, lest it should consume you.

Our God, we will trust thee. Shall we not find thee equal to our faith? One day we shall laugh ourselves to scorn that we looked for so little from thee, for thy giving will not be limited by our hoping. O thou of little faith!

"In everything," says St. Paul, "In everything, by prayer and supplication, with thanksgiving, let your requests be made known unto God."

For this *everything*, nothing is too small. And surely for his *everything*, nothing can be too great. When the Son of man comes and finds too much faith on the earth, may God in his mercy slay us. Meantime, we will hope and trust.

Do you count it a great faith to believe what God has said? It seems to me, I repeat, a little faith. To believe what he has *not* said is faith indeed! For that comes of believing in *him*!

Let us then dare something. Let us not always be unbelieving children: Let us keep in mind that the Lord, not forbidding those who insist on seeing before they will believe, blesses those who have not seen and yet have believed—those who trust in him more than that, who believe without the sight of the eyes, without the hearing of the ears. It is dullhearted, unchildlike people who are always reminding God of his promises. Those promises are good to reveal what God is. But if they think them good as binding God, let them have it so for the hardness of their hearts. They prefer the Word to the Spirit.

But let *us* dare to look beyond, to the "uncovenanted mercies of

God." Those are the mercies beyond our height, beyond our depth, beyond our reach. We know in whom we have believed, and we look for that which has not entered into the heart of man to conceive.

Shall God's thoughts be surpassed by man's thoughts? God's giving by man's asking? God's creation by man's imagination?

No. Let us climb to the height of our Alpine hopes. Let us leave them behind and ascend the spear-pointed Himalayas of our aspirations. Still we shall find the depth of God's sapphire above us. Still we shall find the heavens higher than the earth, and his thoughts and his ways higher than our thoughts and our ways.

Ah, Lord! Be thou in all our being. We dare not think that some things are not for thy beholding, some questions not to be asked of thee. For are we not all thine—utterly thine? Our very passions we hold up to thee, and say, "Behold, Lord! Think about us, for thou hast made us." We would not escape from our history by fleeing into the wilderness, by hiding our heads in the sands of forgetfulness, or the repentance that comes of pain, or the lethargy of hopelessness. We take it, as our very life in our hand, and flee with it unto thee. Triumphant is the answer which thou holdest for every doubt. But thou shalt at least find faith in the earth, O Lord, if thou comest to look for it now—the faith of ignorant but hoping children, who know that they do not know, and believe that thou knowest.[1]

DARE WE IMAGINE THEE AS GOOD AS WE HOPE THOU ART?

(A Fictional Selection from *The Musician's Quest*
and *Robert Falconer*)

Robert consequently began to make efforts toward the saving of his soul, a most rational and prudent exercise but hardly Christian in its nature. His imagination began to busy itself concerning the dire consequences of not entering into the refuge of faith. He made many frantic efforts to believe that he believed and took to keeping the Sabbath very carefully—that is, he went to church three times, never said a word on any subject unconnected with religion, read only religious books, never whistled, stopped thinking of his lost fiddle, and so on—all the time feeling that God was ready to pounce on him if he failed once.

But even through the horrible vapors of these vain endeavors, which denied God altogether as the maker of the world and denied Robert of his soul and heart and brain, there broke a little light from the dim windows of the few books that came his way. In one of these he read a story of a cherub who repents of making a choice with Satan, mourns over his apostasy, and haunts unseen the steps of our Savior. He would gladly return to his lost duties in heaven if only he might. The doubtful situation was left unsolved in the volume, and thus remained unsolved in Robert's mind as well. Would poor Abaddon be forgiven and taken home again?

By Robert's own instincts, he felt there could be no question of his being forgiven. But according to what he had been taught, there could be no question of his perdition. Having no one to talk to, he questioned with himself on the matter, usually siding with the instinctively correct half of himself which supported the merciful view of the case. For all his efforts at keeping the Sabbath had, in his own honest judgment, failed so entirely that he had now come to believe himself not one of those elected for salvation. Therefore, this situation with the fallen angel was no mere mental exercise; for all he knew he might find himself in such a postion one day—out of the fold and wanting to get back in.

He made one attempt to open the subject with Shargar.

"Shargar, what do you think?" he said suddenly one day. "If a devil were to repent, would God forgive him?"

"There's no saying what folk would do till once they've tried," returned Shargar cautiously.

Robert did not care to resume the question with one who so circumspectly refused to take a view of the matter.[2]

He made an attempt with his grandmother.

One Sunday, after trying for a time to revolve his thoughts in due orbit around the mind of the Rev. Hugh MacCleary, as projected in a sermon which he had botched up out of a commentary, Robert failed at last and flew off into what the said gentleman would have pronounced "very dangerous speculation, seeing no man is to go beyond what is written in the Bible, which contains not only the truth, but the whole truth, and nothing but the truth, for this time and all future time—both here and in the world to come." Some such sentence, at least, was in his sermon that day, and the preacher no doubt supposed St. Matthew, not St. Matthew Henry, accountable for its origination. In the limbo into which Robert's spirit then flew, it had been sorely exercised about the substitution of the sufferings of Christ for those which humanity must else have endured while ages rolled on—mere ripples on the ocean of eternity.[3]

After dinner, when the table had been cleared by Betty, they drew their chairs to the fire and Robert began reading, as was the custom, to his grandmother out of the family Bible while Shargar sat listening. Robert had not read long, however, before he looked up and asked. "Wasn't that a mean trick of Joseph, Grandmother, to put that cup, and a silver one too, into Benjamin's sack?"

"Laddie, take care what ye say aboot Joseph, for he was a type o' Christ."

"How was that, Grandmother?"

"They sold him t' the Ishmaelites for silver, as Judas did t' the Lord."

"Did he bear the sins of them that sold him?"

"Ye could say, i' a way, he did, for he was sore afflicted before he made it up t' be the king's right hand. And then he kept a whole heap o' punishment off his brothers."

"So, Grandmother, other folk than Christ might suffer for the sins of their neighbors?"

"Ay, laddie, many a one has t' do that. But not t' make atonement, ye know. Nothing but the suffering o' the spotless could do that. The Lord wouldn't be satisfied wi' less than that. It must be the innocent t' suffer for the guilty."

"I understand that," said Robert, who had heard it so often that he had not yet thought of trying to understand it. "But if we get to the good place, we'll all be innocent, won't we, Grannie?"

"Ay, we will—washed spotless an' pure an' clean an' dressed i' the wedding garment an' set down at the table wi' him an' wi' his Father. That's them that believes i' him, ye know."

"Of course, Grannie—Well, you see, I have been thinking of a plan for almost emptying hell."

"What's i' the boy's head now? Truth, ye shouldn't be meddling wi' such subjects, laddie!"

"I don't want to say anything to vex you, Grannie. I'll go on with the chapter."

"Oh, go on wi' what ye were going t' say. Ye won't say much wrong before I'll cry *stop*," said Mrs. Falconer, curious to know what had been moving in the boy's mind, but watching him like a cat, ready to spring on the first visible hair of the old Adam.

Robert, for his part, recalling the outbreak of terrible grief which he had heard from his grandmother on that memorable night, truly thought that his project would bring comfort to a mind burdened with such care. Thus he went on with the explaining of his plan.

"All of them that sits down to the supper of the Lamb will sit there because Christ suffered the punishment due to their sins—won't they, Grannie?"

"Doubtless, laddie."

"But it'll be weighing hard on their hearts to be sitting there eating and drinking and talking away and enjoying themselves when every now and then there'll come a sigh of wailing up from the bad place, and the smell of burning hard to stand."

"What put that int' yer head, laddie? There's no reason t' think that hell's so near heaven as that. The Lord forbid it."

"Well, but, Grannie, they'll know all the same, whether they smell it or not. And I can't help thinking that the farther away I thought they were, the worse it would be to think about them. Indeed, it would be worse."

"What are ye driving at, laddie? I can't understand ye," said Mrs. Falconer, feeling very uncomfortable and yet curious to hear what would come next. "I don't imagine we'd hae t' think much—"

But here I presume the thought of the added desolation of her Andrew if she were to forget him, as well as his Father in heaven, stopped the flow of her words. She paused, and Robert took up his parable and went on, first with yet another question.

"Do you think, Grannie, that a body would be allowed to speak a word in public there—at the big, long table, I mean?"

"Why not, if it were done wi' modesty an' for a good reason. But really, laddie, I doubt ye're rambling altogether. Ye heard nothing like that today from Mr. MacCleary."

"No, no, he said nothing about it. But maybe I'll go and ask him though."

"What aboot?"

"What I'm going to tell you, Grannie."

"Well, tell away an' hae done wi' it. I'm growing tired o' it."

It was something else than tired she was growing.

"Well, I'm going to try as hard as I can to make it there."

"I hope ye will. Strive an' pray. Resist the Devil. Walk i' the light. Trust not t' yerself, but trust i' Christ an' his salvation."

"Ay, ay, Grannie. Well—"

"Aren't ye done yet?"

"No. I'm but just beginning."

"Beginning, are ye? Humph!"

"Well, if I make it there, the very first night I sit down with the rest of them I'm going to stand up and say—that is if the Master at the head of the table doesn't tell me to sit down— 'Brothers and sisters, listen to me for one minute, and—O Lord, if I say something wrong, just take the speech from me and I'll sit down dumb and rebuked. We're all here by grace and not by merit, except his, as you all know better than me because you have been here longer than me. But it's just tugging at my heart to think of them that's down there. Now we have no merit, and they have no merit. So why are we here and them there? But now we're washed clean and innocent. So now, when there's no punishment left on us, it seems to me that we might bear some of the sins of them that has too many. I call upon each and every one of you that has a friend or neighbor down yonder to rise up and taste not a bite nor drink a drink till we go up together to the foot of the throne and pray the Lord to let us go and do as the Master did before us, and bear the griefs and carry their sorrows down in hell there. And if they repent it may be that they will get remission of their sins and come up here with us at last, and sit down with us at this table—all through the merits of our Savior Jesus Christ, at the head of the table there.' "

"No, Robert, let's hae no more o' this. Ye know as well as I do that them that goes *there*, their doom is fixed an' nothing can alter it. An' we're not t' allow our imaginations t' carry beyond the Scripture. We have our own salvation t' work out wi' fear an' trembling. We hae nothing t' do wi' what's hidden. Only see that ye make it there yerself. That's enough for ye t' mind."

After tea, Mrs. Falconer sent Shargar to church with Betty. When Robert and she were alone together, "Laddie," she said, "ye must beware o' judging the Almighty. What looks t' ye like a wrong may be a right. We don't know all things. An' he's— he's not dead yet—I don't believe that he is—an' he may make it there yet."

Her voice failed her. And Robert had nothing to say. He had all his say before.

"Pray, Robert, pray for yer father, laddie," she resumed, "for we hae good reason t' be anxious about him. Pray while there's life an' hope. Give the Lord no rest. Pray t' him night an' day, as I do, that he would lead him t' see the error o' his ways an' turn t' the Lord who's ready t' pardon. If yer mother had lived, I would hae more hope, I confess, for she was a good lady an' pretty sweet-tongued. But it was the care o' her heart aboot him that shortened her days. An' all that'll be laid upon him: he'll hae t' account for it. Eh, Robert, my man, be a good lad an' serve the Lord wi' all yer heart, an' soul, an' strength, an' mind. For if ye go wrong, yer own father will hae t' bear nobody knows how much punishment, for he's done nothing t' bring ye up i' the way ye should go. For the sake o' yer poor father, hold t' the right road. It may spare him a pang or two at the bad place. Eh, if the Lord would only take me an' let him go!"

Involuntarily and unconsciously the grandmother's love was adopting the hope which she had denounced in her grandson. Robert saw it, but was never one to push a victory. He said nothing. Only a tear or two at the memory of the wayward man he remembered rolled down his cheeks. His grandmother, herself weeping silently, took her neatly folded handkerchief from her pocket and wiped her grandson's fresh cheeks, then wiped her own withered face. And from that moment Robert knew that he loved her.

Then followed the Sabbath-evening prayer. They knelt down together and she uttered a long, extemporary prayer, full of Scripture phrases but not the less earnest and simple, for it flowed from a heart of goodness. Then Robert had to pray after her, loud in her ear, that she might hear him thoroughly, so that he often felt as if he were praying to her and not to God at all.

She had begun to teach him to pray so early in his life that the custom reached beyond the confines of his memory. At first he had had to repeat the words after her. Then she made him construct his own utterances, now and then giving him a suggestion when he fell silent, or putting a phrase into what she considered more suitable language.

On the present occasion, after she had ended her petitions with those for Jews and pagans and for the "Pope o' Rome," she turned to Robert with the usual, "Now, Robert," and Robert began. But after he had gone on for some time with the ordinary phrases, he turned all at once into a new track. Instead of praying in general terms for "those that would not walk in the right way," he said, "O Lord! Save my father," and there paused.

"If it be thy will," suggested his grandmother.

But Robert remained silent. His grandmother repeated the clause.

"I'm trying, Grandmother," said Robert, "but I can't say it. I dare not say an *if* about it. It would be like giving in to his damnation. We *must have* him saved, Grannie!"

"Laddie, laddie! Hold yer tongue!" remonstrated Mrs. Falconer in a tone of distress. "O Lord, forgive him. He's young an' doesn't know better yet. He can't understand thy ways, nor for that matter can I pretend t' understand them myself. But thou art all light an' i' thee is no darkness at all. An' thy light comes int' our blind eyes an' makes them blinder yet. But, O Lord, if it would please thee t' hear our prayer—eh! how we would praise thee! An' my Andrew would praise thee more than ninety an' nine o' them that need no repentance."

A long pause followed. An then the only words that would come were. "For Christ's sake, Amen."

They rose from their knees and Mrs. Falconer sat down by her fire, with her feet on her little wooden stool, and began to quietly review her past life and follow her son through all conditions and circumstances to her imaginable. And when the world to come arose before her, clad in all the glories which her fancy, chilled by education and years, could supply, it was but to vanish in the gloom of the remembrance of poor Andrew with whom she dared not hope to share it.

She felt bound to go on believing as she had been taught, for sometimes the most original mind has the strongest sense of law upon it. Obedience was indeed an essential element of her creed. But she had not yet been sufficiently impressed with the truth that while obedience is the law of the kingdom, it is of considerable importance that which is obeyed should in truth be the will of God.[4]

The Beauty of Holiness

I love thy skies and sunny mists,
Thy fields, thy mountains hoar,
Thy wind that bloweth where it lists—
Thy will, I love it more.

I love thy hidden truth to seek
All round, in sea, on shore;
The arts whereby like gods we speak—
Thy will to me is more.

I love thy men and women, Lord,
The children round thy door;
Calm thoughts that inward strength afford—
Thy will, O Lord, is more.

But when thy will my life doth hold,
Thine to the very core,
The world, which that same will did mould,
I love, then, ten times more!

8

GOD CREATOR OF THE WILL

And God said, Let us make man in our image, after our likeness.
Genesis 1:26

Separation—The Path to True Unity

All things are possible with God, but all things are not easy. It is
easy for him *to be*, for there he has to do with his own perfect
will. It is not easy for him to create—that is, after the grand
fashion which alone will satisfy his glorious heart and will, the fashion
in which he is now creating us. In the very nature of being (that is,
God), it must be hard—and divine history shows how hard—to create
that which shall not be himself, yet like himself.

The problem is, so far to separate from himself that which must yet
on him be ever and always and utterly dependent, that it shall have
the existence of an individual, and be able to turn and regard him—
choose him, and say, "I will arise and go to my Father," and so develop
in itself the highest *divine* of which it is capable: the will for the good
against the evil, the will to be one with the life whence it has come,
the will to shape in its own life the ring of eternity, to be the thing the
Maker thought of when he willed, before he began to work its being.

I imagine the difficulty of doing this thing, of effecting this creation,
this separation from himself such that *will* in the creature shall be
possible—I imagine, I say, the difficulty of such creation so great, that
for it God must begin inconceivably far back in the infinitesimal regions
of beginnings, to set in motion the division from himself which in its

grand result should be individuality, consciousness, choice, and conscious choice—choice at last pure, being the choice of the right, the true, the divinely harmonious.

Hence the final end is oneness—an impossibility without it. For there can be no unity, no delight of love, no harmony, no good in being, where there is but one.

Two at least are needed for oneness; and the greater the number of individuals, the greater, the lovelier, the richer, the diviner is the possible unity.

God's Sacrifice to Give Divine Life

God is life, and the will-source of life.

In the outflowing of that life, I know him. I know nothing deeper in him than love, nor believe there is in him anything deeper than love—nay, that there can be anything deeper than love.

The being of God is love, therefore creation. From all eternity he has been creating. As he saw it was not good for man to be alone, so God has never been alone himself; from all eternity the Father has had the Son, and in the never-begun existence of that Son I imagine an easy outgoing of the Father's nature; while to make other beings—beings like us—I imagine the labor of God an eternal labor. Speaking after our poor human fashions of thought, I imagine that God has never been contented to be alone even with the Son of his love, the prime and perfect idea of humanity, but that God has from the first willed and labored to give existence to other creatures who should be blessed with his blessedness—creatures whom he is now and always has been developing into likeness with that Son.

God knew what it would all cost—not energy of will alone, or merely that utterance and separation from himself, but sore suffering such as we cannot imagine, and could only be God's—in the bringing out, call it birth or development, of the God-life in the individual soul. This suffering is always renewed, a labor thwarted ever by that soul itself, compelling God to take, still at the cost of suffering, the not absolute best, only the best possible means left him by the resistance of his creature. Man finds it hard to get what he wants, because he does not want the best. God finds it hard to give, because he would give the best, and man will not take it. What Jesus did, was what the Father is always doing. The suffering he endured was that of the Father from the foundation of the world, reaching its climax in the person of his Son.

God always provides the sacrifice; the sacrifice is himself. He is always, and has ever been, sacrificing himself to and for his creatures. It lies in the very essence of his creation of them.

If Jesus suffered for men, it was because his Father suffers for men. Only Jesus came close to men through his body and their senses, that he might bring their spirits close to his Father and their Father, so giving them life, and losing what could be lost of his own. He is God our Savior. The God and Father of Jesus Christ could never possibly be satisfied with less than giving himself to his own!

Not the lovingest heart that ever beat can even reflect the length and breadth and depth and height of that love of God, which shows itself in his Son—one, and of one mind, with himself. The whole history is a divine agony to give divine life to creatures. The outcome of that agony, the victory of that creative and again creative energy, will be radiant life, the flower of which is joy unspeakable. Every child will look into the eyes of the Father, and the eyes of the Father will receive the child with an infinite embrace.

The Will—Door to Oneness With God

What is our practical relation to the life original? If we did not make ourselves, how can we do anything at the unknown roots of our being?

It is by the will of the self-existent God that we live.

So the links of unity between ourselves, who *cannot* create life, and him who *has* created it, must already exist. They must only require to be brought together. For the link in our being with which to close the circle of immortal oneness with the Father, we must search the deepest of man's nature; there only, in all assurance, it can be found.

And there we do find it!

For the *will* is the deepest, the strongest, the divinest thing in man. So, I assume, it is in God, too, for we find it in Jesus Christ. Here, and here only, in the relation of the two wills, can a man come into vital contact with the All-in-all.

When a man can and does entirely say, "Not my will, but thine be done," when he so wills the will of God as to do it, then is he one with God—one, as a true son with a true Father. When a man wills that his being be conformed to the being of his origin, which is the life of his life, causing and bearing his life, therefore absolutely and only of its kind, one with it more and deeper than words or figures can say—to the life which is itself, only more of itself, and more than itself, causing itself—when the man thus accepts his own causing life, *and sets himself to live the will of that causing life*, humbly eager after the privileges of his origin, thus receiving God, he becomes, in the act, a partaker of the divine nature, a true son of the living God, and an heir of all he possesses.

By the obedience of a son, he receives into himself the very life of the Father.[1]

Man's Highest Creation

Men speak of the so-called *creations* of the human intellect or of the human imagination. But there is nothing man can do that comes half so near the true "making," the true creativity of the Maker as the ordering of his own way. There is only one thing that is higher, the highest creation of which man is capable, and that is to will the will of the Father. That act indeed contains within it an element of the purely creative, and when man does will such, then he is most like God.

To do what we ought, as children of God, is an altogether higher, more divine, more potent, more creative thing, than to write the grandest poem, paint the most beautiful picture, carve the mightiest statue, build the most magnificent temple, dream out the most enchanting symphony.[2]

All betterment must be radical, for a man can know nothing of the roots of his being. His existence is God's; his betterment must be God's too—God's through honest exercise of that which is highest in man, his own will, God's best handiwork. By actively willing the will of God and doing what of it lies within his power, the man takes the share offered him in his own making, in his own becoming. In willing actively and operatively to become what he was made to be, he becomes creative—so far as a man may. In this way also he becomes like his Father in heaven.[3]

The High Life of Obedience

Obedience is the joining of the links of the eternal round. Obedience is but the other side of the creative will. Will is God's will; obedience is man's will; the two make one.

God, the Root-life, knowing well the thousand troubles it would bring upon him, has created, and goes on creating other lives, that, though incapable of self-being, they may, by willed obedience, share in the bliss of his essential self-ordained being. If we do the will of God, eternal life is ours—no mere continuity of existence, for that in itself is worthless as hell, but a being that is one with the essential Life, and so within reach to fill with the abundant and endless outgoings of his love.

Our souls shall be vessels ever growing, and ever as they grow, filled with the more and more life proceeding from the Father and the Son, from God the ordaining, and God the obedient. The delight of the being, the abundance of the life he came that we might have, we can never know until we have it. But even now to the holy fancy it may sometimes seem too glorious to support—as if we must die of very life—of more being than we could bear—to awake to a yet higher life, and be filled with a wine which our souls were heretofore too weak to hold!

To be for one moment aware of such pure simple love toward but one of my fellows as I trust I shall one day have toward each, must of itself bring a sense of life such as the utmost effort of my imagination can but feebly shadow now—a mighty glory of consciousness! There would be, even in that one love, in the simple purity of a single affection such as we were created to generate and intended to cherish toward all, an expansion of life inexpressible, unutterable. For we are made for love, not for self. Our neighbor is our refuge; self is our demon-foe.

Every man is the image of God to every man, and in proportion as we love him, we shall know the sacred fact. The most precious thing to a human soul is every other human soul. One day we shall know this more clearly. And if it be so between man and man, how will it not be between the man and his Maker, between the child and his eternal Father, between the created and the creating Life?

Must not the glory of existence be endlessly redoubled in the infinite love of the creature—for all love is infinite—to the infinite God, the great one life, that whom is no other—only shadows, lovely shadows of him!⁴

Choosing to Partake of the Divine Nature

Because we have come out of the divine nature, which chooses to be divine, we must *choose* to be divine, to be of God, to be one with God, loving and living as he loves and lives, and so be partakers of the divine nature. Otherwise we perish.

Man cannot originate this life. It must be shown him, and he must choose it. God is the Father of Jesus and of us—of every possibility of our being. But while God is the Father of his children, Jesus is the father of their sonship, for in him is made the life which is sonship to the Father—the recognition, in fact and life, that the Father has his claim upon his sons and daughters.

We are not and cannot become true sons and daughters without our will willing his will, our doing following his making. It was the will of Jesus to be the thing God willed and meant him, that made him the true Son of God. He was not the Son of God because he could not help it, but because he willed to be in himself the Son that he was in the divine idea.

So with us: we must *be* the sons we are. We must be sons and daughters in our will. And we can be sons and daughters, saved into the bliss of our being, only by choosing God for the Father he is, and doing his will—yielding ourselves true sons and daughters to the absolute Father.

Therein lies human bliss—only and essential.

The working out of this our salvation must involve pain, and the handing of it down to them that are below must ever involve pain. But the eternal form of the will of God in and for us is intensity of bliss.[5]

BIRTH OF THE WILL

(A Fictional Selection from *The Peasant Girl's Dream*)

What was passing in the soul of Francis Gordon, I can only indicate; I cannot show in detail. The most mysterious of all vital movements, a generation, a transition, was there—how initiated, God only knows. Francis knew neither whence it came nor whither it went. He was being reborn from above. The change was in himself; the birth was that of his will. It was his own highest action, therefore all God's. He was passing from death into life, and knew it no more than the babe knows that he is being born. The change was into a new state of being, of the very existence of which most men are incredulous, for it is beyond preconception, capable only of being experienced. Thorough as is the change, the man knows himself the same man, and yet would rather cease to be than return to what he was. The unknown germ in him, the root of his being, yea, his very being itself, the holy thing which is his intrinsic substance, hitherto unknown to his consciousness, has begun to declare itself. The caterpillar is passing into the butterfly. It is a change in which God is the potent presence, but which the man or woman must will into being or remain the jailer who prisons in loathsomeness his own God-born self, and chokes the fountain of his own liberty.

Francis knew nothing of all this. He only felt that he must knock at the door behind which Kirsty lived. Kirsty could not open the door to him, but there was One who could, and Francis could knock!

"God help me!" he cried, as he lay on his face to live where once he had lain on his face to die. For the rising again is the sepulcher. The world itself is one vast sepulcher for the heavenly resurrection. We are all busy within the walls of our tomb burying our dead that the corruptible may perish, and the incorruptible go free.

Francis Gordon came out of that earth house a risen man. His will was born. He climbed to the spot where Kirsty and he had sat together, and there, with the vast clear heaven over his head, threw himself once more on his face and lifted up his heart to the heart from whence he came.[6]

This World

Thy world is made to fit thine own,
  A nursery for thy children small,
The playground-footstool of thy throne,
  Thy solemn school-room, Father of all!
When day is done, in twilight's gloom,
We pass into thy presence-room.

Because from selfishness and wrath,
  Our cold and hot extremes of ill,
We grope and stagger on the path—
  Thou tell'st us from thy holy hill,
With icy storms and sunshine rude,
That we are all unripe in good.

Because of snaky things that creep
  Through our soul's sea, dim-undulant,
Thou fill'st the mystery of thy deep
  With faces heartless, grim, and gaunt;
That we may know how ugly seem
The things our spirit-oceans teem.

Because of half-way things that hold
  Good names,
    and have a poisonous breath—
Prudence that is but trust in gold,
  And faith that is but fear of death—
Amongst thy flowers, the lovely brood,
Thou sendest some that are not good.

Thou stay'st thy hand from finishing things
  To make thy child love the complete;
Full many a flower comes up thy springs
  Unshamed in imperfection sweet;
That through good all, and good in part,
Thy work be perfect in the heart.

Because, in careless confidence,
  So oft we leave the narrow way,
Its borders thorny hedges fence,
  Beyond them marshy deeps affray;
But farther on, the heavenly road
Lies through the gardens of our God.

Because thy sheep so often will
  Forsake the meadow cool and damp
To climb the stony, grassless hill,
  Or wallow in the slimy swamp,
Thy sicknesses, where'er they roam,
Go after them to bring them home.

One day, all fear, all ugliness,
  All pain, all discord, dumb or loud,
All selfishness, and all distress,
  Will melt like low-spread
    morning cloud,
And heart and brain be free from thrall,
Because thou, God, art all in all!

9

JESUS, SON IN HIS FATHER'S HOUSE

He went into a mountain apart to pray: and when evening was come, he was there alone.

Matthew 14:25

More Man Than We, Therefore, at Home

Jesus was no stranger who did not know his way about in the world. The world was his home because it was his Father's house. Even when a boy, he could be no lost child, but was with his Father all the time.

Here we find one of the main things wherein the Lord differs from us: we are not at home in this great universe, our Father's house. We ought to be, and one day we shall be, but we are not yet.

This reveals Jesus to be more than man, by revealing him more man than we. We are not complete men, we are not anything near it, and are therefore out of harmony, more or less, with everything in the house of our birth and habitation. Always struggling to make our home in the world, we have not yet succeeded. We are not at home in it, because we are not at home with the Lord of the house, the Father of the family, not one with our elder Brother, who is his right hand. It is only the son, the daughter, that abideth ever in the house. When we are true children, if not the world, then the universe will be our home, felt and known as such, the house we are satisfied with, and would not change.

Hence, until then, the hard struggle, the constant strife we hold with *nature*—as we call the things of our Father, a strife invaluable for our development, at the same time manifesting us not yet men enough to be lords of the house built for us to live in. We cannot govern or command in it as did the Lord, because we are not at one with his Father, therefore neither in harmony with his things, nor rulers over them. Our best power in regard to them is but to find out wonderful facts concerning them and their relations and turn these facts to our uses on systems of our own. For we discover what we seem to discover by working inward from without, while God works outward from within. We shall never really understand the world until we see it in the direction in which God works making it—namely from within outward.

This of course we cannot do until we are one with Him. In the meantime, so much are both we and his things his, that we can err concerning them only as he has made it possible for us to err. We can wander only in the direction of the truth—only to find that we can find nothing.

The Liberty of Jesus Among the Things of His Father

Think for a moment how Jesus was at home among the things of his Father.

What was his place of prayer? Not the temple, but the mountaintop.

Where does he find symbols whereby to speak of what goes on in the mind and before the face of his Father in heaven?

Not in the temple. Not in its rites, not on its altars, not in its Holy of Holies. Rather he finds them in the world and its lovely, lowly facts—on the roadside, in the field, in the vineyard, in the garden, in the house, in the family, and in the commonest of affairs: the lighting of the lamp, the leavening of the meal, the neighbor's borrowing, the losing of a coin, the straying of a sheep.

See how he drives the devils from the souls and bodies of men, as we the wolves from our sheepfolds!

The world has for him no chamber of terror. He walks to the door of the sepulcher, the sealed cellar of his Father's house, and calls forth its four days dead. The roughest of the world's servants do not make him wince; none of them is so arrogant as to disobey him. He falls asleep in the midst of the storm that threatens to swallow his boat. Hear how, on that same occasion, he rebukes his disciples! What, the children to tremble at a gust of wind in the house! God's little ones afraid of a storm! Hear him tell the watery floor to be still! See how the wandering creatures under it come at his call! See how the world's water turns to wine! How its bread grows more bread at his word! See how he goes from the house for a while, and returning with fresh power, takes what shape he pleases, walks through its closed doors, and goes up and down its invisible stairs!

All his life he was among his Father's things, either in heaven or in the world—not only when his parents found him in the temple at Jerusalem.

He is still among his Father's things, everywhere about in the world, everywhere throughout the wide universe. Whatever he laid aside to come to us, to whatever limitations he stooped, he dealt with the things about him in such a lordly, childlike manner as made it clear they were not strange to him, but the things of his Father.

He claimed none of them as his own, would not have had one of them his except through his Father. Only as his Father's could he enjoy them—only as coming forth from the Father, and full of the Father's thought and nature. That the things were his Father's made them precious things to him. He had no care for having, as men count having. All his having was in the Father.[1]

To be lord of space, a man must be free of all bonds to place. To be heir of all things, his heart must have no *things* in it. He must be like him who makes things, not like one who would put everything in his pocket. He must stand on the upper, not the lower side of them. He must be as the man who makes poems, not the man who gathers books of verse.

God, having made a sunset, lets it pass and makes such a sunset no more. He has no picture gallery, no library. What if in heaven men shall be so busy growing that they have not time to write or read![2]

I wonder if Jesus ever put anything in his pocket. I doubt he even had one. Did he ever say, "This is mine, not yours?" Did he not say, "All things are mine, therefore they are yours"?

Oh, for his liberty among the things of the Father! Only by knowing them as the things of our Father can we escape enslaving ourselves to them. Through the false, the infernal idea of *having*, of *possessing* them, we make them our tyrants, make the relation between them and us an evil thing.

Seeing Things as the Father Meant Them

The world was a blessed place to Jesus, because everything in it was his Father's.

What pain must it have been to him to see his brothers so vilely misuse the Father's house by grasping, each for himself, at the family's things! If the knowledge that a spot in the landscape retains in it some pollution suffices to disturb our pleasure in the whole, how must it not have been with him, how must it not be with him now, in regard to the disfigurements and defilements caused by the greed of men, by their haste to be rich, in his Father's lovely house!

Whoever has gazed on flower or cloud, whoever can recall poorest memory of the trail of glory that hung about his childhood, must have some faint idea how his Father's house and the things in it always looked, and must still look, to the Lord. With Jesus there is no fading into the light of common day. He has never lost his childhood, the very essence of childhood being nearness to the Father and the outgoing of his creative love. With that insight of his eternal childhood, he must see everything as the Father means it.

The child sees things as the Father means him to see them, as he thought of them when he uttered them. For God is not only the Father of the child, but of the childhood that constitutes him a child; therefore, the childness is of the divine nature.

The child may not indeed be capable of looking into the Father's method, but he can in a measure understand his work. He has therefore free entrance to his study and workshop both, and is welcome to find out what he can, with fullest liberty to ask him questions. Jesus saw things just as his Father saw them in his creative imagination, when willing them out to the eyes of his children. But because he saw them perfectly, would his love for them be the less? Would familiarity ever destroy his sense of wonder at things essentially wonderful because essentially divine?

I think not. To cease to wonder is to fall from the childlike to the commonplace—most undivine of all intellectual moods. Our nature can never be at home among things that are not wonderful to us.[3]

Obedience Makes Us Inheritors of All Things

It is only in God that the soul has room.

In knowing him is life and its gladness. The secret of your own heart you can never know. But you can know him who knows its secrets.

As this world of delight surrounds and enters your bodily frame, so does God surround your soul and live in it. To be at home with the awful source of your being, through the childlike faith which he not only permits, but requires, and is ever teaching you, or rather seeking to rouse up in you, is the only cure for such feelings as those that may at any moment trouble you.

Do not say it is too high for you. God made you in his own image, therefore capable of understanding him. For this final end he sent his Son, that the Father might with him come into you, and dwell with you.[4]

Could we see things always as we have sometimes seen them—and as one day we must always see them, only far better—would we ever know dullness? To the same homeness which Jesus felt in his Father's world, I think all we humans are destined to rise. Though so many of us now are ignorant of what kind of home we need, what a home we are capable of having, we too shall inherit the earth with the Son eternal, doing with it as we would—willing with the will of the Father.

To such a home as we now inhabit, only perfected, and perfectly beheld, we are traveling—never to reach it except by the obedience that makes us the children, therefore the heirs of God. And, thank God! there the Father does not die that the children may inherit; for—bliss of heaven!—we inherit *with* the Father.

Jesus' parents found him in the temple. But they never *really* found him, nor shall we, until he entered the *true* temple—their own adoring hearts.[5]

There Are No Ordinary Things

The ideas of Christianity are so grand, so high, and the things all around us in life so ordinary. They seem to contradict each other from morning to night—in our minds, I mean.

Do you ever find yourself wondering which is the true: a loving, caring Father, or the grinding of cruel poverty?

What does nature have in common with the Bible and its notions of spirituality?

Yet when we begin to think such thoughts, there we are wrong. For nature has a thousand things! The very wind on my face seems to rouse me to fresh effort after a pure, healthy life! Then there is the sunrise! The snowdrop in the snow! There is the butterfly! And the rain of summer and the clearing of the sky after a storm! There is the hen gathering her chicks under her wing!

I doubt whether anything is in fact *ordinary* except in our own mistrusting nature.[6]

CHURCH OF ALL CHURCHES

(A Fictional Selection from *The Laird's Inheritance*)

That night Cosmo could not sleep. It was a warm summer night, though not yet summer—a soft dewy night, full of genial magic and growth. He dressed himself and went out. It was deliciously cool and damp, but with no shiver. The stars were bright. There was no moon, but the night was yet so far from dark that it seemed conscious throughout of some distant light that illumined it without shine. And his heart felt like the night, as if it held a deeper life than he could ever know.

He wandered about till he came to the field where he had been with his father the day before. He was not thinking actively; any effort would break the spell in which he moved! For the moment he would be but a human plant, gathering comfort from the soft coolness and the dew when the sun had ceased his demands. The coolness and the dew sank into him and made his soul long for the thing that waits the asking.

He came to the spot where his father and he had prayed together, and there he knelt and lifted up his face to the stars. Oh, mighty, true church of all churches—where the Son of Man prayed! In the temple made by man's hands he taught, but here, under the starry roof, was his house of prayer, church where not a mark is to be seen of human hand! This was the church of God's building, the only fitting type of a yet greater, a yet holier church, whose stars are the burning eyes of self-forgetting love, whose worship is a ceaseless ministration of self-forgetting deeds—the one real ideal church, the body of the living Christ, built of the hearts and souls of men and women out of every nation and every creed, through all time and over all the world, redeemed alike from Judaism, paganism, and all the false Christianities that darken and dishonor the true.

Cosmo knelt and looked up. Something awoke within him, and he lifted up his heart, sending his soul aloft through the invisible.[7]

A Prayer

Thou who mad'st the mighty clock
Of the great world go;
Mad'st its pendulum swing and rock,
Ceaseless to and fro;
Thou whose will doth push and draw
Every orb in heaven,
Help me move by higher law
In my spirit graven.

Like a planet let me swing—
With intention strong;
In my orbit rushing sing
Jubilant along;
Help me answer in my course
To my seasons due;
Lord of every stayless force,
Make my Willing true.

10

GOD THE CREATOR AND RULER OF NATURE

And he arose, and rebuked the wind, and said unto the sea, Peace, be still. And the wind ceased, and there was a great calm. And he said unto them, Why are ye so fearful? How is it that ye have no faith? And they feared exceedingly, and said one to another, What manner of man is this, that even the wind and the sea obey him?

Mark 4:39–41

Through Miracles We Know God

I venture to write on our Lord's miracles in the belief that, seeing they are one of the modes in which his unseen life found expression, through them we are bound to arrive at some knowledge of that life. For he has come, Jesus, the Word of God, that we may know God. Every word of his, then, which helps us to know him, helps us to know God. Therefore, we must understand, as far as we may, every one of his words and every one of his actions. I believe this is the immediate end of our creation. And I believe that this will at length result in the unraveling for us of what must now, more or less, appear to every man the knotted and twisted coil of the universe.

It seems to me that it needs no great power of faith to believe in the miracles. There are far harder things to believe. For a man is not required to believe in them except as believing in Jesus. If a man can believe that there is a God, he may well believe that, having made creatures capable of hungering and thirsting for him, he must be capable of speaking a word to guide them in their feeling after him. And if he is a grand God, a God worthy of being God, he will speak the clearest grandest word of guidance he can utter intelligibly to his creatures. For us, that word must simply be the gathering of all the expressions of his visible works into an infinite human face, which was in the beginning with God. It follows that it would be but natural to expect that the deeds of this one great messenger, the infinite human carrying within him the essence of God, should be just the works of the Father done in little.

If Jesus came to reveal his Father in miniature, as it were, to tone down his great voice, which, too loud for men to hear aright, could but sound to them as inarticulate thundering, into such a still small voice as might enter their human ears in welcome human speech, then the works that his Father does so widely, so grandly, that they transcend the vision of men, the Son must do briefly and sharply before their eyes.

This, I think, is the true nature of the miracles, an epitome of God's processes in nature beheld in immediate connection with their source—a source as yet lost to the eyes and too often to the hearts of men in the far-receding gradations of continuous law. That men might see the will of God at work, Jesus did the works of his Father thus.

Here I suppose the objection will be raised, "But do you not thus place the miracles in dignity below the ordinary processes of nature?"

I answer: the miracles are mightier far than the goings on of nature *as beheld by common eyes.* There is nothing so miraculous in nature *if* it is dissociated from a living Will.

But the miracles are surely less than those mighty goings on of nature when nature is seen as it truly is—with God beheld at the heart of all its infinite and intricate workings!

In the name of him who delighted to say, "My Father is greater than I," I will say that his miracles in bread and wine were far less grand and less beautiful than the works of the Father they represented, in making the grain to grow in the valleys, and the grapes to drink the sunlight on the hillsides of the world, with all their infinitudes of tender gradation and delicate mystery of birth. But the Son of the Father be praised, who, as it were, condensed these mysteries before us and let us see the precious gifts coming at once from gracious hands—hands that love could kiss and nails could wound.

The Root of Miracles—Obedience

There are some who would perhaps find it more possible to accept the New Testament story if the miracles did not stand in the way.

But perhaps it would be easier for them to accept both if they could once look into the true heart of these miracles. So long as they regard only the surface of them, they will see only a violation of the laws of nature. When they behold the heart of them, they will recognize there at least a possible fulfillment of her deepest laws.

Let us recognize the works of the Father as epitomized in the miracles of the Son. What in the hands of the Father are the mighty motions and progresses and conquests of life, in the hands of the Son are miracles. I do not myself believe that he valued the working of these miracles as he valued the utterance of the truth in words. But all that he did had the one root, *obedience*, in which alone can any son be free.

And what is the highest obedience? Simply a following of the Father—a doing of what the Father does. Every true father wills that his child should be as he is in his deepest love, in his highest hope. All that Jesus does is of his Father. What we see in the Son is of the Father. What his works mean concerning him, they mean concerning the Father.[1]

God's Higher Laws

I will try, in a few words, to give the ground on which I find it possible to accept the miracles.

How God creates, no man can tell. But as man is made in God's image, he may think about God's work, and dim analogies may arise out of the depth of his nature which have some resemblance to the way in which God works. Everything is because God thinks it into being. Can it then be very hard to believe that he should alter by a thought any form or appearance of things about us?

"It is inconsistent to work otherwise than by law," you say. "Even God himself is bound by his own laws."

True. I heartily agree.

But we know so little of his "laws," as we call them, that we cannot say what is essential in them. We know so little of true law that we cannot certainly say what would be an infringement of this or that law. That which at first sight appears as such, may be but the operating of a higher law which rightly dominates the other.

It is the law, as we call it, that a stone should fall to the ground.

But then a man may place his hand beneath the stone, and, if his hand be strong enough, it is the law that the stone will *not* fall to the ground. The law has been lawfully prevented from working its full end.

In similar ways God might stop the working of one law by the intervention of another. Such intervention, if not understood by us, would be what we would call a miracle.

Possibly a different condition of the earth, producible according to law, might cause everything to fly off from its surface instead of seeking it. The question is whether or not we can believe that the usual laws might be set aside by laws including higher principles and wider operations.

All I have to answer is, "Give me good reason, and I can." Another may say, "What seems good reason to you, does not to me." I answer, "We are both accountable to that Being who has lighted in us the candle of judgment. To him alone we stand or fall. But there must be a final way of right, toward which every willing heart is led, and which no one can find who does not seek it."

All I want to show here is a conceivable region in which a miracle might take place without any violence done to the order of things. Our power of belief depends greatly on our power of imagining a region in which such things might be.

But let us beware lest what we call faith be but the mere assent of a mind that has cared and thought so little about the objects of its so-called faith that it has never seen the difficulties they involve. Some such believers are the worst antagonists of true faith—the children of the Pharisees of old.

If someone says we ought not to try to understand realms in which we have no experience, I answer that there is in me a necessity, a desire for something beyond the shriveling mockery of my own poor self. I grant we ought to accept nothing for which we cannot see the probability of some sufficient reason, but, thank God, this sufficient reason is not limited to the small realm of experience. To suppose that it was would change the hope of life into a poor struggle with events and things and chances—to doom the Psyche to perpetual imprisonment in the worm. I desire the higher; I care not to live for the lower.

A higher condition of harmony with law may one day enable us to do things that must now *appear* an interruption of law. I believe it is in virtue of the absolute harmony in Him, his perfect righteousness, that God can create at all. If man were in harmony with this, if he too were righteous, he would inherit of his Father something in degree correspondent to the creative power in God. Were that the case, the world man inhabits, which is but an extension of his body, would, I think, be subject to him in a way surpassing his wildest dreams of dominion, for it would be the perfect dominion of holy law—a virtue flowing to and from him through the channel of a perfect obedience.

Jesus, the Complete Man

I suspect that our Lord in all his dominion over nature set forth only the complete man—man as God means him one day to be.

In all the cases of the miracles of Jesus, the restoration, I think, of an original law is foreshown—the supremacy of righteous man. While a man cannot order his own house as he would, something is wrong in him, and therefore in his house. I think a true man should be able to rule winds and waters and loaves and fishes, for he comes of the Father who made the house for him.

Had Jesus not been capable of these things, he might have been the best of men, but he could not have been either the perfect man or the perfect God.

Man is not master in his own house because he is not master in himself, because he is not a law unto himself, is not himself obedient to the law by which he exists. Harmony, that is law, alone is power. Discord is weakness. Only God is perfect, living, self-existent law.

Why should Jesus not know where the fishes were, or even make them come at his will?

If in the human form of Jesus, God visited his people, he would naturally show himself Lord over their circumstances. He will not lord it over their minds. They themselves must see and choose and acknowledge the lordship which makes them free. There was no grand display, only the simple doing of what at the time was needful. He had no ambition to show himself the best of men. He came to reveal the Father.

No miracle was needful for himself. He saw the root of the matter—the care of God. But he revealed this root in a few rare and hastened flowers to the eyes that could not see to the root. In him, there is perfect submission to lower law. But he would occasionally reveal the Father to the children by the introduction of higher laws operating in the upper regions, not separated from ours by an impassable gulf—rather connected by gently ascending stairs, many of whose gradations he could blend in one descent.

He revealed the Father as being *under* no law, but as law itself, and the cause of the laws we know, the cause of all harmony because he himself is *the* harmony. Men had to be delivered not only from the fear of suffering and death, but from the fear—which is a kind of worship—of nature. Nature herself must be shown to be subject to the Father and to him whom the Father had sent. Men must believe in the great works of the Father through the little works of the Son; all that he showed was little to what God was doing. They had to be helped to see that it was God who did such things as often as they were done. He it is who causes the corn to grow for man. He gives every fish that a man eats.

Even if things are terrible, yet they are God's, and the Lord will still the storm because of their faith in him—tame a storm, as a man might tame a wild beast, for his Father measures the waters in the hollow of his hand, and men are miserable not to know it.

For Jesus himself, his faith is enough. He sleeps on his pillow, and does not even dream of perishing.[2]

GOD ON THE MOUNTAIN

(A Fictional Selection from *Sir Gibbie*)

U p and up the hill went Gibbie. The path ceased altogether; but when *up* is the word in one's mind—and *up* had grown almost a fixed idea with Gibbie—he can seldom be in doubt whether he is going right, even where there is no track. Indeed in all more arduous ways, men leave no track behind them, no finger-post—there is always but the steepness. He climbed and climbed. The mountain grew steeper and barer as he went, and he became absorbed in his climbing. All at once he discovered that he had lost the stream, where or when he could not tell. All below and around him was red granite rock, scattered over with the chips and splinters detached by air and wind, water and stream, light and heat and cold. Glashgar was only about three thousand feet in height but it was the steepest of its group—a huge rock that, even in the midst of masses, suggested solidity.

Not once while he ascended had the idea come to him that by and by he should be able to climb no farther. For aught he knew there were oat cakes and milk and sheep and collie dogs even higher and higher still. Not until he actually stood upon the peak did he know that there was the earthly *hitherto*—the final obstacle of unobstancy, the everywhere which, from excess of perviousness, was to human foot impervious. The sun was about two hours toward the west, when Gibbie, his little legs almost as active as ever, surmounted the final slope. Running up like a child that would scale heaven, he stood on the bare round, the head of the mountain, and saw, with an invading shock of amazement, and at first of disappointment, that there was no going higher; in every direction the slope was downward. He had never been on the top of anything before. He had always been in the hollows of things. Now the whole world lay beneath him. It was cold; in some of the shadows lay snow— weary exile from both the sky and the sea, and the ways of them—captive in the fetters of the cold—prisoner to the mountain top; but Gibbie felt no cold. In a glow with the climb, which at the last had been hard, his lungs filled with the heavenly air, and his soul with the feeling that he was above everything that was uplifted on the very crown of the earth; he stood in his rags, a fluttering scarecrow, the conqueror of height, the discoverer of immensity, the monarch of space. Nobody knew of such marvel but him! Gibbie had never even heard the word *poetry*, but none the less he was the very stuff out of which poems grow, and now all the latent poetry in him was set swaying and heaving—an ocean inarticulate because unobstructed—a might that could make no music, no thunder of waves, because it had no shore, no rocks of thought against which to break in speech. He sat down on the topmost point; and slowly in the silence and the loneliness, from the unknown fountains of the eternal consciousness, the heart of the child filled. Above him towered infinitude, immensity, potent on his mind through shape to his eye in a soaring dome of blue—the one visible symbol informed and insouled of the eternal, to reveal itself thereby. In it, center and life, lorded the great sun, beginning to cast shadows to the south and east from the endless heaps of the world, that lifted themselves in all directions. Down their sides ran the stream, down busily, hasting away through every valley to the Daur, which bore them back to the ocean-heart—through woods and meadows, park and waste, rocks and willowy marsh. Behind the valleys rose mountains; and behind the mountains, other mountains, more and more, each swathed in its own mystery; and beyond all hung the curtain-depth of the sky-gulf. Gibbie sat and gazed, and dreamed and gazed. The mighty city that had been to him the universe was dropped and lost, like a thing that was now nobody's, in far indistinguishable distance; and he who had lost it, had climbed upon the throne of the world. The air was still when a breath awoke, it but touched his cheek like the down of a feather, and the stillness was there again. The stillness grew great, and slowly descended upon him. It deepened and deepened. Surely it would deepen to a voice!—it was about to speak! It was as if a great single thought was the substance of the silence, and was all over and around him, and closer to him than his clothes, than his body, than his hands. I am describing the indescribable, and compelled to make it too definite for belief. In colder speech, an experience had come to the child; a link in the chain of his development glided over the windlass of his uplifting; a change passed upon him. In after years when Gibbie had the idea of God, when he had learned to think about him, to desire his presence, to believe that a will of love enveloped his will, as the brooding hen spreads her wings over her eggs—as often as the thought of God came to him, it came in the shape of the silence on the top of Glashgar.[3]

Mother Nature

Beautiful mother is busy all day,
So busy she neither can sing nor say;
But lovely thoughts, in a ceaseless flow,
Through her eyes, and her ears, and her bosom go—
Motion, sight, and sound, and scent,
Weaving a royal, rich content.

When night is come, and her children sleep,
Beautiful mother her watch doth keep;
With glowing stars in her dusky hair
Down she sits to her music rare;
And her instrument that never fails,
Is the hearts and throats of her nightingales.

RULER OF THE STORM

(A Fictional Selection from *The Baronet's Song*
and *Sir Gibbie*)

E ver since he became a dweller in the air of Glashgar and
mindful of his first visit thereto and his grand experience on
that occasion, Gibbie had been in the habit—as often as he saw
reason to expect a thunderstorm—of ascending the mountain
and there on the crest of the granite peak to await the arrival of
the tumult.

Toward the evening of a wondrously fine day in the beginning of August, a perfect day of summer in her matronly beauty,

it began to rain. All the next day the slopes and stairs of Glashgar were swept with heavy showers, driven slanting in strong gusts of wind from the northwest.

Gibbie drove his sheep to the refuge of a pen on the lower slope of a valley that ran at right angles to the wind. He then went home and, having told Robert what he had done and eaten his supper, set out in the early falling light to ascend the mountain. A great thunderstorm was at hand and was calling him. It was almost dark before he reached the top, but he knew the surface of Glashgar nearly as well as the floor of the cottage. Just as he had fought his way to the crest of the peak in the face of one of the fiercest of the blasts, a sudden rush of fire made the heavens like the smoke-filled vault of an oven, and at once the thunder followed in a succession of single, sharp explosions without any roll between. The mountain shook with the windy shocks, but the first of the thunderstorm was the worst, and it soon passed. The wind and the rain continued, and the darkness was filled with the rush of water wildly tearing down the sides of the moutain. Thus heaven and earth held communication in torrents all the night. To the ears and heart of Gibbie their noises were a mass of broken music. Every spring and autumn the floods came, and he knew them, and they were welcome to him in their seasons.

It required some care to find his way down through the darkness and the waters to the cottage, but as he was neither in fear nor in haste, he was in little danger. His hands and feet could pick out the path where his eyes were useless. When at length he reached his bed, it was not for a long time to sleep, but to lie awake and listen to the raging of the wind all about, above and below the cottage and the rushing of the streams down past it on every side.

He woke and it was morning. He rose and, dressing hastily, opened the door. What a picture of grey storm rose outspread before him! The wind fiercely invaded the cottage, thick charged with waterdrops. Stepping out he shut the door in haste lest it should blow upon the old people in bed and wake them. He could not see far on any side for the rain that fell and the mist and steam that arose, upon which the wind seemed to have no power; but wherever he did see, there water was running down. Upon the mountain he went—he could hardly have told why. It was a wild, hopeless scene—as if God had turned His face away from the world and all nature was therefore drowned in tears. Gibbie stood gazing and thinking.

That moment Glashgar gave a great heave under him, then rocked and shook from side to side a little and settled down still and steady. The next instant came an explosion followed by a frightful roaring and hurling, as of mingled water and stones. On the side of the mountain beneath him he saw what through the mist looked like a cloud of smoke or dust rising to a height. He darted toward it. As he drew nearer, the cloud seemed to condense, and presently he saw plainly enough that it was a great column of water shooting up and out from the face of the hill. The mountain was cracked, and through the crack and down the hill a river was shooting a sheer cataract, raving and tearing and carrying stones and rocks with it like foam.[4]

Suddenly Gibbie, in the midst of his astonishment and awful delight, noted the path of the new stream, and from his knowledge of the face of the mountain, perceived that its course was direct for the cottage. Down the hill he shot after it, as if it were a wild beast that his fault had freed from its cage. He was not terrified. One believing like him in the perfect Love and perfect Will of a Father of men, as the fact of facts, fears nothing. Fear is faithlessness. But there is so little that is worthy the name of faith, that such a confidence will appear to most not merely incredible but heartless. The Lord himself seems not to have been very hopeful about us, for he said, When the Son of man cometh shall he find faith on the earth? A perfect faith would lift us absolutely above fear. It is in the cracks, crannies, and gulfy faults of our belief, the gaps that are not faith, that the snow of apprehension settles and the ice of unkindness forms.[5]

I Know What Beauty Is

Yea, Beauty's regnant All I know—
  The imperial head, the thoughtful eyes;
  The God-imprisoned harmonies
That out in gracious motions go.

But I leave all, O Son of man,
  Put off my shoes, and come to thee!
  Most lovely thou of all I see,
Most potent thou of all that can!

As child forsakes his favourite toy,
  His sisters' sport, his new-found nest,
  And, climbing to his mother's breast,
Enjoys yet more his late-left joy—

I lose to find. On fair-browed bride
  Fair pearls their fairest light afford;
  So, gathered round thy glory, Lord,
All glory else is glorified.

I know what beauty is, for thou
  Hast set the world within my heart;
  Of me thou madest it a part;
I never loved it more than now.

I know the Sabbath afternoons;
  The light asleep upon the graves:
  Against the sky the poplar waves;
The river murmurs organ tunes.

I know the spring with bud and bell;
  The hush in summer woods at night;
  Autumn, when trees let in more light;
Fantastic winter's lovely spell.

I know the rapture music gives,
  Its mystery of ordered tones;
  Dream-muffled soul, it loves and moans,
And, half-alive, comes in and lives.

And verse I know, whose concord high
  Of thought and music lifts the soul
  Where many a glimmering starry shoal
Glides through the Godhead's living sky.

11

GOD'S BEING REFLECTED IN NATURE

*For the invisible things of him from the creation of the world are clearly
seen, being understood by the things that are made.*

Romans 1:20

The Embodied Character of God

I f the world is God's, every true man and woman ought to feel at
home in it.
Something is wrong if the calm of the summer night does not
sink into the heart, for it embodies the peace of God. Something is
wrong in the man to whom the sunrise is not a divine glory, for therein
is embodied the truth, the simplicity, and the might of the Maker.
When all is true in us, we shall feel the visible presence of God's
watchful eye and loving hand. For the things that he works are their
signs and symbols, their clothing in fact. Alongside the gentle meeting
of earth and sky, in the witnessing colors of the west, in the wind that
so gently visits our cheek, in the great burst of a new morning, the
sordid affairs of mammon sink to the bottom of things and have little
more interest.[1]

Nature, the Live Truth

The appearances of nature are the truths of nature, far deeper than
any scientific discoveries in and concerning them. The show of things
is that for which God cares most, for their show is the face of far deeper

things than they; we see in them, in a distant way, as in a glass darkly, the face of the unseen. It is through their show, not through their analysis, that we enter into their deepest truths. What they say to the childlike soul is the truest thing to be gathered of them.

To know a primrose is a higher thing than to know all the botany of it—just as to know Christ is an infinitely higher thing than to know all theology, all that is said about his person, or babbled about his work.

The body of man does not exist for the sake of its hidden secrets; its hidden secrets exist for the sake of its outside—for the face and the form in which dwells revelation. Its outside points the way to the deepest form of it.

So nature as well exists primarily for her face, her look, her appeals to the heart and the imagination, her simple service to human need, and not for the secrets to be discovered in her and turned to man's farther use. What in the name of God is our knowledge of the elements of the atmosphere to our knowledge of the elements of nature? What are its oxygen, its hydrogen, its nitrogen, its carbonic acid, its ozone, and all the possible rest, to the blowing of the wind on our faces? What is the analysis of water to the babble of a running stream? What is any knowledge of things to the heart, beside its child-play with the Eternal!

And by an infinite decomposition, if we could take everything apart in a perfectly understood manner, we should know nothing more of what a thing really is, for, the moment we decompose it, it ceases to be, and all its meaning is vanished.

Infinitely more than astronomy can do for us is done by the mere aspect and changes of the vault over our heads. Think for a moment what would be our idea of greatness, of God, of infinitude, of aspiration, if, instead of a blue, far withdrawn, light-spangled firmament, we were born and reared under a flat white ceiling!

I would not be supposed to depreciate the labors of science, but I say its discoveries are unspeakably less precious than the merest gifts of nature, those which, from morning to night, we take unthinking from her hands. One day, I trust, we shall be able to enter into their secrets from within them—by natural contact between our heart and theirs. When we are one with God, we may well understand in an hour things that no man of science, prosecuting his investigations from the surface with all the aids that keenest human intellect can supply, would reach in the longest lifetime.

Whether such power will ever come to any man in this world, or can come only in some state of existence beyond it, matters nothing to me; the question does not interest me. Life is one, and things will be then what they are now, for God is one and the same there and here.

And I shall be the same there that I am here, however larger the life with which it may please the Father of my being to endow me.[2]

Mystery in the World

There exists a mystery in the world, and in all the looks of it—a mystery because of a meaning. There is a jubilance in every sunrise, a sober sadness in every sunset. There is a whispering of strange secrets in the wind of the twilight and an unknown bliss in the song of the lark.

We cannot help but be aware of a something beyond it all, now and then filling our minds and hearts with wonder, and compelling us to ask, "What can it all mean?"

The flowers *live*.

They come from the same heart as man himself, and are sent to be his companions and ministers. There is something divinely magical, because profoundly human, in them. Our feeling for many of them doubtless comes from certain associations from childhood. But how did they get hold of us even in childhood? Why do they enter our souls at all?

It is because the flowers are joyous, inarticulate children, come with vague messages from the Father of all. If I confess that what they say to me sometimes makes me weep, how can I call my feeling for them anything but love?

And the flowers are only one example. All nature, from the mountains to the sea to the fog that hangs so low on the hills, the heather in August, the hot, the cold, the rain—everything speaks, like the flower, messages from God, the Father of the universe.

The eternal may have a thousand forms of which we know nothing yet![3]

The beautiful things around us are the expressions of God's face, or, as in Faust, the garment whereby we see the deity. Is God's sun more beautiful than God himself? Has he not left it to us as a symbol of his own life-giving light?[4]

It Is Springtime in God's World

I walked home one winter's Sunday morning after church. It was a lovely day. The sun shone so warm that you could not help thinking of what God would be able to do before long—draw primroses and buttercups out of the earth by force of sweet persuasive influences. But in the shadows lay fine webs of laces of ice, so delicately lovely that one could not but be glad of the cold that made the water able to please itself by taking such graceful forms.

And I wondered over again, for the hundredth time, what could be the principle which, in the wildest, most lawless, fantastically chaotic, apparently capricious work of nature, always kept it beautiful. The beauty of holiness must be at the heart of it somehow, I thought. Because our God is so free from stain, so loving, so unselfish, so good, so altogether what he wants us to be, so holy, therefore all his works declare him in beauty; his fingers can touch nothing but to mold it into loveliness; and even the play of his elements is in grace and tenderness of form.

And then I thought how the sun, at the farthest point from us, had begun to come back toward us, looked upon us with a hopeful smile, and was like the Lord when he visited his people as a little one of themselves, to grow upon the earth until it should blossom as the rose in the light of his presence.

"Ah, Lord," I said in my heart, "draw near unto thy people. It is springtime with thy world, but yet we have cold winds and bitter hail, and pinched voices forbidding them that follow thee and follow not with us. Draw nearer, Sun of Righteousness, and make the trees burgeon, and the flowers blossom, and the voices grow mellow and glad, so that all shall join in praising thee, and find thereby that harmony is better than unison. Let it be summer, O Lord, if it ever may be summer in this court of the Gentiles. But thou hast told us that thy kingdom cometh within us, and so thy joy must come within us too. Draw nigh then, Lord, to those to whom thou wilt draw nigh; and others beholding their welfare will seek to share therein too, and seeing their good works will glorify their Father in heaven."[5]

SOMEONE MUST MEAN IT ALL

(A Fictional Selection from *The Musician's Quest*)

The grassy bank of the gently flowing river was one of Robert's favorite haunts, and one Saturday afternoon at the end of July, when the westering sun was hotter than at midday, he went down to the lower end of a favorite field where the river was confined by a dam and plunged from the bank into the deep water. After a swim of half an hour, he ascended the higher part of the field and lay down to bask in the sun. In his ears was the hush rather than the rush of the water over the dam and the occasional murmur of a belt of trees that skirted the border of the field.

He lay gazing up into the depth of the sky, rendered deeper and bluer by the masses of white cloud that hung almost motionless below it. A gentle wind, laden with pine odors from the sun-heated trees behind him, flapped its tight wing in his face. And all at once the humanity of the world smote his heart. The great sky towered up over him, and its divinity entered his soul; a strange longing after something "he knew not nor could name" awoke within him. followed by the pang of a sudden fear that there was no such thing as that which he sought.

Suddenly the voice of Shargar broke the spell, calling to him from afar to come and see a great salmon that lay by a stone in the water. But once aroused, the feeling that had come over him was never stilled; the desire never left him, sometimes growing to a passion that was relieved only by a flood of tears.

Strange as it may sound to those who have never thought of such things except in connection with Sundays and Bibles and churches and sermons, that which was now working in Falconer's mind was the first dull and faint movement of the greatest need that the human heart possesses—the need of God. There must be truth in the scent of that pinewood; someone must mean it. There must be a glory in those heavens that depends not upon our imagination; some power greater than they must dwell in them. Some spirit must move in that wind that haunts us with a kind of human sorrow; some soul must look up to us from the eye of that starry flower.

Little did Robert think that such was his need—that his soul was searching after One whose form was constantly presented to him, but as constantly obscured by the words without knowledge spoken in the religious assemblies of the land. Little did he realize that he was longing without knowing it on Saturday for that from which on the Sunday he would be repelled, again without knowing it.

For weeks the mood broken by the voice of his companion did not return, though the forms of nature were after that full of a pleasure he had never known before. He loved the grass; the water was more gracious to him; he would leave his bed early that he might gaze on the clouds of the east with their borders gold-blasted with sunrise; he would linger in the fields, that the amber and purple and green and red of the sunset might not escape after the sun unseen. And as long as he felt the mystery, the revelation of the mystery lay before and not behind him.[6]

That Holy Thing

They all were looking for a king
     To slay their foes, and lift them high:
Thou cam'st a little baby thing
     That made a woman cry.

O son of man, to right my lot
     Nought but thy presence can avail;
Yet on the road thy wheels are not,
     Nor on the sea thy sail!

My fancied ways why shouldst thou heed?
     Thou com'st down thine own secret stair;
Com'st down to answer all my need,
     Yea, every bygone prayer!

12

*J*ESUS THE SERVANT

He poured water into a basin, and began to wash the disciples' feet.

John 13:5

The Upside-Down Pyramid of God's Kingdom

Reflect a moment on Matthew's words in the twentieth chapter of his Gospel: "But Jesus called them unto him and said, 'Ye know that the princes of the Gentiles exercise dominion over them, and they that are great exercise authority upon them. But it should not be so among you: but whosoever will be great among you, let him be your minister; and whosoever will be chief among you, let him be your servant: even as the Son of Man came not to be ministered unto, but to minister, and to give his life a ransom for many.' "

How little this scripture is believed! People think, if they think about it at all, that this is very well in the church, but, as things go in the world, it won't do. At least their actions imply this, for every man is struggling to get above the other. There is a continual jostling, and crowding, and buzzing, and striving to get what we wrongly call *ahead*.

But it is not to be so if we would enter the kingdom of heaven. The Lord said, "It shall not be so among you."

The notion of rank in the world is like a pyramid; the higher you go up, the fewer there are above you whom you must serve, and the more you are served by those beneath you. All who are under serve those who are above, until you come to the apex, and there stands someone who has to do no service, but whom all the others have to serve.

In the kingdom of heaven, however, the figure is exactly reversed. The pyramid is upside-down. The Son of Man lies at the inverted apex of the pyramid. He upholds, and serves, and ministers unto all, and they who would be high in his kingdom must go near him, at the bottom, to uphold and minister to all they can uphold and minister unto.

There is no other law of precedence, no other law of rank and position in God's kingdom.

And that is the *only* kingdom. The other kingdom, that of this world, passes away.

Serving—for Truth's Sake

The man who seeks this rank of which I have spoken must be honest to follow it. It will not do to say, "I want to be great, therefore I will serve." A man will not get at it so. He must seek it for the truth's sake, for the love of his fellows, for the worship of God, for the delight in what is good.

In the kingdom of heaven people do not think whether they are promoted. They are so absorbed in the delight and glory of the goodness that is round about them that they learn not to think about themselves at all. It is the bad in us that makes us think about ourselves. It is necessary for us, because there is bad in us, to think about ourselves. But as we go on, we think less and less about ourselves, until at last we are possessed with the spirit of truth, the spirit of the kingdom, and live in gladness and in peace. We are prouder of our brothers and sisters than of ourselves; we delight in them.

The Lord says that "the Son of Man came not to be ministered unto." He was, of course, ministered unto, and even now we bring to him the burnt offerings of our very spirits.

But he did not come for that. It was to help us that he came. We are told also that he is the express image of the Father. Then what he does, the Father must do.

Do not think of God only as being always over our heads, merely throwing over us a widespread benevolence. Can you imagine the tenderness of a mother's heart, taking her child to soothe and minister to it. That is like God; that *is* God. It is God's way.

His hand is not only over us, but recollect what David said: "His hand was upon me . . . wherever I go, God is there—beneath me, before me, his hand is upon me; if I go to sleep, he is there; when I go down to the dead, he is there."

Everywhere is God. The earth underneath us is his hand upholding us; the waters are in the hollow of it. Every spring-fountain of gladness about us is his making and his delight. He tends us and cares for us;

he is close to us, breathing into our nostrils the breath of life, and breathing into our spirit this thought and that thought to make us look up and recognize the love and care around us.

But what a poor thing for the little baby would it be if it were to be constantly tended thus tenderly and preciously by its mother, but if it were never to open its eyes to look up and see the mother's face bending over it. To recognize and know this lovingkindness, and to stand up in it strong and glad; this is the ministration of God unto us.[1]

The necessities of our deepest nature do not allow us contentment in mere personal satisfaction. We were not made to live alone.

I well remember feeling as a child that I did not want God to love me if he did not love everybody. I had been taught that God chooses some but not others. My very being recoiled from the hint of such a false idea. Even were I one of the few, the chosen, the elect, I could not accept love from such a God. The kind of love I needed was essential to my nature—the same love that *all* men needed, the love that belonged to them as the children of the Father, a love he could not give me unless he gave it to all men.[2]

Daily Ministration—Door to the Kingdom

Do you ever think, "I could worship God if he were so-and-so?" Do you imagine that God is not as good, as perfect, as absolutely all-in-all as your thoughts can imagine? There is no way we can conceive of his wondrous goodness; he will not disappoint us; he will far exceed our wildest thoughts of goodness! Use all the words and symbols that we have in nature, in human relations, in the family—all our symbols of grace and tenderness, of lovingkindness between man and man, and between man and woman, and between woman and woman, but you can never come up to the thought of what God's loving ministration to us is.

When our Lord came, he let us see how his Father was doing this always. In giving his life he consummated and crowned it all. But it was his life that he gave for us—his whole being, his whole strength, his whole energy.

But how are we to learn this ministration?

I will tell you where it begins.

Most of us are forced to work. If you do not see that the commonest things of life—what we do from day to day—belong to the plan of God, you have got to learn it. Most of us have to work, and infinitely better is that for us than if we were not forced to work, but not a very fine thing unless it goes to something farther. We must work, then, and what is our work?

It is always, in some form, doing something for other people. It is doing; it is ministration in some shape or other.

It may not be so-called "Christian service," but all work is a serving. God's hand is in the commonest of everyday affairs. And one of the laws by which God intends that the world should go is that one man should be serviceable and useful and kind to another.

Thus, any man or woman who does honest work in service to another, who does a thing well, and who seeks diligently and kindly to serve his neighbor, and who tries to do what he has been given to do better, that man or woman is doing God's service.

Of course, this goes a great deal farther. We have endless opportunities of showing ourselves neighbors to the man or woman or child who comes near us. That is the true reality of serving God, on a far higher plane than mere diligent work to receive our wages. The deepest reward, if "reward" is a word that can be used at all in such a relation, ought to be the service we render our brothers and sisters. The Lord is serving us every moment, and he says, "If I have washed your feet, so you ought to wash one another's feet."

Service Is Present Obedience

There are some, when just beginning to learn this, who look about in a blind kind of way, thinking, "I wish I could serve God. I do not know what to do! How is it to be begun? What shall I do to find out? Where is there something for me to do?" Looking about for something grand, something, no doubt, also recognized by men, they ignore the service God has already put right in front of them. And he can give them nothing more to do until they do that.

Where does such service begin?

It begins where it began with Jesus, who was, and still is, a servant.

Service is obedience, or it is nothing. We obey God by serving our neighbor—just as Jesus did—by getting underneath the pyramid rather than seeking to climb to the top of it. Our Lord came to give his life, and to minister to all in obedience to his Father's will. We call him equal with God. Of course we do not pretend to explain it. We know that God is greater than he, because Jesus said so. But somehow we can worship him with our God, and we need not try to distinguish more than is necessary about it.

But observe his obedience to the Father. Jesus was not the ruler there. He did not give the commands; he obeyed them. And yet we say, he is God! In the kingdom of heaven, obedience is as divine in its essence as command. With regard to humanity, obedience is far more divine in its essence than command. It is not the ruling being who is most like God; it is the man who ministers to his fellow.

Obedience is the grandest thing in the world to begin with. Yes, and we shall end with it too.

Do you want to know how to minister, how to be a servant like Jesus was a servant?

Begin by obeying!

Obey everyone who has a right to command you. But above all, look to what our Lord has said, and find out what he wants you to do out of what he left behind. Obedience to that will make you part of the grand scheme and way of God in this world. Take your place in God's kingdom by so doing.

In obedience is salvation, in service is dignity—salvation from yourself, dignity before God and man.

Try it, and see whether you will not feel in yourself the beginning of being cleansed when you say, "I will seek no more to be above my fellows, but I will seek to minister to them, doing my work in God's name for them."

Let us go forth and do this service of God in ministering to our fellows, and so helping God in his work of upholding and glorifying and saving all.[3]

Whose Servant Are You?

"You cannot serve God and mammon."

Who said this? Is he not the Lord by whose name you are called, in whose name your churches are built, and who will at last judge every one of us? And yet how many of you are trying your hardest to do the very thing your Master tells you is impossible? I appeal to your own conscience. Are you not striving to serve God and mammon?

Do you say to yourselves that it cannot be? Surely if a man strove hard to serve both God and mammon, he would soon see that it was impossible. It is not easy to serve God, but it is easy to serve wealth. Surely the incompatibility of the two endeavors must quickly become apparent. But there is no strife in you. With *ease* you serve mammon every day and hour of your lives. But for God you do not even ask yourselves the question whether or not you are serving him at all.

Let us consider for a moment the God you often do not serve, and then the mammon you do serve, even without knowing it. The God you do not serve is the Father of lights, the source of love, the Maker of man and woman, the Head of the great family, the Father of father-hood and motherhood, the Life-giver who would die to preserve his children but would rather slay them than they should live as slaves of evil, the God who can neither think, nor do, nor endure anything mean or unfair, the God of poetry and music and every marvel, the God of the mountaintops and the rivers that run from the snows of death to make the earth joyous with life, the God of the valley and the wheat field, the God who has set love between youth and maiden, the God and Father of our Lord Jesus Christ, the Perfect, the God whom Christ knew, of whom he declared that to know him was eternal life.

The mammon you all too often serve is not a mere negation but a positive Death. His temple is a darkness, a black hollow, ever hungry, in the heart of man. His wages are death, but he calls them life, and many believe him. I will tell you some of the marks of his service, a few of the badges of his household for he has no visible temple. No man bends the knee to him; it is only his soul, his manhood, that the worshiper casts in the dust before him.

When a man talks of the joys of making money, or boasts of number one, meaning himself, then he is a servant of mammon. If when you make a bargain, you think only of yourself and your own gain, you are a servant of mammon. If in the church you would say to the rich man, "Sit here in a good place," and to the poor man, "Stand there," you are a mammon server. If you favor the company of the popular and those whom men call well-to-do, then you are serving mammon and not God. If your hope of well-being in times to come rests upon your houses or lands or business or savings, and not upon the living God, whether you are friendly and kind or a churl whom no one loves, you are equally a server of mammon. If the loss of your goods would take from you the joy of your life, then you serve mammon. If with your words you confess that God is the only good, and yet you live as if he had sent you into the world to make yourself rich before you die; if it will add a pang to the pains of your death to think that you have to leave your fair house, your trees, your horses, your shop, your books all behind you, then you are a server of mammon and far truer to your real master than he will prove to you.

The moment the breath is out of your body, your master has already deserted you. And of all that for which you did rejoice, that which gave you such power over your fellows, there is not left so much as a spike of thistledown for the wind to blow from your sight. For all you had there is nothing to show.

Some of you are no doubt saying in your hearts, "Preach to yourself, and practice your own preaching!"

And you say well. And so I mean to do, lest having preached to others I should myself be a castaway. But let me continue.

Money is not mammon. It is God's invention. It is good and the gift of God. If it were not for money and the need of it, there would not be half the friendships in the world. It is powerful for good when divinely used. Give it plenty of air, and it is sweet as the hawthorn. But shut it up, and it rots and breeds worms. Like the earth itself, like the heart and mind of man, it must be broken and turned, not heaped together and neglected.

Money is an angel of mercy, whose wings are full of balm and dews and refreshings. But when you lay hold of him, pluck his wings, pen him in a yard, and fall down and worship him, then with the blessed vengeance of God his Master, he deals plague and confusion and terror to stop the idolatry. If I misuse or waste or hoard it, I pray my Master to see to it and punish me. I would undergo the pain of any fire rather than be given over to the disgusting idol!

Friends, don't be the slave of materialism, of greed, of selfishness. Be wary. Don't hoard the gold when it is in your purse. Instead, in God's name, spend—and spend more. Take heed *how* you spend. But take heed that you *do* spend. Be as the sun in heaven; let your money be your rays, your angels of life and love and deliverance. Be a candle of the Lord to spread his light through the world. If until now you have radiated darkness in any fashion, humble yourself; then arise and shine.

But if you are poor, then don't mourn over your purse when it is empty. He who desires more than God wills him to have, he also is a servant of mammon, for he trusts in what God has made and not in God himself. He who laments what God has taken from him, he is a servant of mammon. He who cannot pray because of the worldly cares pressing in on him is a servant of mammon.

Certain men love and trust their horses more than the God who made both them *and* their horses. None the less confidently will they expound on the doctrine of God. But a man who does not surrender his soul to the living God and live in him, his religion is worth the splinter of a straw. A man's views on the things of God can be trusted only to the extent that man is himself walking with God.

Friends, cast your idol into the furnace. Melt your mammon down, coin him up, make God's money of him, and send him out to do God's work. Make of him cups to carry the gift of God, the water of life, through the world—in lovingkindness to the oppressed, in rest to the weary who have borne the burden and heat of the day, in joy to the heavy-hearted, in laughter to the dull-spirited. Let them all be glad with reason and merry without gloating.

Ah, what gifts in music, in drama, in the story, in the picture, in books, in flowers and friendly feasting, what true gifts might not the mammon of unrighteousness, changed back into the money of God, give to men and women, bone of our bone, flesh of our flesh! How would you not spend your money for the Lord if he need it from your hand?

He *does* need it, for he that spends it upon the least of his fellows spends it upon the Lord.

Hold fast to God with one hand while you open wide the other to your neighbor—that is true religion and undefiled, that is to live the life Jesus came to teach us about and to demonstrate to us.

Lord, defend us from mammon. Hold your temple against his foul invasion. Purify our money with your air and your sun that it may be our slave, and you our Master. Amen.[4]

Sweeper of the Floor

Methought that in a solemn church I stood.
Its marble acres, worn with knees and feet,
Lay spread from door to door, from street to street.
Midway the form hung high upon the rood
Of him who gave his life to be our good;
Beyond, priests flitted, bowed, and murmured meet,
Among the candles shining still and sweet.
Men came and went, and worshipped as they could—
And still their dust a woman with her broom,
Bowed to her work, kept sweeping to the door.
Then saw I, slow through all the pillared gloom,
Across the church a silent figure come:
"Daughter," it said, "thou sweepest well my floor!"
It is the Lord! I cried, and saw no more.

DIVINE SERVICE

(A Fictional Selection from *The Curate's Awakening*)

Later that afternoon Wingfold took the draper to see Polwarth. The dwarf allowed Wingfold to help him in getting tea, and the conversation, as will be the case where all are in earnest, quickly found the right channel.

It is not often in life that such conversations occur. In most discussions, each man has some point to maintain, and his object is to justify his own thesis and disprove his neighbor's. He may have originally adopted his thesis because of some sign of truth in it, but his mode of supporting it is generally to block up every cranny in his soul at which more truth might enter. In the present case, unusual as it is for as many as three truth-loving men to come together on the face of this planet, here were three simply set on uttering truth they had seen and gaining sight of truth as yet hidden from them.

I shall attempt only a general impression of the result of their evening's discussion.

"I have been trying hard to follow you, Mr. Polwarth," acknowledged the draper, after his host had for a while had the talk to himself, "but I cannot get hold of it. Would you tell me what you mean by divine service? I think you use the phrase in some different sense from what I have been accustomed to."

"When I use the phrase *divine service*," explained Polwarth, "I mean nothing whatever about the church or its observance. I mean simply serving God. Shall I make the church a temple of idolatrous worship by supposing that it exists for the sake of supplying some need that God has, or of gratifying some taste in him, that I there listen to his Word, say prayers to him, and sing his praises for his benefit? Shall I degrade the sanctity of the closet, hallowed in the words of Jesus, by shutting myself behind its door in the vain fancy of doing something there that God requires of me as a sacred *observance*? Shall I foolishly imagine that to exercise the highest and loveliest privilege of my existence, that of pouring forth my whole heart in prayer into the heart of him who is accountable for me, who has glorified me with his own image—in my soul, gentlemen, sadly disfigured as it is in my body!—shall I call *that* serving God?"

"But," interjected Drew, "is not God pleased that a man should pour out his soul to him?"

"Yes, doubtless. But is the child who sits by his father's knee and looks up into his father's face *serving* that father because the heart of the father delights to look down upon the child? And shall the moment of my deepest repose, the moment when I serve myself with the life of the universe, be called serving my God? What would you think of a child who said, 'I am very useful to my father, for when I ask him for something, or tell him I love him, it gives him such pleasure'? When my child would serve me, he sees some need I have, jumps from his seat at my knee, finds that which will meet my need, and is my eager, happy servant; he has done something for his father. His seat by my knee is love, delight, well-being, peace—not service, however pleasing in my eyes. Do not talk of public worship as divine service. Search the prophets and you will find observances, fasts and sacrifices and solemn feasts of the temple were regarded by God's holy men with loathing and scorn just because by the people they were regarded as *divine service*."

"But," speculated Mr. Drew, "I can't help thinking that if the phrase ever was used in that sense, there is no meaning of that kind attached to it now: service stands merely for the forms of public worship."

"If there were no such thing as *divine service* in the true sense of the word, then it would scarcely be worthwhile to quarrel with its misapplication. But I believe that true and genuine service may be given to the living God. And for the development of the divine nature in man, it is necessary that he should do something for God. And it is not hard to discover how, for God is in every creature and in their needs. Therefore, Jesus says that whatever is done to one of his little ones is done to him. And if the soul of a believer be the temple of the Spirit, then is not the place of that man's labor—his shop, his bank, his laboratory, his school, his factory—the temple of Jesus Christ, where the spirit of the man is at work? Mr. Drew, your shop is the temple of your service where the Lord Christ ought to be throned. Your counter ought to be his altar, and everything laid on it with intent of doing as you can for your neighbor, in the name of Christ Jesus."

The little prophet's face glowed as he stopped. But neither of his companions spoke.

Polwarth went on, "You will not become a rich man, but by so doing you will be saved from growing too rich and you will be a fellow worker with God for the salvation of his world."

"I must live; I cannot give my goods away," murmured Mr. Drew, thinking about all he had heard.

"Giving them away would be easy," added Polwarth. "No, a harder task is yours, Mr. Drew—to make your business profitable to you, and at the same time to be not only just, but interested in, and careful of, and caring for your neighbor—as a servant of the God of bounty who gives to all men liberally. Your calling is to do the best for your neighbor that you reasonably can."

"But who is to determine what is reasonable?" asked Drew.

"The man himself, thinking in the presence of Jesus Christ. There is a holy moderation which is of God, and he will gladly reveal it to you."

"There won't be many fortunes made by that rule, Mr. Polwarth."

"Very few," admitted the dwarf.[5]

The Consoler

On an Engraving of Scheffer's Christus Consolator.

What human form is this? What form divine?
And who are these that gaze upon his face
Mild, beautiful, and full of heavenly grace,
With whose reflected light the gazers shine?
Saviour, who does not know it to be thine?
Who does not long to fill a gazer's place?
And yet there is no time, there is no space
To keep away thy servants from thy shrine!
Here if we kneel, and watch with faithful eyes,
Thou art not too far for faithful eyes to see,
Thou art not too far to turn and look on me,
To speak to me, and to receive my sighs.
Therefore forever I forget the skies,
And find an everlasting Sun in thee.

Oh let us never leave that happy throng!
From that low attitude of love not cease!
In all the world there is no other peace,
In all the world no other shield from wrong.
But chiefly, Saviour, for thy feet we long—
For no vain quiet, for no pride's increase—
But that, being weak, and thou divinely strong,
Us from our hateful selves thou mayst release.
We wander from thy fold's free holy air,
Forget thy looks, and take our fill of sin!
But if thou keep us evermore within,
We never surely can forget thee there—
Breathing thy breath, thy white robe given to wear,
And loving thee for all thou didst die to win!

To speak of him in language of our own,
Is not for us too daringly to try;
But, Saviour, we can read thy history
Upon the faces round thy humble throne;
And as the flower among the grass makes known
What summer suns have warmed it from the sky,
As every human smile and human sigh
Is witness that we do not live alone,
So in that company—in those sweet tears,
The firstborn of a rugged melted heart,
In those gaunt chains forever torn apart,
And in the words that weeping mother hears,
We read the story of two thousand years,
And know thee somewhat, Saviour, as thou art.

13

*J*ESUS THE MEEK AND LOWLY

Take my yoke upon you, and learn of me; for I am meek and lowly in heart; and ye shall find rest unto your souls. For my yoke is easy, and my burden is light.

Matthew 11:29–30

How God Reveals His Best Things

The Lord's words can be so interesting. But their very familiarity in our ears can cause us to miss their import.

Consider his statement in Matthew 11 just prior to that written above: "I thank thee, O Father, Lord of heaven and earth, because thou hast hid these things from the wise and prudent, and hast revealed them unto babes. Even so, Father: for so it seemed good in thy sight."

It is curious, is it not, how the things of God are always inverted in importance from the things of man. The Lord makes no complaint against the wise and prudent. He merely recognizes that they are not those to whom his Father reveals his best things, for which fact and the reasons of it, he thanks, or praises, his Father. *I bless thy will; I see that thou art right; I am of one mind with thee;* something of each of these phases of meaning seems to belong to the Greek word.

"But why not reveal true things first to the wise? Are they not the fittest to receive them?"

Only if these spiritual truths and the wisdom of so-called "wise" men lie in the same region—not otherwise. In fact, the wisdom of this world, meaning by the term, the philosophy of prudence, self-protection, precaution, especially *unfits* a man for receiving what the Father has to reveal. In proportion to our care about our own well-being is our capacity diminished to understand and welcome the care of the Father. The wise and prudent, with all their energy of thought, could never see the things of the Father sufficiently to recognize them as true. Their sagacity labors in earthly things, and so fills their minds with their own questions and conclusions, that they cannot see the eternal foundations God has laid in man, or the consequent necessities of their own nature.

Wise and prudent religious men interpret the great heart of God, not by their own hearts, but by their intellects. Then, postponing the obedience that alone can give power to the understanding, they press upon men's minds their low interpretations of the will of the Father, instead of by their own example impressing the doing of that will upon their hearts. They are the slaves of the letter in all its weakness and imperfection—and will be until the Spirit of the Word, the Spirit of obedience, shall set them free.

Terribly has the gospel of Jesus suffered in the mouths of the wise and prudent! How would it be faring now had its first messages been committed to persons of great repute, instead of those simple fishermen? From the first we should have had a system founded on a human interpretation of the divine gospel, instead of the gospel itself. As it is, we have had one dull miserable human system after another usurping its place. But, thank God, the gospel remains!

Had the wise and prudent been the confidants of God, the letter would at once have usurped the place of the spirit, and a system of religion, with its rickety, malodorous plan of salvation, would have been put in the place of a living Christ. The great Brother, the human God, the eternal Son, the living One, would have been utterly hidden from the tearful eyes and aching hearts of the weary and heavy laden.

But the Father revealed his things to babes, because the babes were his own little ones, uncorrupted by the wisdom or the care of this world, and therefore able to receive them. The babes are near enough whence they come to understand a little how things go in the presence of their Father in heaven, and thereby to interpret the words of the Son. Quickly will the Father seal the old bond when the Son himself, the first of the babes, the one perfect babe of God, comes to lead the children out of the lovely "shadows of eternity" into the land of the "white celestial thought." As God is the one, only, real Father, so is it only to God that anyone can be a perfect child. Only in his garden can childhood blossom.

Jesus Shows Us How to Be Children

Having thanked his Father, Jesus turns to his disciples and tells them that he knows the Father, being his Son, and that he only can reveal the Father to the rest of his children: "No man knoweth the Son, but the Father; neither knoweth any man the Father save the Son, and he to whomsoever the Son will reveal him." It is almost as if his mention of the babes brought his thoughts back to himself and his Father, between whom lay the secret of all life. The relation of the Father and the Son contains the idea of the universe.

No man, when first he comes to himself, can have any true knowledge of God. He can have only desire for such knowledge. The Father must draw nearer to him. He therefore sends his firstborn, who does know him, is exactly like him, and can represent him perfectly. Drawn to the Son, the children receive him, and then he is able to reveal the Father to them.

No wisdom of the wise can find out God. The simplicity of the whole natural relation is too deep for the philosopher. The Son alone can reveal God; the child alone understands him.

The Elder Brother accompanies the younger, and makes him yet more a child like himself. He interpenetrates his willing companion with his obedient glory. He lets him see how he delights in his Father, and lets him know that God is his Father too. He rouses in his little brother and sister the sense of their Father's will. And the younger, as he hears and obeys, begins to see that his Elder Brother must be the very image of their Father. He becomes more and more of a child, and more and more the Son reveals to him the Father. For he knows that to know the Father is the one thing every child of the Father needs, the one thing to fill the divine gulf of his necessity. To see the Father is the cry of every child-heart in the universe of the Father.

Comfort yourselves then, brothers and sisters. He to whom the Son will reveal him shall know the Father, and the Son came to us that he might reveal him. "Eternal Brother," we cry, "show us the Father. Be thyself to us, that in thee we may know him. We too are his children. Let the other children share with thee in the things of the Father."

Not Our Yoke, but His

Having spoken to his Father first, and then to his disciples, the Lord turns to the whole world and lets his heart overflow: "Come unto me all ye that labor and are heavy laden, and I will give you rest." His call reaches to the very ends of the earth. He calls those who are weary, those who do not even know that ignorance of the Father is the cause of all their labor and the heaviness of their burden.

This is the Lord's own form of his gospel, more intensely personal and direct, and at the same time of wide inclusion. "I have rest because I know the Father," he says. "Be meek and lowly of heart toward him as I am. Let him lay his yoke upon you as he lays it on me. I do his will, not my own. Take on you the yoke that I wear; be his child like me; become a babe to whom he can reveal his wonders. Then shall you too find rest for your souls. You shall have the same peace I have; you will be weary and heavy laden no more. I find my yoke easy, my burden light."

We must not imagine that when the Lord says, "Take my yoke upon you," he means for us to take a yoke *like* his; we must take on us the *very* yoke that he himself is carrying. The intent of his words is this: "Take the other end of *my* yoke, doing as I do, being as I am."

Think of it a moment: to walk in the same yoke with the Son of Man, doing the same labor with him! Nothing less than this is offered the man who would have rest in his soul, is required of the man who would know the Father, is by the Lord pressed upon him to whom he would give the same peace which pervades and sustains his own eternal heart.

But a yoke is for drawing. And what load is the Lord pulling? With what is the cart laden which he would have us help him draw?

With what but the will of the eternal, the perfect Father?

How should the Father honor the Son, but by giving him his will to embody in deed, by making him hand to his Father's heart—and hardest of all, in bringing home his children! Especially in drawing this load must his yokefellow share. How to draw it, he must learn of him who draws by his side.

Whoever, in the commonest duties that fall to him, does as the Father would have him do, bears his yoke along with Jesus; and the Father takes his help for the redemption of the world—for the deliverance of men from the slavery of their own rubbish-laden wagons, into the liberty of God's husbandmen.

Bearing the same yoke with Jesus, the man and woman learn to walk step by step with him, drawing the cart laden with the will of the Father of both, and rejoicing with the joy of Jesus. The glory of existence is to take up its burden, and exist for Existence eternal and supreme—for the Father who does his divine and perfect best to impart his glad life to us, making us sharers of that nature which is bliss, and that labor which is peace.

He lives for us; we must live for him. The little ones must take their full share in the great Father's work; his work is the business of the family.

The Wonderful Burden!

Does your soul jump, does your brain tremble at the thought of such a burden as the will of the eternally creating, eternally saving God?

"How shall mortal man walk in such a yoke?" you say, "even with the Son of God bearing it also?"

Why, brother, sister, it is the only burden bearable—the only burden that can be borne of mortal man. Under any other, even the lightest, he must at last sink, worn out and weary, his very soul gray with sickness.

He on whom the other half of the burden lays, with the weight of God's creation to redeem, says, "The yoke I bear is easy; the burden I draw is light." And this he said knowing the death he was soon to die. The yoke did not gall his neck; the burden did not overstrain his muscles; neither did the goal on Calvary frighten him away from the straight way thither. He had the will of the Father to work out, and that was his strength as well as his joy. He had the same will as his Father. To him the one thing worth living for was the share the love of his Father gave him in his work. He loved his Father even to the death of the cross, and eternally beyond it.

When we give ourselves up to the Father as the Son gave himself, we shall not only find our yoke easy and our burden light, but that they communicate ease and lightness. Not only will they not make us weary, but they will give us rest from all other weariness.

Let us not waste a moment in asking how this can be; the only way to know that is to take the yoke on us. That rest is a secret for every heart to know, for never a tongue to tell. Only by having it can we know it. If it seems impossible to take the yoke on us, let us attempt the impossible: let us lay hold of the yoke, and bow our heads, and try to get our necks under it. If we give our Father the opportunity, he will help and not fail us. He is helping us every moment when we least think we need his help.

When or how much his creatures can do or bear, only God understands. But when it seems most impossible to do or bear, we must be most confident that he will neither demand too much, nor fail with the vital Creator-help. That help will be there when needed—that is, the moment it can be of help. To be able beforehand to imagine ourselves doing or bearing, we have neither claim nor need.

It is vain to think that any weariness, however caused, any burden, however slight, may be got rid of otherwise than by bowing the neck to the yoke of the Father's will. There can be no other rest for heart and soul that he has created. From every burden, from every anxiety, from all dread of shame or loss, even loss of love itself, that yoke will set us free.[1]

To One Unsatisfied

When, with all the loved around thee,
Still, thy heart says, "I am lonely,"
It is well; the truth hath found thee:
Rest is with the Father only.

COME, AND YOU SHALL FIND REST

(A Fictional Selection from *The Curate's Awakening*)

As Wingfold walked back to his lodgings, he found a new element mingling in his thoughts. Human suffering laid hold upon him in a way that was new to him. He realized there were hearts in the world from whose agony broke terrible cries, hearts which produced sad faces like Miss Lingard's. Such hearts might be groaning and writhing in any of the houses he passed, and even if he knew the hearts, he could do nothing for their relief. What multitudes there must be in the world—how many even in Glaston—whose hearts were overwhelmed, who knew their own bitterness, and yet had no friend radiant enough to bring sunshine into their shady places! He fell into a mournful mood over the troubles of his race. Though always a kind-hearted fellow, he had not been used to thinking about such things; he had experienced troubles enough of his own. But now that he had begun to hope, he saw a glimmer of light somewhere at the end of the dark cave in which he had all at once discovered that he was buried alive. He began also to feel how wretched those must be who were groping on without any hope in their dark eyes.

If he had never committed any crime, he had yet done enough wrong to understand the misery of shame and dishonor. How much more miserable must those be who had committed some terrible deed? What relief, what hope was there for them? What a breeding nest of cares and pains was the human heart! Oh, surely it needed some refuge! If no Savior had yet come, the tortured world of human hearts cried aloud for one. The world certainly needed a Savior to whom anyone might go, at any moment, without a journey, without letters or commendations or credentials. And yet, what was the good of the pardon such a one might give if still the consciousness of the deeds of sin or the misery of loneliness kept on stinging? And who would wish one he loved to grow callous to a sin he had committed?

But if there was a God—such a God as, according to the Christian story, had sent his own son into the world, had given him to appear among us, clothed in the garb of humanity, to take all the consequences of being the son of obedience among the children of disobedience, engulfing their wrongs in his infinite forgiveness, and winnng them back, by slow and unpromising and tedious renewal, to the heart of his father, surely such a God would not have created them knowing that some of them would commit such horrible sins from which he could not redeem them. And as he thought, the word rose in his mind, *"Come unto me, all you that labor and are heavy laden, and I will give you rest."*

His heart filled! He pondered the words. When he got home, he sought and found them in the book. *Did a man ever really say them?* he wondered to himself. Such words they were! If a man did utter them, either he was the most presumptuous of mortals, or *he could do what he said.*

All the rest of the week his mind was full of thoughts like these. Again and again the suffering face of Helen Lingard arose, bringing with it the growing suspicion that behind it must lie some oppressive secret. When he raised his head on Sunday and cast his eyes around on his congregation, they rested for one brief moment on her troubled countenance whose reflection so often lately had looked out from the mirror of his memory. Next they flitted across the satisfied, healthy, clever face of her cousin, behind which plainly sat a seared conscience in an easy chair. The third moment they saw the pevish autumnal visage of Mrs. Ramshorn. The next they roved a little, then rested on the draper's good-humored face on which brooded a cloud of thoughtfulness. Last of all they found the faces of both the dwarfs. It was the first time he had seen Rachel there, and it struck him that her face expressed greater suffering than he had read in it before. *She ought to be in bed rather than church*, he thought. The same seemed to be the case with her uncle's countenance also.

With these fleeting observations came the conclusion that the pulpit was a wonderful watchtower from which to study human nature, for people lay bare more of their real nature and condition to the man in the pulpit than they know. Their faces had fallen into the shape of their minds, for the church had an isolating as well as a congregating power. This all flashed through the curate's mind in the briefest of moments before he began to speak. The tears rose in his eyes as he gazed, and his heart swelled toward his own flock, as if his spirit would break forth in a flood of tenderness. Then he quickly began to speak.

As usual his voice trembled at first, but then gathered strength as it found its way. This is a good deal like what he said:

"The marvelous man who is reported to have appeared in Palestine, teaching and preaching, seems to have suffered far more from sympathy with the inward sorrows of his race than from pity for their bodily pains. These last could he not have swept from the earth with a word? And yet it seems to have been mostly, if not always, only in answer to prayer that he healed them. Even then he did so for the sake of some deeper spiritual healing that should go with the bodily cure. His tears could not have flowed for the dead man whom he was about to call from the tomb. What source could they have but compassion and pitiful sympathy for the dead man's sisters and friends in their sorrows?

"Yet are there not more terrible troubles than mourning a death? There is the weight of conscious wrong-being and wrong-doing: that is the gravestone that needs to be rolled away before a man can rise to life. The guilt of sin, that is the great weight which rests upon us. Call to mind how Jesus used to forgive men's sins, thus lifting from their hearts the crushing load that paralyzed them—the repentant woman who wept sore-hearted from very love, the publicans who knew they were despised because they were despicable. With him they sought and found shelter. He received them, and the life within them rose up, and the light shone—despite shame and self-reproach. If God be for us, who can be against us? In his name they rose from the hell of their own heart's condemnation, and went forth into truth and strength and hope. They heard and believed and obeyed his words. And of all words that ever were spoken, were there ever any gentler, tenderer, humbler, lovelier than these? *'Come unto me all ye that labor and are heavy laden, and I will give you rest. Take my yoke upon you, and learn of me; for I am meek and lowly in heart: and you shall find rest for your souls. For my yoke is easy, and my burden is light.'*

"Surely these words, could they but be believed, are such as every human heart might gladly hear! You who call yourselves Christians profess to believe such rest is available, yet how many of you take no single step toward him who says 'Come,' lift not an eye to see whether a face of mercy may not be gazing down upon you? Is it that you do not believe there ever was such a man they call Jesus? Or is it that you are doubtful concerning the whole significance of his life? If the man said the words, he must have at least believed he could fulfill them. Who that knows anything about him can for a moment say that this man did not believe what he spoke?

"Hear me, my friends; I dare not yet say I know there is a Father. I can only say with my whole heart I hope we indeed have a Father in heaven. But this man says *he knows*. If he tells me he knows, I must listen and observe that it is his own best he wants to give; no bribe to obedience to his will, but the assurance of bliss if we will but do as he does. He wants us to have peace—*his* peace—peace from the same source as his. For what does he mean by, 'Take my yoke upon you and learn of me'? He does not mean, *Wear the yoke I lay upon you*. I do not say he might not have said what amounts to the same thing at other times, but that is not the truth he would convey in these words. He means, *Take upon you the yoke that I wear; learn to do as I do, who submits everything and refers everything to the will of my Father. Yea, have my will only insofar as I carry out his will; be meek and lowly in heart, and you shall find rest for your souls.* With all the grief of humanity in his heart, in the face of the death that awaited him, he yet says, 'For my yoke, the yoke I wear, is easy, the burden I bear is light.'

"What made that yoke easy—that burden light? That it was the will of the Father. If a man answer, 'Any good man who believed in a god might say the same thing, and I do not see how that can help me,' my reply is that this man says, 'Come unto me, and I will give you rest'—asserting the power to give perfect help to him that comes. No one else can do that. Does all this seem too far away, my friends, and very distant from the things about us? The things close by do not give you peace. Peace has to come from somewhere else. And do not our souls themselves cry out for a nobler, better, more beautiful life?"

Long before he came to a close, Wingfold was blind to all before him. He felt only the general suffering of the human soul. He did not see that Helen was sobbing convulsively. The word had touched her and had unsealed the fountain of tears, if not of faith. Neither did he see the curl on the lip of Bascombe, or the glance of annoyance which, every now and then, he cast upon the bent head beside him. What on earth are you crying about? flashed in Bascombe's eyes, but Helen did not see them. One or two more in the congregation were weeping, and here and there shone a face in which the light seemed to prevent the tears. Polwarth shone and Rachel wept. For the rest, the congregation listened only with varying degrees of attention and indifference. The majority looked as if neither Wingfold nor anyone else ever meant anything—at least in the pulpit.[2]

Blessed Are the Meek, For They Shall Inherit the Earth

A quiet heart, submissive, meek,
Father, do thou bestow,
Which more than granted, will not seek
To have, or give, or know.

Each little hill then holds its gift
Forth to my joying eyes;
Each mighty mountain then doth lift
My spirit to the skies.

Lo, then the running water sounds
With gladsome, secret things!
The silent water more abounds,
And more the hidden springs.

Live murmurs then the trees will blend
With all the feathered song;
The waving grass low tribute lend
Earth's music to prolong.

The sun will cast great crowns of light
On waves that anthems roar;
The dusky billows break at night
In flashes on the shore.

Each harebell, each white lily's cup,
The hum of hidden bee,
Yea, every odour floating up,
The insect revelry—

Each hue, each harmony divine
The holy world about,
Its soul will send forth into mine,
My soul to widen out.

And thus the great earth I shall hold,
A perfect gift of thine;
Richer by these, a thousandfold,
Than if broad lands were mine.

14

*J*ESUS THE CHILDLIKE

Except ye be converted, and become as little children, ye shall not enter into the kingdom of heaven.

Matthew 18:3

Essential Childhood

There are two scriptures we must look at. The first is from Mark: "And he sat down, and called the twelve, and saith unto them, 'If any man desire to be first, the same shall be last of all, and servant of all.' He took a child, and set him in the midst of them: and when he had taken him in his arms, he said unto them, 'Whosoever shall receive one of such children in my name, receiveth me: and whosoever shall receive me, receiveth not me, but him that sent me' " (Mark 9: 35–37).

This passage records a lesson our Lord gave his disciples against ambition, against emulation.

It is not for the sake of setting forth this lesson that I write about these words of our Lord, but for the sake of a truth, a revelation about God's character, in which his great argument reaches its height. The lesson lay, not in the humanity of the disciples, but in the *childhood* of the child. And it led to the enunciation of a yet higher truth, upon which it was founded, and from which indeed it sprung.

Nothing is required of man that is not first in God. It is because God is perfect that we are required to be perfect. And it is for the revelation of God to all human souls, that they may be saved by knowing him, and so becoming like him, that a child was thus chosen and set before them in the gospel. He who, in giving the cup of water or the embrace, comes into contact with the essential childhood of the child—that is, embraces the *childlike* humanity of it—is a partaker of the meaning, that is, the blessedness of this passage. It is the recognition of childhood as divine that will show the disciple how vain the strife after relative place or honor is in the great kingdom.

For he says *in my name.* This means *as representing me;* and, therefore, *as being like me.* Our Lord could not commission anyone to be received in his name who could not more or less represent him. He had just been telling the disciples that they must become like this child. And now, when he tells them to receive such a little child in his name, it must surely imply something in common between them all—something in which the child and Jesus meet—something in which the child and the disciples meet. What else can that be than the spiritual childhood?

It is not blind and arbitrary obedience alone that the Lord will have, but obedience to the *truth.*

He who receives a child in the name of Jesus does so perceiving, wherein Jesus and the child are one, what is common to them. He must not only see that reality of loveliness in the child which constitutes true childhood, but must perceive that the child is like Jesus, or rather, that the Lord is like the child, and may be embraced, yes, is embraced, by every heart childlike enough to embrace a child for the sake of his childness.

For the blessedness is the perceiving of the truth. The blessing is the truth itself, the God-known truth that the Lord has the heart of a child.

To receive a child in the name of Jesus is to receive Jesus; to receive Jesus is to receive God; therefore to receive the child is to receive God himself.

Kingdom Truth—God Is Like the Child

The second scripture tells us a great deal about the kingdom of heaven.

"Verily I say unto you, except ye be converted, and become as little children, ye shall not enter into the kingdom of heaven. Whosoever therefore shall humble himself as this little child, the same is greatest in the kingdom of heaven. And whosoever shall receive one such little child in my name receiveth me" (Matthew 18:3–5).

What is the kingdom of Christ?

A rule of love, of truth—a rule of service.

The king is the chief servant in it. "The kings of the earth have dominion: it shall not be so among you . . . the Son of Man came to minister."

So he that would be greatest among them, and come nearest the King himself, must be the servant of all. If to enter into this kingdom we must become children, the spirit of children must be its pervading spirit throughout, from lowly subject to lowliest king.

The lesson added by St. Luke to the presentation of the child is: "For he that is least among you all, the same shall be great." St. Matthew says: "Whosoever shall humble himself as this little child, the same is greatest in the kingdom of heaven."

Hence the sign that passes between king and subject. The subject kneels in homage to the kings of the earth; the heavenly king takes his subject in his arms. This is the all-pervading relation of the kingdom.

To receive the child because God receives it is one thing; to receive it because it is *like* God is another. The former will do little to destroy ambition, but the latter strikes at the very root of emulation. As soon as service is done for the honor and not for the service-sake, the doer is that moment outside the kingdom. But when we receive the child in the name of Christ, the very childhood that we receive into our arms is humanity. We love its humanity in its childhood, for childhood is the deepest heart of humanity—its divine heart; and so in the name of Jesus we receive all humanity. Therefore, although the lesson is not about humanity, but about childhood, it returns upon our race, and we receive our race with wider arms and deeper heart.

But to advance now to the highest point of this teaching of our Lord: "He that receiveth me receiveth him that sent me." To receive a child in the name of God is to receive God himself.

How do we receive him?

As alone he can be received: by knowing him as he is. To know him is to have him in us. And that we may know him, let us now receive this revelation of him, in the words of our Lord himself. Here is the argument of highest import founded upon the teaching of our Master in the utterance before us.

God is represented in Jesus, because God is like Jesus. Jesus is represented in the child, because Jesus is like the child. Therefore God is represented in the child, because he is like the child.

God is childlike. In the true vision of this fact lies the receiving of God in the child.

If the Lord meant this—that is, if this be a truth—he that is able to receive it will receive it; he that hath ears to hear it will hear it. For our Lord's arguments are for the presentation of the truth, and the truth carries its own conviction to him who is able to receive it.[1]

Growing Into Childhood

The same thing is lovely in the child and the Ancient of days. Some scholars and critics foolishly object that the Master taught what others had taught before him, as if he should not be the wise householder with his old things as well as new. Such men recognize the old things. The new they do not understand, therefore do not consider.

Who first taught that the mighty God, the Lord, the maker of heaven and earth, was like a child?

Who first said, "Love one another as I have loved you"?

Who first dared to say, "He that overcometh shall sit down with me on my throne even as I overcame and am set down with my Father on his throne"?

Who first taught men that the creature who would but be a true creature should share the glory of his Creator, sitting with him, on his throne?[2]

There is a childhood into which we have to grow, just as there is a childhood which we must leave behind. Most of us, as we are leaving the one, as yet have scarce an inkling of the other.

One is a childishness from which but few of those who are counted wisest among men have freed themselves. The other is a childlikeness, which is the highest gain of humanity.[3]

The Christmas Child

"Little one, who straight hast come
Down the heavenly stair,
Tell us all about your home,
And the father there."

"He is such a one as I,
Like as like can be.
Do his will, and, by and by,
Home and him you'll see."

ARMS OF THE ETERNAL

(A Fictional Selection from *The Minister's Restoration*)

O nce more out in the country, the beauties of the world began to work the will of their Maker upon Isy's poor lacerated soul. And afar in its hidden depths the process of healing was already begun. Sorrow would often return unbidden, would at times even rise like a crested wave and threaten despair, but the Real and the True, long hidden from her by false treatment and by the lying judgments of men and women, was now at length beginning to reveal himself to her tear-blinded vision. Hope was lifting a feeble head above the tangled weeds of the subsiding deluge, and before long the girl would be able to see and understand how little the Father, whose judgment in the truth of things, cares what at any time his child may have been or done the moment that child gives herself up to be made what he would have her! Looking down into the hearts of men, he sees differences there of which the self-important world takes no heed. For indeed, many that count themselves of the first, he sees the last—and what he sees, alone is. Kings and emperors may be utterly forgotten, while a gutter-child, a thief, a girl who in this world never had even a notion of purity, may lie smiling in the arms of the Eternal, while the head of a lordly house that still flourishes like a green baytree, may be wandering about with the dogs beyond the walls of the city.

In the open world, the power of the present God began at once to influence Isobel, for there, although dimly, she yet looked into his open face, sketched vaguely in the mighty something we call nature—chiefly on the great vault we call heaven. Shapely but undefined; perfect in form, yet limitless in depth; blue and persistent, yet ever evading capture by human heart in human eye; this sphere of fashioned boundlessness, of definite shapelessness, called up in her heart the formless children of upheavedness—grandeur, namely, and awe, hope and desire: all rushed together toward the dawn of the unspeakable One, who, dwelling in that heaven, is above all heavens; mighty and unchangeable, yet childlike; inexorable, yet tender as never was mother; devoted as never yet was any child except one. Isy, indeed, understood little of all this; yet she wept, she knew not why; and it was not for sorrow.[4]

A Song in the Night

I would I were an angel strong,
An angel of the sun, hasting along!

I would I were just come awake,
A child outbursting from night's dusky brake!

Or lark whose inward, upward fate
Mocks every wall that masks the heavenly gate!

Or hopeful cock whose clarion clear
Shrills ten times ere a film of dawn appear!

Or but a glowworm: even then
My light would come straight from the Light of Men!

I am a dead seed, dark and slow:
Father of larks and children, make me grow.

15

GOD IS LIGHT

God is light, and in him is no darkness at all.

1 John 1:5

Good News for the Heart

E very man must read the Word for himself. One may read it in one shape, another in another: all will be right if it be indeed the Word (Jesus) they read, and they read it by the lamp of obedience. He who is willing to do the will of the Father shall know the truth of the teaching of Jesus. The Spirit is "given to them that obey him."

Let us hear how John reads the Word in his version of the gospel: *"This then is the message,"* he says, *"which we have heard of him, and declare unto you, that God is light, and in him is no darkness at all."*

Ah, my heart, this is indeed good news for you!

This *is* Gospel! If God be light, what more, what else can I seek than God, than God himself!

Away with your doctrines! I am saved—for God is my light!

My God, I come to you. That you should be yourself is enough for time and eternity, for my soul and all its endless need.

Whatever seems to me darkness, that I will not believe of my God. If I should mistake, and call that darkness which is light, will he not reveal the matter to me, setting it in the light that lights every man, showing me that I saw but the husk of the thing, not the kernel? Will he not break open the shell for me, and let the truth of it, his thought, stream out upon me?

God is light far beyond what we can see. God means us to be jubilant in the fact that he is light. If I am not honest enough, if the eye in me be not single enough, then, Living Light, purge my eyes from their darkness, that they may let the light in, and so I become an inheritor, with your other children, of that light which is your God-head, and makes your creatures need to worship you. "In your light we shall see light."

In proportion, as we have the image of Christ mirrored in us, we shall know what is and what is not light. No being, for himself or for another, needs fear the light of God. All fear of the light comes of the darkness; it will vanish as we are more and more interpenetrated with the light.

An Ever-Enlarging Enough

There is no loveliness, nothing that makes man dear to his brother man, that is not in God, only it is infinitely better in God.

He is God our Savior. Jesus is our Savior because God is our Savior. He is the God of comfort and consolation. He will soothe and satisfy his children better than any mother her infant.

The only thing he will not give them this: He will not leave them to stay in the dark. If a child cries, "I want the darkness," and complains that God will not give it, yet God will not give it. He gives what his child needs—often by refusing what the child asks. If his child says, "I will not be good; I prefer to die; let me die!" God's dealing with that child will be as if he said, "No; I have the right to content you, not by giving you your own will but mine, which is your one good. You shall not die; you shall live to thank me that I would not answer your prayer."

There are good things God must delay giving, until his child has a pocket to hold them—until God gets his child to make that pocket. God must first make him fit to receive and to have. There is no part of our nature that shall not be satisfied—and that not by lessening it, but by enlarging it to embrace an ever-enlarging enough.[1]

The only refuge from heathenish representations of God under Christian forms, the only refuge from man's blinding and paralysing theories, from the dead, wooden shapes substituted for the living forms of human love and hope and aspiration, from the interpretations which render Scripture as dry as a speech in Chancery—surely the one refuge from all these evils is the Son of Man.

For no misrepresentation and no misconception can destroy the beauty of that face which the marring of sorrow has elevated into the region of reality, beyond the marring of irreverent speculation and scholastic definition. From the God of man's paintings, we turn to the man of God's being, and he leads us to the true God, the radiation of whose glory we first see in him.[2]

While there is a wonderful simplicity in God, much about him has been obscured by the traditions of men. We are surrounded with things difficult to understand. The way most people take is to look away, lest they should find out they have to understand them.

Some people are constantly rubbing at their skylights, but if they do not keep their other windows clean also, there will not be much light in the house.

God, like his body, the light, is all about us, and prefers to shine in upon us sideways, for we could not endure the power of his vertical glory. No mortal man can see God and live, and he who does not love his brother, whom he has seen, will not love his God, whom he has not seen. He will come to us in the morning through the eyes of a child when we have been gazing all night at the stars in vain.[3]

Come to God, then, my brother, my sister, with all your desires and instincts, all your lofty ideals, all your longing for purity and unselfishness, all your yearning to love and be true, all your aspirations after self-forgetfulness and child-life in the breath of the Father. Come to him with all your weaknesses, all your shames, all your futilities; with all your helplessness over your own thoughts; with all your failures, yes, the sick sense of having missed the tide of true affairs. Come to him with all your doubts, fears, dishonesties, meanness, paltriness, misjudgments, weariness, disappointments, and staleness. Be sure he will take you with all your miserable brood into the care of his limitless heart!

For he is light, and in him is no darkness at all.

Light Must Destroy Darkness

If he were a king, a governor, if the only name that described him were The Almighty, you might well doubt whether there could be light enough in him for you and your darkness. But he is your Father, and more your Father than the word can mean in any lips but his who said, "my Father and your Father, my God and your God." And such a Father *is* light, an infinite, perfect light. He is light, and in him is no darkness at all. If anything seems to be in him that you cannot be content with, be sure that the ripening of your love to your fellows and to him, the source of your being, will make you at length know that anything else than just what he is would have been to you an endless loss. Be not afraid to build upon the rock, Christ, with your holy imagination. Let no one persuade you that there is in him a little darkness, because of something he has said which his creature interprets as darkness.

No man is condemned for anything he has done; he is condemned for continuing to do wrong. He is condemned for not coming out of the darkness, for not coming to the light, the living God, who sent the light, his Son, into the world to guide him home.

God gives every man time. There is a light that lightens sage and savage, but the glory of God in the face of Jesus may not have shined on this sage or that savage. The condemnation is of those who, having seen Jesus, refuse to come to him, or pretend to come to him but do not the things he says. "All manner of sin and blasphemy," the Lord said, "shall be forgiven unto men; but the blasphemy against the Spirit shall not be forgiven." God speaks, as it were, in this manner: "I forgive you everything. Not a word more shall be said about your sins—only come out of them. Come out of the darkness of your exile. Come into the light of your home, of your birthright, and do evil no more. Lie no more, cheat no more, oppress no more, slander no more, envy no more, be neither greedy nor vain. Love your neighbor as I love you. Be my good child; trust in your Father. I am light. Come to me, and you shall see things as I see them, and hate the evil things. I will make you love the thing that now you call good and love not. I forgive all the past."

"I thank you, Lord, for forgiving me," says his child who does not yet love the light, "but I prefer staying in the darkness: forgive me that too."

"No; that cannot be," replies the Lord of light. "The one thing that cannot be forgiven is the sin of choosing to be evil, of refusing deliverance. It is impossible to forgive that sin. It would be to take part in it. To side with wrong against right, with murder against life, cannot be forgiven. The thing that is past I pass, but he who goes on doing the same, annihilates my forgiveness, makes it of no effect. Let a man have committed any sin whatever, I forgive him. But to choose to go on sinning—how can I forgive that? It would be to nourish and cherish evil! It would be to let my creation go to ruin. If a man refuses to come out of his sin, he must suffer the vengeance of a love that would be no love if it left him there. Shall I allow my creatures to be the thing my soul hates?"

There is no excuse for this refusal. If we were punished for every fault, there would be no end, no respite. But God passes by all he can. He passes by and forgets a thousand sins, yes, tens of thousands, forgiving them all—only we must begin to be good, begin to do evil no more. He who refuses must be punished and punished, punished through all the ages, punished until he gives way, yields, and comes to the light, that his deeds may be seen by himself to be what they are, and be by himself reproved, and the Father at last have his child again. For the man who in this world resists to the full, there may be, perhaps, a whole age or era in the history of the universe during which his sin shall not be forgiven. But *never* can it be forgiven until he repents. How can they who will not repent be forgiven, except in the sense that God does and will do all he can to make them repent? Who knows but such sin may need for its cure the continuous punishment of an aeon?

There are three conceivable kinds of punishment—first, that of mere retribution, which I take to be entirely and only human—therefore, indeed, more properly *inhuman*, for that which is not divine is not essential to humanity, and is of evil. Second, that which works repentance. And third, that which refines and purifies, working for holiness. But the punishment which falls on those whom the Lord loves because they have repented is a very different thing from the punishment that falls on those whom he loves indeed but cannot forgive, because they hold fast by their sins.

As God's essential nature *is* love, so he *is* light. There can be, by his very nature, no darkness in him. Therefore, the closer his creatures come to him, the more the remaining darkness must be burned out of them by the light of God's approaching presence.[4]

Enlighten Us, O Father of Lights!

(An Interpretation of God's Radiance in Verse)

LIGHT

Firstborn of the creating Voice!
Minister of God's Spirit, who wast sent
Waiting upon him first, what time he went
Moving about mid the tumultuous noise
Of each unpiloted element
Upon the face of the void formless deep!
Thou who didst come unbodied and alone
Ere yet the sun was set his rule to keep,
Or ever the moon shone,
Or e'er the wandering star-flocks forth were driven!
Thou garment of the Invisible, whose skirt
Sweeps, glory-giving, over earth and heaven!
Thou comforter, be with me as thou wert
When first I longed for words, to be
A radiant garment for my thought, like thee!

We lay us down in sorrow,
Wrapt in the old mantle of our mother Night;
In vexing dreams we strive until the morrow;
Grief lifts our eyelids up—and lo, the light!
The sunlight on the wall! And visions rise
Of shining leaves that make sweet melodies;
Of wind-borne waves with thee upon their crests;
Of rippled sands on which thou rainest down;
Of quiet lakes that smooth for thee their breasts;
Of clouds that show thy glory as their own;
O joy! O joy! The visions are gone by!
Light, gladness, motion, are reality!

Thou art the god of earth. The skylark springs
Far up to catch thy glory on his wings;
And thou dost bless him first that highest soars.
The bee comes forth to see thee; and the flowers
Worship thee all day long, and through the skies
Follow thy journey with their earnest eyes.
River of life, thou pourest on the woods,
And on thy waves float out the wakening buds;
The trees lean toward thee, and, in loving pain,
Keep turning still to see thee yet again;
South sides of pines, haunted all day by thee,
Bear violins that tremble humanly.
And nothing in thine eyes is mean or low:
Where'er thou art, on every side,
All things are glorified;
And where thou canst not come, there thou dost throw
Beautiful shadows, made out of the dark,
That else were shapeless; now it bears thy mark.

Thou plaything of the child,
When from the water's surface thou dost spring,
Thyself upon his chamber ceiling fling,
And there, in mazy dance and motion wild,
Disport thyself—etherial, undefiled,
Capricious, like the thinkings of the child!
I am a child again, to think of thee
In thy consummate glee.
How I would play with thee, athirst to climb
On sloping ladders of thy moted beams,
When through the gray dust darting in long streams!
How marvel at the dusky glimmering red,
With which my closed fingers thou hadst made
Like rainy clouds that curtain the sun's bed!
And how I loved thee always in the moon!
But most about the harvest-time,
When corn and moonlight made a mellow tune,
And thou wast grave and tender as a cooing dove!
And then the stars that flashed cold, deathless love!
And the ghost-stars that shimmered in the tide!
And more mysterious earthly stars,
That shone from windows of the hill and glen—
Thee prisoned in with lattice-bars,

Mingling with household love and rest of weary men!
And still I am a child, thank God!—to spy
Thee starry stream from bit of broken glass
Upon the brown earth undescribed,
Is a found thing to me, a gladness high,
A spark that lights joy's altar-fire within,
A thought of hope to prophecy akin,
That from my spirit fruitless will not pass.

Thou art the joy of age:
Thy sun is dear when long the shadow falls.
Forth to its friendliness the old man crawls,
And, like the bird hung out in his poor cage
To gather song from radiance, in his chair
Sits by the door; and sitteth there
His soul within him, like a child that lies
Half dreaming, with half-open eyes,
At close of a long afternoon in summer—
High ruins round him, ancient ruins, where
The raven is almost the only comer—
Half dreams, half broods, in wonderment
At thy celestial ascent
Through rifted loop to light upon the gold
That waves its bloom in some high airy rent:
So dreams the old man's soul, that is not old,
But sleepy mid the ruins that enfold.

What soul-like changes, evanescent moods,
Upon the face of the still passive earth,
Its hills, and fields, and woods,
Thou with thy seasons and thy hours art ever calling forth!
Even like a lord of music bent
Over his instrument,
Giving to carol, not to tempest birth!
When, clear as holiness, the morning ray
Casts the rock's dewy darkness at its feet,
Mottling with shadows all the mountain gray;
When, at the hour of sovereign noon,
Infinite silent cataracts sheet
Shadowless through the air of thunder-breeding June;
When now a yellower glory slanting passes
'Twixt longer shadows o'er the meadow grasses;

And now the moon lifts up her shining shield,
High on the peak of a cloud-hill revealed;
Now crescent, low, wandering sun-dazed away,
Unconscious of her own star-mingled ray,

    Of operative single power,
And simple unity the one emblem,
Yet all the colours that our passionate eyes devour,
In rainbow, moonbow, or in opal gem,
Are the melodious descant of divided thee.
Lo thee in yellow sands! Lo thee
In the blue air and sea!
In the green corn, with scarlet poppies lit,
Thy half-souls parted, patient thou dost sit.
Lo thee in dying triumphs of the west!
Lo thee in dewdrop's tiny breast!
Thee on the vast white cloud that floats away,
Bearing upon its skirt a brown moon-ray!
Gold-regent, thou dost spendthrift throw
Thy hoardless wealth of gleam and glow!
The thousand hues and shades upon the flowers
Are all the pastime of thy leisure hours;
The jewelled ores in mines that hidden be,
Are dead till touched by thee.

    Everywhere,
Thou art lancing through the air!
Every atom from another
Takes thee, gives thee to his brother;
Continually,
Thou art wetting the wet sea,
Bathing its sluggish woods below,
Making the salt flowers bud and blow;
Silently,
Workest thou, and ardently,
Waking from the night of nought
Into being and to thought;
Influences
Every beam of thine dispenses,
Potent, subtle, reaching far,
Shooting different from each star.
Not an iron rod can lie

In circle of thy beamy eye,
But its look doth change it so
That it cannot choose but show
Thou, the worker, hast been there;
Yea, sometimes, on substance rare,
Thou dost leave thy ghostly mark
Even in what men call the dark.
Ever doing, ever showing,
Thou dost set our hearts a glowing—
Universal something sent
To shadow forth the Excellent!

When the firstborn affections—
Those winged seekers of the world within,
That search about in all directions,
Some bright thing for themselves to win—
Through pathless woods, through home-bred fogs,
Through stony plains, through treacherous bogs,
Long, long, have followed faces fair,
Fair soul-less faces, vanished into air,
And darkness is around them and above,
Desolate of aught to love,
And through the gloom on every side,
Strange dismal forms are dim described,
And the air is as the breath
From the lips of void-eyed Death,
And the knees are bowed in prayer
To the Stronger than despair—
Then the ever-lifted cry,
Give us light, or we shall die,
Cometh to the Father's ears,
And he hearkens, and he hears:—
As some slow sun would glimmer forth
From sunless winter of the north,
We, hardly trusting hopeful eyes,
Discern and doubt the opening skies.
From a misty gray that lies on
Our dim future's far horizon,
It grows a fresh aurora, sent
Up the spirit's firmament,
Telling, through the vapours dun,
Of the coming, coming sun!

'Tis Truth awaking in the soul!
His Righteousness to make us whole!
And what shall we, this Truth receiving,
Though with but a faint believing,
Call it but eternal Light?
'Tis the morning, 'twas the night!

All things most excellent
Are likened unto thee, excellent thing!
Yea, he who from the Father forth was sent,
Came like a lamp, to bring,
Across the winds and wastes of night,
The everlasting light.
Hail, Word of God, the telling of his thought!
Hail, Light of God, the making-visible!
Hail, far-transcending glory brought
In human form with man to dwell—
Thy dazzling gone; thy power not less
To show, irradiate, and bless;
The gathering of the primal rays divine
Informing chaos, to a pure sunshine!

Gentle winds through forests calling!
Bright birds through the thick leaves glancing!
Solemn waves on seashores falling!
White sails on blue waters dancing!
Mountain streams glad music giving!
Children in the clear pool laving!
Yellow corn and green grass waving!
Long-haired, bright-eyed maidens living!
Light, O radiant, it is thou!
Light!—we know our Father now!

Father of Lights, high-lost, unspeakable,
On whom no changing shadow ever fell!
Thy light we know not, are content to see;
Thee we know not, and are content to be!—
Nay, nay! until we know thee, not content are we!
But, when thy wisdom cannot be expressed,
Shall we imagine darkness in thy breast?
Our hearts awake and witness loud for thee!
The very shadows on our souls that lie,

Good witness to the light supernal bear;
The something 'twixt us and the sky
Could cast no shadow if light were not there!
If children tremble in the night,
It is because their God is light!
The shining of the common day
Is mystery still, howe'er it ebb and flow—
Behind the seeing orb, the secret lies:
Thy living light's eternal play,
Its motions, whence or whither, who shall know?—
Behind the life itself, its fountains rise!
In thee, the Light, the darkness hath no place;
And we have seen thee in the Savior's face.

Enlighten me, O Light!—why art thou such?
Why art thou awful to our eyes, and sweet?
Cherished as love, and slaying with a touch?
Why in thee do the known and unknown meet?
Why swift and tender, strong and delicate?
Simple as truth, yet manifold in might?
Why does one love thee, and another hate?
Why cleave my words to the portals of my speech
When I a goodly matter would indite?
Why mounts my thought of thee beyond my reach?
—In vain to follow thee, I thee beseech,
For God is light.

GOD'S NATURE FEEDS US, THOUGH WE KNOW IT NOT

(A Fictional Selection from *The Baron's Apprenticeship*)

One of the benefits of illness is that, either from general weakness or from the brain's being cast into a state of rest, habits are broken for a time; and more simple, childlike, and natural modes of thought and feeling come into action, whereby right has a better chance. Some sicknesses may well open windows into the unseen. A man's self-stereotyped thinking is unfavorable to revelation; his mind works too strongly in its familiar channels. But illness, in weakening these habits and breaking down these channels, strengthens more primary and original modes of vision. More open to the influences of the divine question are those who are not frozen in their own dullness, cased in their own habits, bound by their own pride to foregone conclusions, or shut up in the completeness of human error, theorizing beyond their knowledge and power.

Having thus in a measure given himself up, Richard began to grow toward the light. What a joy to think that a man may, while still unsure about God, yet be coming close to him! How else should we be saved at all? For God alone is our salvation; to know him is salvation. He is in us all the time, otherwise we could never move to seek him. Only in faith can we be saved: there is no good but him, and not to be one with that good by obedience is to be unsaved; but the poorest *desire* to draw near to him *is* an approach to him. Very unsure of him we may be; how should we be sure of what we do not yet know? But the unsureness does not nullify the approach. A man may not be sure that the sun has risen, may not be sure that the sun will ever rise, yet he has the good of what light there is. Richard was fed from the heart of God without knowing that he was partaking of the Spirit of God. He had been partaking of the creation of God all his life. The world had been feeding him with its beauty and essential truth, with the sweetness of its air, and the vastness of its sky of freedom.

But now he had begun, in the words of St. Peter, to be a partaker of the divine nature. He had started on a voyage of self-discovery. Richard was beginning to feel in his deepest nature—where alone it can be felt—his need of God.[5]

O Wind of God

O wind of God, that blowest in the mind,
  Blow, blow and wake the gentle spring in me;
Blow, swifter blow, a strong warm summer wind,
  Till all the flowers with eyes come out to see;
  Blow till the fruit hangs red on every tree,
And our high-soaring song-larks meet thy dove—
High the imperfect soars, descends the perfect love!

Blow not the less though winter cometh then;
  Blow, wind of God, blow hither changes keen;
Let the spring creep into the ground again,
  The flowers close all their eyes and not be seen:
  All lives in thee that ever once hath been!
Blow, fill my upper air with icy storms;
Breathe cold, O wind of God, and kill my cankerworms.

16

GOD THE FEARSOME

And when I saw him, I fell at his feet as dead. And he laid his right hand upon me, saying unto me, Fear not; I am the first and the last: I am he that liveth.

Revelation 1:17–18

We Fear God Because We Do Not Know Him

Fear is a wholesome element in the human economy. They are silly who would banish it from all association with religion. True, there is no religion in fear; religion is love, and love casts out fear. But until a man has love, it is well he should have fear. So long as there are wild beasts about, it is better to be afraid than secure.[1]

Fear always clouds the first beginnings of coming to know God.

So long as love is imperfect, there is room for fear. The thing that is unknown, yet known to exist, will always be more or less formidable. When it is known as immeasurably greater than we, and as having claims and making demands on us, and the more vaguely these are apprehended, the more room there is for anxiety.

And when the conscience is not clear, this anxiety may well mount to terror.

Where it is possible that fear should exist, it is well it should exist, cause continual uneasiness, and be cast out by nothing less than love. In him who does not know God, and must be anything but satisfied with himself, fear toward God is as reasonable as it is natural and serves powerfully toward the development of his true humanity. Until love, which is the truth toward God, is able to cast out fear, it is well that fear should hold. It is a bond, however poor, between that which is and that which creates—a bond that must be broken, but a bond that can be broken only by the tightening of an infinitely closer bond.

In truth, God must be terrible to those who are far from him; for they fear he will do—yes, he is doing—with them what they do not, cannot desire, and can ill endure. That which is the power and worth of life they must be, or die; and the vague consciousness of this makes them afraid. They love their poor existence as it is; God loves it as it must be. And they fear him.

God will not abolish this human fear except with the truth of his own being. Although he loves them utterly, he does not tell them there is nothing in him to make them afraid. While they are such as they are, there is much in him that can only frighten them. They ought, they do well, to fear him. It is only in proportion as we approach the capacity of seeing and understanding that our individuality can be perfected only in the love of our neighbor, and that our being can find its end only in oneness with the Source from which it came; in proportion, I do not say as we see these things, but as we near the possibility of seeing them, will our terror at the God of our life abate.

Fear Vanishes Before the Fire-Core of the Universe

The fire of God, which is his essential being, his love, his creative power, is a fire unlike its earthly symbol in this, that it is only at a distance it burns—that the farther from him, the worse it burns, and that when we turn and begin to approach him, the burning begins to change to comfort, which will grow to such bliss that the heart at length cries out with a gladness no other gladness can reach.

The glory of being, the essence of life and its joy, must, like the sun, consume the dead and send corruption down to the dust. That which it burns in the soul is not of the soul, yet so close to the soul is the foul fungus growth sprung from and subsisting upon it, that the burning of it is felt through every spiritual nerve. When the evil parasites are consumed away, that is when the man yields his self and all that self's low world and returns to his Lord and God, then that which before he was aware of only as burning, he will feel as love, comfort, strength—an eternal, ever-growing life in him. For now he lives, and life cannot hurt life. It can only destroy death, which needs and ought to be destroyed: God is life essential, eternal, and death cannot live in his sight. For death is corruption and has no existence in itself, living only in the decay of the things of life.

If then any child of the Father finds that he is afraid before him, let him make haste—let him not linger to put on any garment, but rush at once in his nakedness, a true child, into the salvation of the Father's arms, the home from which he was sent that he might learn that it was home. What father would not rejoice to see his child running to his embrace? How much more will not the Father of our spirits, who seeks nothing but his children themselves, receive us with open arms!

Endless must be our terror, until we come heart to heart with the Fire-core of the universe, the First and the Last and the Living One!

But oh, the joy to be told, by Power himself, the First and the Last, the Living One—told what we can indeed then see *must* be true, but which we are so slow to believe—that the cure for trembling is the presence of Power; that fear cannot stand before Strength; that the visible God is the destruction of death; that the one and only safety in the universe is the perfect nearness of the Living One! God is being! Death is nowhere![2]

SEEING GOD'S LIGHT THROUGH A CLOUD OF FEAR

(A Fictional Selection from *The Highlander's Last Song*)

But things were not as they should be. Something was required of her. Did God want her to do something? She had never thought whether he required anything of her. She must be a better girl! Then she would have God with her and not be afraid.

All the time it was God near her who was making her unhappy and ordering her thoughts so. For as the Son of Man came not to bring peace on earth but a sword, so the first visit of God to the human soul is generally in a cloud of fear and doubt, rising from the soul itself at his approach. The sun is the dispeller of clouds, yet often he must look through a fog if he would visit the earth at all. The child, not being a son, does not know his Father. He may know that God is called a father; but what the word means he does not know. How, then, should he understand when the Father comes to deliver him from his paltry self and give him life indeed![3]

The Sheep and the Goats

The thousand streets of London gray
  Repel all country sights;
But bar not winds upon their way,
Nor quench the scent of new-mown hay
  In depth of summer nights.

And here and there an open spot,
  Still bare to light and dark,
With grass receives the wanderer hot;
There trees are growing, houses not—
  They call the place a park.

Soft creatures, with ungentle guides,
  God's sheep from hill and plain,
Flow thitherward in fitful tides,
There weary lie on woolly sides,
  Or crop the grass amain.

And from dark alley, yard, and den,
  In ragged skirts and coats,
Come thither children of poor men,
Wild things, untaught of word or pen—
  The little human goats.

In Regent's Park, one cloudless day,
  An overdriven sheep,
Come a hard, long, and dusty way,
Throbbing with thirst and hotness lay,
  A panting woollen heap.

But help is nearer than we know
  For ills of every name:
Ragged enough to scare the crow,
But with a heart to pity woe,
  A quick-eyed urchin came.

Little he knew of field or fold,
  Yet knew what ailed; his cap
Was ready cup for water cold;
Though creased, and stained, and very old,
  'Twas not much torn, good hap!

Shaping the rim and crown he went,
  Till crown from rim was deep;
The water gushed from pore and rent,
Before he came one half was spent—
  The other saved the sheep.

O little goat, born, bred in ill,
  Unwashed, half-fed, unshorn,
Thou to the sheep from breezy hill
Wast bishop, pastor, what you will,
  In London dry and lorn!

And let priests say the thing they please,
  My faith, though poor and dim,
Thinks he will say who always sees,
In doing it to one of these
  Thou didst it unto him.

17

GOD THE RIGHTEOUS

. . . that I may win Christ, and be found in him, not having mine own righteousness, which is of the law, but that which is through the faith of Christ, the righteousness which is of God by faith.

Philippians 3: 8–9

Neither Doing nor Knowing but Being

What is the righteousness which is of God by faith? It is simply the thing that God wants every man to be, wrought out in him by constant obedient contact with God himself. It is not an attribute either of God or man, but a fact of character in God and in man. It is God's righteousness wrought out in us, so that as he is righteous, we too are righteous.

It does not consist in obeying this or that law, not even the keeping of every law, so that no hairsbreadth did we run counter to one of them. To be righteous is to be such a heart, soul, mind, and will, as would recoil with horror from the lightest possible breach of any law of God. It is to be so in love with what is fair and right as to make it impossible for a person to do anything that is less than absolutely righteous. It is not the love of righteousness in the abstract that makes anyone righteous, but such a love of fair play toward everyone with whom we come into contact, that anything less than fulfilling, with a clear joy, our divine relation to him or her, is impossible.[1]

More powerful than all powers is *being*. *To be* is more powerful than even *to do*. Action may be hypocrisy, but being is the thing itself and the parent of action.

If by neglect of its wings an eagle should sink to become a sparrow, it would then recognize only the laws of sparrow life. For the sparrows of humanity do not generally believe in a consuming fire and an outer darkness, where all that will be left is an ever renewed "alas!" The "alas" is that they neglected their wings, neglected to try to see beyond their own horizons, neglected to do the words of him who alone is life. It is truth and not serenity that a man's nature requires of him. It is help, not the leaving of cards at doors, that will be recognized as the test. It is love, and no amount of flattery, that will prosper. Differences wide as that between a gentleman and a cad will contract to a hairs-breadth in that day. The customs of the trade and the picking of pockets will go together, with the greater excuse for the greater need and the less knowledge. Liars the most gentlemanlike and the most rowdy will go as liars just the same. The first shall be last, and the last first.[2]

Loving Rightness not Doctrines

The righteousness of God goes far beyond mere deeds, and requires of us love and helping mercy as our highest obligation and justice to our fellowman.

Our relations with others—God first, and then our neighbor in order and degree—must one day become, as in true nature they are, the gladness of our being. Nothing will then ever appear good for us that is not in harmony with those blessed relations. Every thought will not merely be just, but will be just because it is something more, because it is live and true. The light of our life, our sole, eternal, and infinite joy, is simply God—God—God—nothing but God, and all his creatures in him. He is all and in all, and all the children of the kingdom know it. God is truth, is life. To be in God is to know him and need no law. Existence will be eternal Godness.

Some will think they would not like such a way of it. But the more we truly know God, the more we will desire him, until at length we live in and for him with all our conscious heart. Before you can judge this, however, you must know at least a little of God as he is, not as you imagine him.

The righteousness which is of God by faith in the source, the prime of that righteousness, is just the same kind of thing as God's righteousness. The righteousness of him who does the will of his Father in heaven is the righteousness of Jesus Christ, is God's own righteousness. The man who has this righteousness, thinks about things as God thinks about them, loves the things that God loves, cares for nothing that God does not care about. The man with God's righteousness does not love a thing merely because it is right, but loves the very rightness in it. He not only loves a thought, but he loves the man in his thinking that thought; he loves the thought alive in the man. He does not take his joy from himself. He feels joy in himself, but it comes to him from others—from God first, and from somebody, anybody, everybody next.

The man who really knows God is, and always will be, content with what God, who is the very self of his self, shall choose for him. He is entirely God's, and not at all his own. His consciousness of himself is the reflex from those about him, not the result of his own turning in of his regard upon himself. It is not the contemplation of what God has made him; it is the being what God has made him and the contemplation of what God himself is, and what he has made his fellows, that gives him his joy. He wants nothing, and feels that he has all things, for he is in the bosom of the Father, and the thoughts of his Father come to him. He knows that if he needs anything, it is his before he asks it; for his Father has willed him, in the might and truth of his fatherhood, to be one with himself.

This then—or something like this, for words are poor to tell the best things—is the righteousness which is of God by faith. What a far and wonderful cry this is from the prevailing theology that is built on a sort of legal fiction, in which Jesus was treated as he was not, in order that we might be treated as what we are not. This doctrine of so-called imputed righteousness would have us remain unrighteous and yet be treated as if we were righteous. For myself, it warms my heart not a bit to be told that God will pretend that I am righteous, when I know I am not. The longing of my heart is to one day, through the work of the spirit of Jesus Christ within me, *be* righteous, as he is righteous.

O Lord, give me a childlike mind and the heart of a child that I might approach thee and that thou might accomplish righteousness within me!

Righteousness not Wrought Through the Intellect

The wise and prudent interprets God by himself and does not understand him. The child interprets God by himself and does understand him. The wise and the prudent must make a system and arrange things in his mind before he can say, *"I believe."* The child sees, believes, obeys—and knows he must be perfect as his Father in heaven is perfect.

If an angel, seeming to come from heaven, told such a child that God had let him off, that he did not require so much of him as complete righteousness, that he could not indeed allow him to be wicked but would let a great deal go by, modifying his demands because it was so hard for him to be altogether good, the true child of God would at once recognize the angel for what it was, woven with its starry brilliancy—a demon from hell.

How God can bring about this righteousness in you, or me, I cannot tell you. Let him do it, and perhaps you will know. If you never know *how*, he will do it nonetheless. He originates the possibility of your being his son, his daughter. He makes you *able* to will it, but *you* must will it.

If he is not doing it in you—that is, if you have as yet prevented him from beginning—why should I tell you, even if I knew the process, how he would do what you will not let him do? And indeed, how should you be able to know? For it must deal with deeper and higher things than you *can* know anything of until the work is at least begun.

Perhaps if you approved of the plans of the glad Creator, you would allow him to make of you something divine. But to teach your intellect what has to be learned by your whole being, what cannot be understood without your whole being, it would do you no good to understand except you understood in your whole being—if this be the province of any man, it is not mine. Let the dead bury their dead, and the dead teach their dead. For me, I will try to wake them.

Awake and Cry to Him!

To those who are awake, I cry: For the sake of your Father and the firstborn among many brethren to whom we belong, for the sake of those he has given us to love the most dearly, let patience have her perfect work. Statue under the chisel of the Sculptor, stand steady to the blows of his mallet. Clay on the wheel, let the fingers of the Divine Potter model you at their will. Obey the Father's lightest word. Hear the Brother who knows you and died for you. Beat down your sin, and trample it to death.

God is righteous, and he is our righteousness. Let his very being fill you with itself! When you sit at home in your house, which is the temple of the Lord, open all your windows to breathe the air of his approach. Set the watcher on your turret, that he may listen out into the dark for the sound of his coming, and your hand be on the latch to open the door at his first knock. Should you open the door and not see him, do not say he did not knock, but understand that he is there, and wants you to go out to him. It may be he has something for you to do for him. Go and do it. And perhaps you will return with a new prayer, to find a new window in your soul.

Never wait for fitter time or place to talk to him. To wait till you go to church, or to your closet, is to make *him* wait. He will listen as you walk in the lane or the crowded street, in a field or in a place of meeting. Remember that the service he requires is not done in any church. He will say to no one, "You never went to church: depart from me, I do not know you." But he will say, "Inasmuch as you never helped one of my Father's children, you have done nothing for me."

Church is *not* the place for divine service. It is a place of prayer, a place of praise, a place to feed upon good things, a place to learn of God, as is every place. It is a place to look in the eyes of your neighbor and love God along with him, as is every place. But the world in which you move, the place of your living and loving and labor, not the church you go to on your day off, is the place of divine service, the place where God works righteousness into your being. Serve your neighbor, and you serve God. Thus will God be able to do his work in your heart.[3]

Cry unto him, "O God!" and it will be enough.

For what are the prayers of the whole universe more than expansions of that one cry? It is not what God can give us, but God that we want. The only comfort is that God is, and I am his, otherwise I should not be at all. The very life of God by which we live is an everlasting eternal giving of himself away. He asserts himself, only, solely, altogether, in an infinite sacrifice of devotion.[4]

THE HOPE OF BECOMING BETTER

(A Fictional Selection from *The Marquis' Secret*)

There is no wrong man can do but against the living Right. Surely you believe, my lady, that there is a living Power of right, who *will* have right done?"

"In plain language, I suppose you mean, do I believe in a god?"

"That is what I mean, if by a god you mean a being who cares about us and loves justice—that is, fair play—one whom, therefore, we wrong to the very heart when we do a thing that is not just."

"I would gladly believe in such a being if things were so that I could. As they are, I confess it seems to be the best thing to doubt it. How can I help doubting it when I see so much suffering, oppression, and cruelty in the world?"

"I used to find that a difficulty. Indeed it troubled me sorely until Mr. Graham helped me see that ease and prosperity and comfort—indeed, the absence of those things you mentioned— are far from what God intends us to have. What if these things, or the lack of them, should be but the means of our gaining something in its very nature so much better that—"

"But why should a being have to suffer for that 'something better' you speak of? What kind of a God would make that 'the means' for our betterment? Your theory is so frightful!"

"But suppose he knows that the barest beginnings of the good he intends would reconcile us to those difficult means and even cause us to choose his will at any expense of suffering?"

Clementina said nothing for a moment. Religious people, she found, could think as boldly as she.

"I tell you, Lady Clementina," said Malcolm, rising and approaching her a step or two, "if I had not the hope of one day being good like God himself, if I thought there was no escape out of the wrong and badness I feel within me, not all the wealth and honors of the world could reconcile me to life."[5]

Foolish Children

Waking in the night to pray,
    Sleeping when the answer comes,
Foolish are we even at play—
    Tearfully we beat our drums!
Cast the good dry bread away,
    Weep, and gather up the crumbs!

"Evermore," while shines the day,
    "Lord," we cry, "thy will be done!"
Soon as evening groweth gray,
    Thy fair will we fain would shun!
"Take, oh, take thy hand away!
    See the horrid dark begun!"

"Thou hast conquered Death," we say,
    "Christ, whom Hades could not keep!"
Then, "Ah, see the pallid clay!
    Death it is," we cry, "not sleep!
Grave, take all. Shut out the Day.
    Sit we on the ground and weep!"

Gathering potsherds all the day,
    Truant children, Lord, we roam;
Fret, and longer want to play,
    When at cool thy voice doth come!—
Elder Brother, lead the way;
    Make us good as we go home.

18

JESUS THE SUBSERVIENT, LIFE-CREATING SON

*All things were made by him; and without him was not any thing made
that was made. In him was life; and the life was the light of men.*

John 1:3–4

Both the Father and the Son Create

Let us look at this passage as, from my reading of the Greek, I think
it ought to be translated: "All things were made through him, and
without him was made not one thing. That which was made in
him was life, and the life was the light of men."

In this grand assertion seems to me to lie, more than shadowed,
the germ of creation and redemption—of all the divine in its relation
to all the human.

I believe that Jesus Christ is the eternal Son of the eternal Father;
that from the first of firstness Jesus is the Son, because God is the
Father—a statement imperfect and unfit because it is an attempt of
human thought to represent that which it cannot grasp.

We must not wonder things away into nothingness, but try to
present them to ourselves after what fashion we are able—our shadows
of the heavenly. For our very beings and understanding and consciousness, though but shadows in regard to any perfection either of outline
or operation, are yet shadows of God's being, his understanding, his
consciousness, and he has cast those shadows. In our shadow-speech
then, and following with my shadow-understanding as best I can, let
us seek to understand the words of the evangelist.

The Father, in creating, brought out of the unseen the things that are seen, and in so doing made essential use of the Son, so that all that exists was created *through* him. What the difference may be between the part in creation of the Father and the part of the Son, who can fully grasp? But let us look closer.

Core of Creation—Obedient Self-Willing

The power by which the Son created the worlds was given him by his Father. But he had in himself an even greater power to be used. There was something made, not *through* but *in* him; something brought into being by himself, without the Father. "That which was made *in* him was life."

What is the *life* the writer intends? What does Christ create in himself apart from the Father, which is correspondent to the creative power of God?

Just this: Jesus has the Father to love. The love of the Son is responsive to the love of the Father. The response to self-existent love is self-abnegating love. The refusal of himself is that in Jesus which corresponds to the creation of God.

His love takes action, it *creates*, in self-abjuration, in the death of self as motive. *That* is the moment of highest creation—in the willing laying down of self into the Father's will, in the drowning of self in the life of God, where it lives only as love.

In that willing yielding of his self is *life* created. Such is the life spoken of by the Apostle John when he said, "That which was made in him was life."

And truly, that life *is* the light of men![1]

The so-called *creations* of the human intellect and of the human imagination are spoken of. But there is nothing man can do that comes half so near the true "making," the true creativity of the Maker, as the ordering of his own way. There is only one thing that is higher—the highest creation of which man is capable—and that is to will the will of the Father. That act indeed contains within it an element of the purely creative, and when man does will such, then he is most like God.

To do what we ought to do, as children of God, is an altogether higher, more divine, more potent, more creative thing than to write the grandest poem, paint the most beautiful picture, carve the mightiest statue, build the most magnificent temple, dream out the most enchanting symphony.[2]

Height of Being—Deathing Oneself Into God

The life of Christ is this—that he does nothing, cares for nothing for his own sake, because he cares with his whole soul for the will, the pleasure of his Father. Because his Father is his Father, therefore he will be his child. The truth in Jesus is his relation to his Father; the righteousness of Jesus is his fulfillment of that relation.

Loving his Father thus with his whole being, Jesus is not merely alive as born of God, but, giving himself with perfect will to God, choosing to die to himself and live to God, he therein creates in himself a new and higher life. And standing upon himself, he has gained the power to awaken life, the divine shadow of his own, in the hearts of his brothers and sisters, who have come from the same birth-home as himself, namely, the heart of his God and our God, his Father and our Father. To will, not from self, but with the Eternal, is to live.

The choice of his own being, in the full knowledge of what he did—this active willing to be the Son of the Father, perfect in obedience—is that in Jesus which responds and corresponds to the self-existence of God. Jesus rose at once to the height of his being, set himself down on the throne of his nature, in the act of subjecting himself to the will of the Father as his only good, the only *reason* for his existence. When he died on the cross, he did, in the wild weather of his outlying provinces in the torture of the body of his revelation, that which he had done at home in glory and gladness. From the infinite beginning—for here I can speak only by contradictions—he completed and held fast the eternal circle of his existence in saying, "Thy will, not mine, be done!" He made himself what he is by *deathing* himself into the will of the eternal Father, through which he was the eternal Son—thus plunging into the fountain of his own life, the everlasting Fatherhood, and taking the Godhead of the Son.

This is the life that was made *in* Jesus: "That which was made in him was life."

This life, self-willed in Jesus, is the one thing that makes such life the eternal life, the true life, possible—no, imperative, essential, to every man, woman, and child, whom the Father has sent into the outer, that they may go back into the inner world, his heart. As the self-existent life of the Father has given us being, so the willed devotion of Jesus is his power to give us eternal life like his own—to enable us to do the same. There is no life for any one, other than the same kind that Jesus has; Jesus' disciple must live by the same absolute devotion of his will to the Father's. Then is the disciple's life one with the life of the Father.

Mutual Devotion of Father and Son

Let us not forget that the devotion of the Son could never have been but for the devotion of the Father, who never seeks his own glory one atom more than does the Son. He is devoted to the Son, and to all his sons and daughters, with a devotion perfect and eternal, with fathomless unselfishness. The whole being and doing of Jesus on earth is the same as his being and doing from all eternity, that whereby he is the blessed Son-God of the Father-God. It is a being like God, a doing of the will of God, a working of the works of God, therefore an unveiling of the Father in the Son, that we may know him. It is the prayer of the Son to the rest of the sons to come back to the Father, to be reconciled to the Father, to behave to the Father as he does.

Jesus seems to me to say: "I know your Father, for he is my Father. He is just like me, only greater and better. He is the only true, original good. I am true because I seek nothing but his will. He only is all in all. Come home with me, and sit with me on the throne of my obedience. Together we will do his will, and be glad with him, for his will is the only good."

The bond of the universe, the chain that holds it together, the one active unity, the harmony of things, the negation of difference, the reconciliation of all forms and all wandering desires, the fact at the root of every vision, is the devotion of the Son to the Father. It is the life of the universe. It is not the fact that God created all things that makes the universe a whole. Rather it is that he through whom he created them loves him perfectly, is eternally content in his Father, is satisfied to be because his Father is with him.

It is not the fact that God is all in all that unites the universe. Rather it is the love of the Son to the Father. For of no onehood comes unity. There can be no oneness where there is only one. For the very beginnings of unity there must be two. Without Christ, therefore, there could be no universe. The reconciliation wrought by Jesus is not the primary source of unity to the world. That reconciliation was the necessary working out of the eternal antecedent fact, the fact making itself potent upon the rest of the family—that God and Christ are one, are Father and Son, the Father loving the Son as only the Father can love, the Son loving the Father as only the Son can love.

The prayer of the Lord for unity between men and the Father and himself springs from the eternal need of love. The more I regard it the more I am lost in the wonder and glory of the thing. The very music that makes the harmony of life lies not in a theory of love, but in the fact of love in the heart of the Father, in the burning love in the hearts of Father and Son. Glory be to the Father and to the Son, and to the Spirit of both, the fatherhood of the Father meeting and blending with the sonhood of the Son, and drawing us up into the glory of their joy, to share in the thoughts of love that pass between them, in their thoughts of delight and rest in each other, in their thoughts of joy in all the little ones. The life of Jesus is the light of men, revealing to them the Father.

Father, Thy Will Be Done!

But the fact that there *is* light is not enough.

We too must have light in ourselves. We too must, like the Life himself, *live*. We can live in no way but that in which Jesus lived, in which life was made in him.

That way is to give up our life.

This is the one supreme action of life possible to us for the making of life in ourselves.

Christ did it of himself, and so became light to us, that we might be able to do it in ourselves, after him, through his originating act. But we must do it ourselves. The help that he has given and gives us every moment, the light and the spirit-working of the Lord, the Spirit, in our hearts, is all there that we may, as we must, do it ourselves. Until then we are not alive; life is not made in us.

The whole strife and labor and agony of the Son with every man is to get him to die as he died. All preaching that aims not at this is a building with wood and hay and stubble.

If I say not with my whole heart, "My father, do with me as thou wilt, only help me against myself and for thee"; if I cannot say, "I am thy child, the inheritor of thy Spirit, let me be thine in any shape the love that is my Father may please to have me"; if we cannot, fully as this, give ourselves to the Father, then we have not yet laid hold upon that for which Christ has laid hold upon us.

When a man or woman truly and perfectly says with Jesus, and as Jesus said it, "Thy will be done," he closes the everlasting life-circle. The life of the Father and the Son flows through him; he is a part of the divine organism. Then is the prayer of the Lord in him fulfilled: "I in them and thou in me, that they may be made perfect in one." The Christ in us is the Spirit of the perfect child toward the perfect Father. The Christ in us is our own true nature made to blossom in us by the Lord, whose life is the light of men that it may become the life of men; for our true nature is childhood to the Father.

Friends, let us arise and live—arise even in the darkest moments of spiritual stupidity, when hope itself sees nothing to hope for. Let us go at once to the Life. Let us comfort ourselves in the thought of the Father and the Son. So long as there dwells harmony, so long as the Son loves the Father with all the love the Father can welcome, all is well with us, his little ones. God is all right. Why should we mind standing in the dark for a minute outside his window?

Of course we miss the *inness*, but there is a bliss of its own in waiting. What if the rain be falling and with wind blowing; what even if the curtain be drawn across the window? Let us say to the Lord, "Jesus, thou art loving the Father in there. Out here we will do his will, patiently waiting until he opens the door. We shall not mind the wind or rain much. Perhaps thou art saying to the Father, 'Thy little ones need some wind and rain: their buds are hard; the flowers do not come out. I cannot get them made blessed without a little more winter-weather.' "

In a word, let us be at peace, because peace is at the heart of things— peace and utter satisfaction between the Father and the Son, in which peace they call us to share; in which peace they promise that at length, when they have their good way with us, we shall share.

Before us, then, lies a bliss unspeakable to every child who will fall in with the perfect imagination of the Father. God's imagination is one with his creative will. The thing that God imagines, that thing exists. When the created falls in with the will of him who "loved him into being," then all is well. From then on the mighty creation goes on in him upon higher and yet higher levels.

Thy will, O God, be done! There is no life but that born of the life that the Word made in himself by doing thy will, which life is the light of men. Through that light is born the life of men—the same life in them that came first into being in Jesus. As he laid down his life, so must men lay down their lives, that as he lives they may live also.[3]

A Song Prayer

Lord Jesus,
Oh, ease us
Of Self that oppresses,
Annoys and distresses
Body and brain
With dull pain!

Thou never,
Since ever,
Save one moment only,
Wast left, or wast lonely:
We are alone,
And make moan.

Far parted,
Dull-hearted,
We wander, sleep-walking,
Mere shadows, dim-stalking:
Orphans we roam,
Far from home.

Oh new man,
Sole human,
God's son and our brother,
Give each to the other—
No one left out
In cold doubt!

High Father,
Oh gather
Thy sons and thy daughters,
Through fires and through waters,
Home to the nest
Of thy breast!

There under
The wonder
Of great wings of healing,
Of love and revealing,
Teach us anew
To sing true.

DISCOVERING WHO GOD IS

(A Fictional Selection from *The Curate's Awakening*)

N o conviction can be got—or if it could be got, would be of any lasting value—through that dealer in secondhand goods, the intellect. If by it we could prove there is a God, it would be of small avail indeed. *We must see him and know him.* And I know of no other way of knowing that there is a God but that which reveals *what* he is—and that way is Jesus Christ as he revealed himself on earth, and as he is revealed afresh to every heart that seeks to know the truth about him."

A pause followed—a solemn one—and then again Polwarth spoke.

"Either the whole frame of existence," he declared, "is a wretched, miserable chaos of a world, or it is an embodied idea growing toward perfection in him who is the one perfect creative Idea, the Father of Lights, who himself suffers that he may bring his many sons and daughters into his own glory."

"But," interjected Wingfold, "—only do not think I am opposing you; I am now in the mental straits you have left so far behind—how am I to know that I have not merely talked myself into the believing of what I would like to be true?"

"Leave that question until you know what that really is which you want to believe. I do not imagine you have yet more than the faintest glimmer of the nature of that which you find yourself doubting. Is a man to refuse to open his curtains lest some flash in his own eyes should deceive him with a vision of morning while it is still night? The truth to the soul is as light to the eyes: you may be deceived, and mistake something else for light, but you can never fail to know the light when it really comes."

"What, then, would you have of me? What am I to *do*?" inquired Wingfold.

"Your business," emphasized Polwarth, "is to acquaint yourself with the man Jesus: he will be to you the one to reveal the Father. Take your New Testament as if you had never seen it before, and read to find out. The point is, there was a man who said he knew God and that if you would give heed to him, you should know him too. The record left of him is indeed scanty, yet enough to disclose what kind of man he was—his principles, his ways of looking at things, his thoughts of his Father and his brothers and the relations between them, of man's business in life, his destiny, and his hopes.[4]

Better Things

Better to smell the violet
Than sip the glowing wine;
Better to hearken to a brook
Than watch a diamond shine.

Better to have a loving friend
Than ten admiring foes;
Better a daisy's earthy root
Than a gorgeous, dying rose.

Better to love in loneliness
Than bask in love all day;
Better the fountain in the heart
Than the fountain by the way.

Better be fed by mother's hand
Than eat alone at will;
Better to trust in God, than say,
My goods my storehouse fill.

Better to be a little wise
Than in knowledge to abound;
Better to teach a child than toil
To fill perfection's round.

Better to sit at some man's feet
Than thrill a listening state;
Better suspect that thou art proud
Than be sure that thou art great.

Better to walk the realm unseen
Than watch the hour's event;
Better the Well done, faithful slave!
Than the air with shoutings rent.

Better to have a quiet grief
Than many turbulent joys;
Better to miss thy manhood's aim
Than sacrifice the boy's.

Better a death when work is done
Than earth's most favoured birth;
Better a child in God's great house
Than the king of all the earth.

19

CHRIST THE LIBERATOR

Stand fast therefore in the liberty wherewith Christ hath made us free.

Galatians 5:1

Freedom Lies in Living the Truth

God is *good*, in the very core and essence of his being. He is good, perfect, complete—for he is love.

I protest against all such teaching as, originating in and fostered by the faithlessness of the human heart, gives the impression that the exceeding goodness of God toward us is not the natural and necessary outcome of his being. The root of every heresy popular in the church draws its nourishment merely and only from the soil of unbelief. The idea that God would be God all the same had he not taken upon himself the divine toil of bringing home his wandering children, had he done nothing to seek and save the lost, is totally false.

That lie would have it that the very idea of God admitting of his being less than he is, less than perfect, less than all-in-all, less than Jesus Christ! Less than love absolute, less than entire unselfishness! They would have it that such a so-called God is deserving of the greater homage.

So it might be, if he were not our Father. But to think of the living God not as our Father is to think of him as nothing like the God we see in Jesus Christ.

It will be answered that we have fallen, and God is thereby freed from any obligation toward us. We have cut ourselves off from him by our sin, and now our reinstatement into his presence must be all our *own* doing.

It is but another lie.

No amount of wrongdoing in a child can ever free a parent from the divine necessity of doing all he can to deliver and liberate his child. The bond between them can never be broken.

Our Lord teaches us that the truth, known by obedience to him, will make us free: our freedom lies in living the truth of our relations to God and man.

In this lies our liberation.

For a man to be alone in the universe would be to be as a slave to unspeakable longings and loneliness. And to speak after the manner of men: God could not be satisfied with himself without doing all that a God and Father could do for the creatures he had made—that is, without doing just what he has done, what he is doing, what he will do, to deliver his sons and daughters, and bring them home with rejoicing.

To answer the cry of the human heart, "Would that I could see him! Would that I might come before him, and look upon him face to face!" He his son, the express image of his person. And again, that we might not be limited in our understanding of God, he took him away. Having seen God, in his absence we understand him better. That we might know God, Jesus came. That we might go to God, he went.

Liberation From Our Selves

If we dare, like Job, to plead with God in any of the heart-eating troubles that arise from the impossibility of loving such misrepresentation of him as is held out to us by our would-be teachers; if we think and speak out before him that which seems to us to be right, will he not be heartily pleased with his children's love of righteousness—with the truth that will not part with him and his righteousness?

For the heart that wants to do and think aright, the heart that seeks to worship him as no tyrant, but as the perfectly, absolutely righteous God, is the delight of the Father. To the heart that will not call that righteousness which it feels to be unjust, but clings to the skirt of his garment, and lifts pleading eyes to his countenance—to that heart he will lay open the riches of his being—riches which it has not entered that heart to conceive. In God's heart, in his very being, lies our help, our deliverance.

O Lord, they tell me I have so offended against thy law that I am threatened to be eternally banished from thy presence. But if thou helpest me not, how can I ever be other than I am? Lord, remember, I was born in sin: how then can I see sin as thou seest it? I have never known myself clean: how can I cleanse myself? Thou must take me as I am and cleanse me. Is it not impossible that I should behold the final goodness of good, the final evilness of evil? How then can I deserve eternal torment? Thou requirest of us to forgive; surely thou forgivest freely! Bound thou mayest be to destroy evil, but art thou bound to keep the sinner alive that thou mayest punish him, even if it make him no better? Sin cannot be deep as life, for thou art the life; and sorrow and pain go deeper than sin, for they reach to the divine in us.

Chastise us, O God, we pray thee, in lovingkindness, and we shall not faint. We have done much that is evil, yea, evil is very deep in us, but we are not all evil; and art not thou thyself, in thy Son, the sacrifice for our sins, the atonement of our breach? Could we ever have come to know good as thou knowest it, save by passing through the sea of sin and the fire of cleansing?

In spite of all our fears and weaknesses and wrongs, thou wilt be to us what thou art—such a perfect Father as no most loving child-heart on earth could invent the thought of! Thou wilt take our sins on thyself, giving us thy life besides. Thou bearest our griefs and carriest our sorrows, and surely thou wilt one day enable us to pay every debt we owe to each other! Thou wilt be to us a right generous, abundant Father! Then truly our hearts shall be jubilant, because thou art what thou art—infinitely beyond all we could imagine. Thou wilt humble and raise us up. Thou hast given thyself to us that, having thee, we may be eternally alive with life. We run within the circle of what men call thy wrath, and find ourselves clasped in the arms of thy love!

Friends, our cross may be heavy, and the Way of Sorrows rough. But we have the right to cry out to God for help. He has spent, and is spending himself to give us our birthright, which is righteousness. Though we shall not be condemned for our sins, we cannot be saved except by leaving them. Though we shall not be condemned for the sins that are past, we shall be condemned if we love the darkness rather than the light and refuse to come to him that we may have life.[1]

Alas, for poor men and women and their aching hearts!

Come, sore heart, and see whether Christ's heart can heal yours. He knows what sighs and tears are, and if he knew no sin himself, the more pitiful must it have been to look on the sighs and tears that guilt wrung from the tortured hearts of his brothers and sisters. Beloved, we *must* get rid of this misery of ours. It is slaying us. It is turning the fair earth into a hell, and our hearts into its fuel.

There stands the Man who says he knows; take him at his word. Go to him who says in the power of his eternal tenderness and his pity, "Come unto me, all ye that labor and are heavy laden, and I will give you rest. Take my yoke upon you, and learn of me; for I am meek and lowly in heart: and you shall find rest for your souls. For my yoke is easy, and my burden is light!"[2]

Oh, God is so true and good and strong and beautiful! The God of mountain lands, and snowdrops, of woman's beauty and man's strength—the God and Father of our Lord Jesus Christ.[3]

God is offering us the one thing we cannot live without—*his own self*. He is offering to liberate us from *our selves*. We must make room for him. We must cleanse our hearts that he may come in. We must do as the Master tells us, who knew all about the Father and the way to him: we must deny ourselves, and take up our cross daily, and follow him. Therein is our liberation.[4]

WHATEVER GOD DOES IS RIGHT

(A Fictional Selection from *The Musician's Quest*)

She felt bound to go on believing as she had been taught, for sometimes the most original mind has the strongest sense of law upon it. Obedience was indeed an essential element of her creed. But she had not yet been sufficiently impressed with the truth that while obedience is the law of the kingdom, it is of considerable importance that that which is obeyed should in truth be the will of God. Mrs. Falconer's submission and obedience led her to accept as the will of God that which was anything but giving him honor to accept as such. Therefore, her love for God was too like the love of the slave or the dog, too little like the love of the child, whose obedience the Father cannot be satisfied with until the child cares for his reason as the highest form of his will. True, the child who most faithfully desires to know the inward will or reason of the Father will be the most ready to obey without it. Only for obedience of this blind kind, it is essential that the apparent command at least be such as he can suppose attributable to the Father. Had Abraham doubted whether it was in any case right to slay his son, he would have been justified in doubting whether God really required it of him and would have been bound to delay action until the arrival of more light. The will of God can never be other than good; but I doubt if any man can ever be sure that a thing is the will of God except by seeing into its nature and character and beholding its goodness. Whatever God does must be right, but are we sure that we know what he does? That which men say he does may be very wrong indeed.[5]

Morning Hymn

O Lord of life, thy quickening voice
  Awakes my morning song!
In gladsome words I would rejoice
  That I to thee belong.

I see thy light, I feel thy wind;
  The world, it is thy word;
Whatever wakes my heart and mind,
  Thy presence is, my Lord.

The living soul which I call me
  Doth love, and long to know;
It is a thought of living thee,
  Nor forth of thee can go.

Therefore I choose my highest part,
  And turn my face to thee;
Therefore I stir my inmost heart
  To worship fervently.

Lord, let me live and will this day—
  Keep rising from the dead;
Lord, make my spirit good and gay—
  Give me my daily bread.

Within my heart, speak, Lord, speak on,
  My heart alive to keep,
Till comes the night, and, labour done,
  In thee I fall asleep.

20

*J*ESUS THE CONCEALER AND ILLUMINATOR OF TRUTH

Unto you it is given to know the mystery of the kingdom of God: but unto them that are without, all these things are done in parables: that seeing they may see, and not perceive; hearing they may hear, and not understand.

Mark 4:11–12

Theological Explainers Hide the Gospel

There is a wonderful thing in the parables, not readily grasped, but indicated by the Lord himself—their unintelligibility to the mere intellect. They are addressed to the conscience and not to the intellect, to the will and not to the imagination.

The parables are strong and direct, but not definite. They are not meant to explain anything, but to rouse a man to the feeling, "I am not what I ought to be."

Many maundering interpretations may be given by the wise, with plentiful loss of labor, while the child who uses them for the necessity of walking in the one path will constantly receive light from them.

The greatest obscuration of the words of the Lord comes from those who give themselves to interpret rather than do them. Theologians have done more to hide the Gospel of Christ than any of its adversaries. It was not for our understanding, but our will, that Christ came. He who does that which he sees, shall understand. He who is set upon understanding rather than doing, shall go on stumbling and mistaking and speaking foolishness. The Gospel itself, and in it the parables of the truth, are to be understood only by those who walk by what they find. It is not intended by the speaker of the parables that any other should know intellectually what, known but intellectually, would be for his injury. When the pilgrim of the truth comes on his journey to the region of the parable, he finds its interpretation. It is not a fruit or a jewel to be stored, but a well springing by the wayside.

Does the Light Blind or Illuminate?

The parables are plainly for the teaching of the truth, and yet the Lord speaks of them as for the concealing of it.

This difficulty may be removed by realizing that they are for the understanding of the man only who is practical—who does the thing he knows, who seeks to understand it practically. They reveal to the live conscience, otherwise not to the keenest intellect—though at the same time they may help to rouse the conscience with glimpses of the truth, where the man is on the borders of waking.

Ignorance may be at once a punishment and a kindness. "Because you will not *do*, you shall not *see*; but it would be worse for you if you did see, not being of the disposition to do."

Such are punished in having the way closed before them. They punish themselves; their own actions (their non-doing of what they ought to see and ought to do) results—as it cannot but result on them— in the keeping of their eyes closed. To say to them certain things so that they could understand them would but harden them more, because they would still not do them. They should have only parables— lanterns of the truth, clear to those who will walk in their light, dark to those who will not.

The former are content to have the light cast upon their way; the latter will have it in their eyes, and thus are unable to use the light properly. For them to have the light would only blind them. For them to *know* would be their worse condemnation. They are not fit to know more. Thus more shall not be given them yet.

They choose the dark. And they shall stay in the dark until they choose to come out of it.[1]

God is visible all around us, but only to the man or woman who *would* see him. Either there is a God and that God is perfect truth and loveliness, or else all poetry and art is but an unsown, unplanted, rootless flower crowning a somewhat symmetrical heap of stones.

The light is there, but not all use it to see with. The man who sees no beauty in the flower's petals, finds no perfume in its breath, may well accord it the parentage of the stones. But the man whose heart swells in looking at it will be ready to think it has roots that reach below them.[2]

Triolet

Oh that men would praise the Lord
For his goodness unto men!
Forth he sends his saving word,
—Oh that men would praise the Lord!—
And from shades of death abhorred
Lifts them up to light again:
Oh that men would praise the Lord
For his goodness unto men!

THE REDEMPTION OF OUR HEARTS, NOT OUR UNDERSTANDINGS

(A Fictional Selection from *The Shepherd's Castle*)

T he shield of God's presence must have been over you."

"How glad I should be to think so! But we have no right to think so till we believe in Christ—and—it is a terrible thing to say—I don't know that I believe."

"Whoever taught you that will have to answer for teaching a terrible lie," said Donal.

"I know he makes his sun to shine and his rain to fall upon the good and the bad, but that is only of this world's things."

"Are you able to worship a God who will give you all the little things he does not care much about, but will not give you help to do the things he wants you to do, but which you do not know how to do?"

"But there are things he cannot do till we believe."

"That is very true. But that does not say that God does not do all that can be done for even the worst of men to help them believe. He finds it very hard to teach us, but he is never tired of trying. Anyone who is willing to be taught of God will be taught, and thoroughly taught by him."

"I am afraid I am doing wrong in listening to you, Mr. Grant. I do wish what you say might be true, but are you not in danger—you will pardon me for saying it—of presumption? How could all the good people be wrong?"

"Because the greater part of the teachers among them have always set themselves more to explain God than to obey him. The gospel is given not to redeem our understanding, but our hearts; that done, and only then, our understanding will be free. If the things be true which I have heard from Sunday to Sunday in church since I came here, then the Lord brought us no salvation at all, but only a change of shape to our miseries. It has not redeemed you, Lady Arctura, and never will. Nothing but Christ himself for your very own teacher and friend and brother, not all the doctrines about him, even if every one of them were true, can save you."

"But how should men know that such is not the true God?"

"If a man desires God, he cannot help knowing enough of him to be capable of learning more. His idea of him cannot be all wrong. But that does not make him fit to teach others all about him—only to go on to learn for himself."

"But you must allow that God hates and punishes sin—and that is a terrible thing."

"It would be ten times more terrible if he did not hate and punish it. Do you think Jesus came to deliver us from the punishment of our sins? He would not have moved a step for that. The terrible thing is to be bad, and all punishment is to help to deliver us from it, nor will it cease till we have given up being bad. God will have us good."[3]

Lessons for a Child

There breathes not a breath of the summer air
But the spirit of love is moving there;
Not a trembling leaf on the shadowy tree,
Flutters with hundreds in harmony,
But that spirit can part its tone from the rest,
And read the life in its beetle's breast.
When the sunshiny butterflies come and go,
Like flowers paying visits to and fro,
Not a single wave of their fanning wings
Is unfelt by the spirit that feeleth all things.
The long-mantled moths that sleep at noon
And rove in the light of the gentler moon;
And the myriad gnats that dance like a wall,
Or a moving column that will not fall;
And the dragon-flies that go burning by,
Shot like a glance from a seeking eye—
There is one being that loves them all:
Not a fly in a spider's web can fall
But he cares for the spider, and cares for the fly;
He cares for you, whether you laugh or cry,
Cares whether your mother smile or sigh.
How he cares for so many, I do not know,
But it would be too strange if he did not so—
Dreadful and dreary for even a fly!
So I cannot wait for the how and why,
But believe that all things are gathered and nursed
In the love of him whose love went first
And made this world—like a huge great nest
For a hen to sit on with feathery breast.

21

GOD IS DUTIFULLY GOOD TO HIS CHILDREN

O that thou wouldest hide me in the grave, that thou wouldest keep me secret, until thy wrath be past, that thou wouldest appoint me a set time, and remember me! . . . all the days of my appointed time will I wait, till my change come. Thou shalt call, and I will answer thee: thou wilt have a desire to the work of thine hands.

Job 14:13–15

God Owes Something to His Creature

T he book of Job seems to me the most daring of poems. Daring yet grand!

The grandeur of Job is that throughout the poem Job pleads his cause with God against all the remonstrance of religious authority, recognizing no one but God. And the grandest of all is this, that he implies, if he does not actually say, that God *owes* something to his creature.

This is the beginning of the greatest discovery of all—that God owes *himself* to the creature he has made in his image, for so God has made him incapable of living without him. This, God's creatures' highest claim upon him, is his divinest gift to them. For the fulfilling of this their claim God has sent his Son, that he may himself, the Father of him and of us, follow into our hearts.

Perhaps the worst thing in a theology constructed out of a man's dull *possible,* and not out of the being and deeds and words of Jesus Christ, is the impression it conveys throughout that God acknowledges no such obligation. Are we not the clay and he the Potter? How can the clay lay claim upon the Potter?

We are the clay, it is true, but *his* clay, spiritual clay, live clay, with needs and desires—clay worth the Son of God's dying for, that it might learn to consent to be shaped unto honor.

We can have no merit; a *merit* is a thing impossible. But God has given us rights. Out of him we have nothing, but created by him, come forth from him, we have even rights toward him—but never *against* him! His whole desire and labor is to make us capable of claiming, and induce us to claim of him the things whose rights he bestowed in creating us. No claim had we to be created; that involves an absurdity. But, being made, we have claims on him who made us; our needs are our claims. A man who will not provide for the hunger of his child is condemned by the whole world.

"Ah, but," says the partisan of God, "the Almighty stands in a relation very different from that of an earthly father; there is no parallel."

I grant it. The man did not create the child; he only yielded to an impulse created in himself. God is infinitely *more* bound to provide for *his* child than any man is to provide for his. God created both the child and his hunger. The relation is infinitely, divinely closer. It is God to whom every hunger, every aspiration, every desire, every longing of our nature is to be referred. He made them all—made us the creatures of a thousand necessities—and have we no claim in him?

We have claims innumerable, infinite. And his one great claim on us is that we should claim our claims of him.

It is terrible to represent God as unrelated to us in the way of appeal to his righteousness. How should he be righteous without owing us anything? Surely he owes us nothing that he does not pay like a God; in every act of his being he lays himself under obligation to his creatures. Oh, the grandeur of his goodness and righteous and fearless unselfishness!

The Child Has a Claim Upon His Father

When doubt and dread invade, and the voice of love in the soul is dumb, what can please the Father better than to hear his child cry to him from whom he came, "Here I am O God! Thou hast made me: give me that which thou hast made me needing." The child's necessity, his weakness, his helplessness, are the strongest of his claims.

And this is just what God desires, that his children should claim their Father.

To what end are all God's dealings with them, all his sufferings with and for and in them, but that they should claim their birthright? Is not their birthright just what he made them for, made in them when he made them? Is not that what he has been putting forth his energy to give them ever since first he began them to be—the divine nature, God himself?

The child has, and must have, a claim on the Father, a claim which it is the joy of the Father's heart to acknowledge. A created need is a created claim. God is the origin of both need and supply, the Father of our necessities, the abundant giver of the good things. Gloriously he meets the claims of his child! The life of Jesus is the heart of his answer, not primarily to the prayers, but to the divine necessities of the children he has sent out into his universe.

Away with the thought that God could have been a perfect, an adorable Creator, doing anything less than he has done for his children! That any other kind of being than Jesus Christ could have been worthy of all-glorifying worship! That his nature demanded less of him than he has done! That his nature of absolute love, absolute self-devotion— could have been without these highest splendors!

Job cries out to his Creator, "Oh that thou wouldest hide me in the grave!" God must love this creature that looks up to him with hungry eyes—hungry for life, for acknowledgment, for justice, for the possibilities of living that life which the making life has made him alive for the sake of living. Let him do with me as he will, cries Job, even to seating me in the ashes. Not the less will I bring forward my claim, assert it—insist upon it—assail with it the ear and the heart of the Father!

Is it not the sweetest music the ear of the Maker can hear—except the word of his perfect Son, "Lo, I come to do thy will, O God!"? We, imperfect children, shall learn to say the same words too. That we may grow capable and say them, and so enter into our birthright, yes, become partakers of the divine nature in its divinest element, that the Son came to us—died for the slaying of our selfishness, the destruction of our mean hollow pride, the waking of our childhood. We are his Father's debtors for our needs, our rights, our claims, and he will have us pay the uttermost farthing. Yes, so true is the Father, he will even compel us, through misery if needful, to put in our claims, for he knows we have eternal need of these things. Without the essential rights of his being, who can live?[1]

Even those who weep and know not why are laying claim to God's fatherhood in the depth of their being. In all human tears is contact of the human soul with the great human soul of God. They are the beginnings of possible communion, nothing less, with the Father of all! Surely God sees the tears and knows the heart he has made. He who will not let us out until we have paid the uttermost farthing rejoices over the offer of the first golden grain in payment. Easy to please is he, hard indeed to satisfy.[2]

ALL IS WELL WHEN WE KNOW WHO GOD IS

(A Fictional Selection from *The Elect Lady*)

Think, ma'am: people that only care to be saved, that is, not to be punished for their sins, are anxious only about themselves, not about God and his glory at all. They talk about the glory of God, but they make it consist in pure selfishness! According to them, he seeks everything for himself; which is dead against the truth of God, a diabolic slander of God. It does not trouble them to believe such things about God; they do not even desire that God should not be like that; they only want to escape him. They dare not say God will not do this or that however clear it be that it would not be fair: they are in terror of contradicting the Bible. They make more of the Bible than of God, and so fail to find the truth of the Bible, and accept things concerning God which are not in the Bible, and are the greatest of insults to him! Dawtie never thinks about saving her soul; she has no fear about her soul; she is anxious only about God and his glory. How the doubts come, God knows; but if she did not love God, they would not be there. Jesus says God will speedily avenge his elect—those that cry day and night to him—which I take to mean that he will soon save them from all such miseries. Free Dawtie from unsureness about God, and she has no fear left. All is well, in the prison or on the throne of God, if he only be what she thinks he is. If any one say that doubt cannot co-exist with faith, I answer, it can with love, and love is the greater of the two, yea is the very heart of faith itself. God's children are not yet God's men and women.[3]

Autumn Song

Autumn clouds are flying, flying
   O'er the waste of blue;
Summer flowers are dying, dying,
   Late so lovely new.
Labouring wains are slowly rolling
   Home with winter grain;
Holy bells are slowly tolling
   Over buried men.

Goldener light sets noon a sleeping
   Like an afternoon;
Colder airs come stealing, creeping
   From the misty moon;
And the leaves, of old age dying,
   Earthy hues put on;
Out on every lone wind sighing
   That their day is gone.

Autumn's sun is sinking, sinking
   Down to winter low;
And our hearts are thinking, thinking
   Of the sleet and snow;
For our sun is slowly sliding
   Down the hill of might;
And no moon is softly gliding
   Up the slope of night.

See the bare fields' pillaged prizes
   Heaped in golden glooms!
See, the earth's outworn sunrises
   Dream in cloudy tombs!
Darkling flowers but wait the blowing
   Of a quickening wind;
And the man, through Death's door going,
   Leaves old Death behind.

Mourn not, then, clear tones that alter;
   Let the gold turn gray;
Feet, though feeble, still may falter
   Toward the better day!
Brother, let not weak faith linger
   O'er a withered thing;
Mark how Autumn's prophet finger
   Burns to hues of Spring.

22

GOD THE BESTOWER OF RIGHTS

Blessed are they that do his commandments, that they may have right to the tree of life, and may enter in through the gates into the city.

Revelation 22:14

Unmerited Rights

When I say, as I have, that God has bestowed upon us *rights*, be it well understood, I do not mean *merits*—of any sort.

We can deserve from him nothing at all, in the sense of any right proceeding from ourselves. All our rights are such as the bounty of love inconceivable has glorified our being with—bestowed for the one purpose of giving the satisfaction, the fulfillment of the same— rights so deep, so high, so delicate, that their satisfaction cannot be given until we desire it—yea, long for it with our deepest desire.

The giver of them came to men, lived with men, and died by the hands of men, that they might possess these rights abundantly. More to fulfill his part God could not do—except indeed what he is still doing every hour, every moment, for every individual.

Our rights are rights with God himself at the heart of them. He could recall them if he pleased, but only by recalling us, by making us cease. While we exist, by the being that is ours, they are ours. If he could not fulfill our rights to us—because we would not have them, that is—if he could not make us such as to care for these rights, which he has given us out of the very depth of his creative being, I think he would have to uncreate us. But as to deserving, that is absurd. He had to die in the endeavor to make us listen and receive. There is no claim on God that springs from us; all is from him.

The Right to Be Compelled

But lest any unchildlike soul might, in arrogance and ignorance, think to stand upon his rights, as it were, *against* God, and demand of him this or that after the will of the flesh, I will lay before such a person some of the things to which he has a right because of the divine germ that is in him.

He has a claim on God, a divine claim, for any pain, any want, any disappointment or misery that would help to show him to himself as the fool he is.

He has a claim to be punished to the last scorpion of the whip, to be spared not one pang that may urge him toward repentance.

He has a claim to be sent out into the outer darkness, whether to what we call hell, or something speechlessly worse, if nothing less will do.

He has a claim to be compelled to repent, to be hedged in on every side, to have one after another of the strong, sharp-toothed sheepdogs of the Great Shepherd sent after him, to thwart him in any desire, foil him in any plan, frustrate him of any hope, until he comes to see at length that nothing will ease his pain, nothing make life a thing worth having, but the presence of the living God within him.

Nothing is noble enough for the desire of the heart of man but oneness with the eternal. For this God must make him yield his very being, that God may enter in and dwell with him.

That the man would enforce or insist upon none of these claims is nothing. For it is not a man who owes them to him, but the eternal God, who, by his own will of right toward the creature he has made, is bound to discharge them. God has to answer to himself for his idea; he has to do with the need of the nature he made, not with the self-born choice of the self-ruined man. God's candle yet burns dim in the man's soul; that candle must one day shine as the sun. For what is the all-pervading dissatisfaction of man's being but an unrecognized hunger after the righteousness of his Father. The soul God made is thus hungering, through the selfish, usurping self, only after low and selfish things, ever trying, but in vain, to fill its narrow content with husks too poor for its poverty-stricken desires. For even that most degraded chamber of the soul, which is the temple of the defiled self, cannot be filled with less than God. Even the usurping self must be miserable until it cease to look at itself in the mirror of Satan and open the door of its innermost closet to the God who means to dwell there, and make peace.[1]

How blessed a thing it is that God will judge us, and man shall now! Where we see no difference, God sees ages of difference. The very thing that appears to us as condemnation may to the eyes of God be grounds for excuse, yea, for partial justification. Only God's excuse is, I suspect, seldom coincident with the excuse man makes for himself. If anyone thinks that God will not search closely into things, I say there could not be such a God.

He will see the uttermost farthing paid. His excuses are as just as his condemnations.[2]

He that has looked on the face of God in Jesus Christ, whose heart overflows, if ever so little, with answering love, sees God standing with full hands to give the abundance for which he created his children, and those children holding back, refusing to take, doubting the God-heart, which knows itself absolute in truth and love.[3]

OBEDIENCE HOLDS OPEN THE DOOR FOR WISDOM

(A Fictional Selection from *Sir Gibbie*)

Now came to the girl a few such days of delight, of freedom, of life, as she had never even dreamed of. She roamed Glashgar with Gibbie, the gentlest, kindest, most interesting of companions. Wherever his sheep went, she went too, and to many places besides—some of them such strange, wild, terrible places, as would have terrified her without him.

How he startled her once by darting off a rock like a seagull, straight, head-foremost, into the Death-pot! She screamed with horror, but he had done it only to amuse her; for, after what seemed to her a fearful time, he came smiling up out of the terrible darkness. What a brave, beautiful boy he was! He never hurt anything, and nothing ever seemed to hurt him. And what a number of things he knew! He showed her things on the mountain, things in the sky, things in the pools and streams wherever they went. He did better than to tell her about them; he made her see them, and then the things themselves told her.

She was not always certain she saw just what he wanted her to see, but she always saw something that made her glad with knowledge. He had a New Testament Janet had given him, which he carried in his pocket, and when she joined him, for he was always out with his sheep hours before she was up, she would generally find him seated on a stone, or lying in the heather, with the little book in his hand, looking solemn and sweet. But the moment he saw her, he would spring merrily up to welcome her. It were indeed an argument against religion as strong as sad, if one of the children the kingdom specially claims could not be possessed by the life of the Son of God without losing his simplicity and joyousness. Those of my readers will be the least inclined to doubt the boy, who, by obedience, had come to know its reward. For obedience alone holds wide the door for the entrance of the spirit of wisdom. There was as little to wonder at in Gibbie as there was much to love and admire, for from the moment when, yet a mere child, he heard there was such a one claiming his obedience, he began to turn to him the hearing ear, the willing heart, the ready hand. The main thing which rendered this devotion more easy and natural to him than to others was, that, more than in most, the love of man had in him prepared the way of the Lord. He who so loved the sons of men was ready to love the Son of Man the moment he heard of him; love makes obedience a joy; and of him who obeys, all heaven is the patrimony—he is fellow-heir with Christ.[4]

Oh Thou of Little Faith

Sad-hearted, be at peace: the snowdrop lies
    Buried in sepulcher of ghastly snow;
But spring is floating up the southern skies,
    And darkling the pale snowdrop waits below.

Let me persuade: in dull December's day
    We scarce believe there is a month of June;
But up the stairs of April and of May
    The hot sun climbeth to the summer's noon.

Yet hear me: I love God, and half I rest.
    O better! God loves thee, so all rest thou.
He is our summer, our dim-visioned Best;—
    And in his heart thy prayer is resting now.

23

OUR TRUSTWORTHY GOD

Trust in the Lord with all thine heart; and lean not unto thine own understanding. In all thy ways acknowledge him, and he shall direct thy paths.

Proverbs 3:5–6

God's Might Implies Goodness

W hich of us has not struggled over Job's plight and sought to understand why God answers him as he does?

When Job calls out to him from the depths of his misery, God gives him no direct explanation of why he has so afflicted him. God justifies Job in his Word. He says Job has spoken what is right concerning him, and then he proceeds to call up before him one after another of the works of his hands. The answer, like many of our Lord's answers, seems addressed not to Job's intellect, but to the revealing, God-like imagination in the man.

The argument implied seems to be this: that if God is so far beyond Job in power, and his works so far beyond his understanding that they fill him with wonder and admiration—the vast might of the creation, the times and the seasons, the marvels of the heavens, the springs of the sea, the gates of death, the animals with their beauties and in-stincts, the strange and awful beasts—then Job, beholding these things, ought to reason that he who could work so grandly beyond his understanding must certainly use wisdom in things that touch man nearer, though they came no nearer his understanding.

In this world, power is no proof of righteousness. But was it likely that he who could create should be unrighteous? Did not all God make move the delight of the beholding man? Might he not therefore trust him to do him justice? In such high affairs as the rights of a live soul, might not matters be involved too high for Job? The Maker of Job was so much greater than Job, that his ways with him might well be beyond his comprehension! God's thoughts were higher than Job's thoughts, as the heavens were higher than the earth.

The true child, the righteous man, will trust absolutely, against all appearances, the God who has created in him the love of righteousness.

God rouses Job's child-heart to trust. All the rest of Job's life on earth, I imagine, his slowly vanishing perplexities would yield him ever-fresh meditations concerning God and his ways, new opportunities of trusting him, as Job grew in all directions into the knowledge of God. His perplexities would thus prove of a divine gift.

A Closed Book of Larger Blessedness

Everything, in truth, we cannot understand is a closed book of larger knowledge and blessedness, whose covers the blessed perplexity urges us to open. There is, there can be, nothing which in itself cannot be righteously known—whether intelligible for us matters nothing. That God knows is enough for me. I shall know, if I can know, and when it is good for me to know.

How much more than Job are we bound, who know him in his Son as Love, to trust God in all the troubling questions that force themselves upon us concerning the motions and results of things!

Job's confusion was much like that of many today when facing the awful contradiction of two such facts staring each other in the face: that God was just, yet at the same time *punishing* a righteous man. The confusion comes from the inability to receive the thought that approving love itself might be inflicting or allowing the torture—that suffering is granted to a righteous man, that he might be made perfect. I can well imagine that at times, as the one moment he doubted God's righteousness, and the next cried aloud, "Though he slay me, yet will I trust him," there must in the chaos have mingled some element of doubt as to the existence of God.

Let not such doubt be supposed a further stage in unbelief. To deny the existence of God may, paradoxical as the statement will at first seem to some, involve less unbelief than the smallest yielding to doubt of his goodness. I say *yielding*, for a man may be haunted with doubts, and only grow thereby in faith. Doubts are the messengers of the Living One to rouse the honest heart. They are the first knock at our door of things that are not yet, but have to be, understood. Theirs in general is the inhospitable reception of angels who do not come in their own likeness.

Doubt must precede every deeper assurance. For uncertainties are what we first see when we look into a region hitherto unknown, unexplored, unannexed.

We Need Assurance of God's Being

In all Job's begging and longing to see God, then, may well be supposed to mingle the mighty desire to be assured of God's being. When he hears the voice of God, though it utters no word of explanation, it is enough to Job to hear it. He knows that God is and that he hears the cry of his creature. That God is there, knowing all about him, and what had befallen him, is enough; Job needs no more to reconcile seeming contradictions. Even if Job could not at first follow his argument, God settled everything for him when, by answering him out of the whirlwind, he showed him that he had not forsaken him.

It is true that nothing but a far closer divine presence can ever make life a thing fit for a son of man, for he is made in the image of God, and it is for him absolutely imperative that he should have in him the reality of which his being is the image. While he does not have it in him, his being, his conscious self, is but a mask.

But for the present, Job, yielding to God, was calmed and satisfied. Perhaps he came at length to see the lack of faith in him, which made him doubt God. To know that our faith is weak is the first step toward its strengthening. To distrust is death; but to know that we are distrusting, and to cry out, is to begin to live—to begin to be made such that we cannot distrust—such that God may do anything with us and we shall never doubt him.

Until doubt is impossible, we are lacking in the true, the childlike, knowledge of God. For either God is such that one *may* distrust him, or he is such that to distrust him is the greatest injustice of which we can be guilty. If then we are able to distrust him, either we know God imperfectly, or we do not know him. Perhaps Job learned something like this. Anyhow, the result of what he had to endure was a greater nearness to God, though all he was required to receive at the moment was the argument from God's loving wisdom in his power, to his loving wisdom in everything else. In a deep sense, power and goodness are one. In the deepest fact they are one.

Seeing God, Job forgets all he wanted to say, all he thought he would say if he could but see him. The close of the poem is grandly abrupt. To justify himself in the presence of him who is righteousness, seems to Job what it is—foolishness. Job had his desire: he saw the face of God—and abhorred himself in dust and ashes. He sought justification; he found self-abhorrence—the best thing, to begin with, the face of God could do for him. Good man as Job was, he had never yet been right near to God. Now God had come near to him, had become very real to him.

We May Trust God—Utterly!

Two things are clearly contained in, and manifest from this portion of scripture: that not every man deserves for his sins to be punished everlastingly from the presence of the Lord; and that the best of men, when he sees the face of God, will know himself vile. God is just. We may trust him. He will never deal with the sinner as if he were capable of sinning the pure sin; yet if the best man be not delivered from himself, that self will sink him into hell.

The prosperity that follows Job's submission is the embodiment of a great truth. Although a man must do right if it send him to Hades, yea, even were it to send him forever to hell itself, yet, while the Lord lives, we need not fear. We *may* trust him. *All* good things must grow out of and hang upon the one central good, the one law of life—the will, the one good, our trustworthy God.[1]

For God to be God, he must be God everywhere, and not a maggot can die any more than a Shakespeare be born without him. He is either enough, that is, all in all, or he is not at all.[2]

Do you dare say I expect too much from God? Is it likely that Jesus will say so of any man or woman when he looks for faith in the earth?[3]

To submit absolutely to God is the only reason: circumstance as well as all being must then bud and blossom as the rose.

And it will! What matter whether in this world or the next, if one day I know my life as a perfect bliss, having neither limitation nor hindrance nor pain nor sorrow more than it can dominate in peace and perfect assurance?[4]

To My Lord and Master

Imagination cannot rise above thee;
Near and afar I see thee, and I love thee;
My misery away from me I thrust it,
For thy perfection I behold, and trust it.

To My God

Oh how oft I wake and find
I have been forgetting thee!
I am never from thy mind:
Thou it is that wakest me.

THINKING OF GOD ARIGHT

(A Fictional Selection from *Donal Grant*)

S he could now think of the Father of Spirits without fear, almost without doubt—think of Him as the root of every delight of the world, at the heart of the horse she rode, in the wind that blew joy into her as she swept through its yielding bosom— think of Him as altogether loving and true, the veritable Father of Jesus Christ, as like Him as like could be like, more like Him than any one other in the universe could be like another—like him as only Eternal Son can be like Eternal Father. No wonder that with this well of living water in her heart she should be glad—merry even, and ready for anything.[5]

The Carpenter

O Lord, at Joseph's humble bench
    Thy hands did handle saw and plane;
Thy hammer nails did drive and clench,
    Avoiding knot and humouring grain.

That thou didst seem, thou wast indeed,
    In sport thy tools thou didst not use;
Nor, helping hind's or fisher's need,
    The labourer's hire, too nice, refuse.

Lord, might I be but as a saw,
    A plane, a chisel, in thy hand!—
No, Lord! I take it back in awe,
    Such prayer for me is far too grand.

I pray, O Master, let me lie,
    As on thy bench the favoured wood;
Thy saw, thy plane, thy chisel ply,
    And work me into something good.

No, no; ambition, holy-high,
    Urges for more than both to pray:
Come in, O Gracious Force, I cry—
    Or workman, share my shed of clay.

Then I, at bench, or desk, or oar,
    With knife or needle, voice or pen,
As thou in Nazareth of yore,
    Shall do the Father's will again.

Thus fashioning a workman rare,
    O Master, this shall be thy fee:
Home to thy Father thou shalt bear
    Another child made like to thee.

24

GOD THE FATHER OF HIS CHILDREN

—the Spirit of adoption, whereby we cry, Abba, Father.
Romans 8:15

Childship

The hardest, gladdest thing in the world is to cry, "Father!" from a full heart.

One of the primary reasons for this, it seems to me, is the so-called doctrine of adoption. When a heart hears that it is not the child of God by origin, but may possibly be merely adopted into his family, its love sinks at once in a cold faint. The word has, I suggest from studying the Greek New Testament, been seriously mistranslated into our English Bibles. I consider Luther much nearer the mark when he translates *adoption* as *kindschaft* or *childship*.

No more than an earthly parent can God be content to have only children: he must have sons and daughters—children of his soul, of his spirit, of his love—not merely in the sense that he loves them, or even that they love him, but in the sense that they love like him, love as he loves. For this he does not adopt them; he dies to give them himself, thereby to raise his own to his heart. He gives them a birth from above. They are born again out of himself and into himself. His children are not his real, true sons and daughters until they think like him, feel with him, judge as he judges, are at home with him, love the same things, seek the same ends. For this are we created; it is the one end of our being, and includes all other ends whatever.

He is our Father all the time, for he is true. But until we respond with the truth of children, he cannot fully reveal the Father to us; there is no place for the dove of tenderness to alight. He is our Father, but we are not yet his children. Because we are his children, we must become his sons and daughters. Nothing will satisfy him, or us, until we be one with our Father!

What else could serve! How else should life ever be good! Because we are the sons of God, we must become the sons of God.

The refusal, and the inability, to look up to God as our Father is the one central wrong in the whole human affair, the one central misery. Recognizing our Father fully will more or less clear away every difficulty in life.

We Choose to Be Children of God

There may be among my readers—alas!—some to whom the word *Father* brings no cheer, no dawn, in whose heart it rouses no tremble of even a vanished emotion. It is hardly likely to be their fault. For though as children we seldom love as we ought, though we often offend, and although the conduct of some children is inexplicable to the parent who loves them, yet if a parent has been but moderately kind, even the son who has grown up a worthless man will now and then feel, in his better moments, some dim reflex of childship, some faintly pleasant, some slightly sorrowful remembrance of the father around whose neck his arms had sometimes clung. In my own childhood and boyhood my father was the refuge from all the ills and pains of life.

Therefore I say to son or daughter who has no pleasure in the name *Father*, you must interpret the word by all that you have missed in life. All that human tenderness can give or desire in nearness and readiness of love, all and infinitely more must be true of the perfect Father—of the maker of fatherhood, the Father of all the fathers of the earth, especially the Father of those who have specially shown a father-heart.

This Father would make to himself sons and daughters indeed— that is, sons and daughters not merely by having come from his heart, but by having returned there—children in virtue of being such as whence they came, such as choose to be what he is. He will have them share in his being and nature—strong wherein he cares for strength, tender and gracious as he is tender and gracious, angry where he is angry.

He has made us, but we have to *be*. All things were made *through* the Word, but that which was made *in* the Word was life, and that life is the light of men. They who live by this light, that is, live as Jesus lived—by obedience, namely, to the Father, have a share in their own making. The light becomes life in them. By obedience they become one with the Godhead. "As many as received him, to them gave he power to become the sons of God." He does not *make* them the sons of God, but he gives them power to become the sons of God. In choosing and obeying the truth, man becomes the true son of the Father of lights.

The Development of Children Into Sons and Daughters

We are the sons of God the moment we lift up our hearts, seeking to be sons—the moment we begin to cry *Father*. But as the world must be redeemed in a few men to begin with; so the soul is redeemed in a few of its thoughts and wants and ways to begin with. It takes a long time to finish the new creation of this redemption. Until our outward condition is that of sons royal, sons divine; so long as the garments of our souls, these mortal bodies, are mean, torn, dragged, and stained, so long as we groan under sickness and weakness and weariness, old age, forgetfulness, and all heavy things, we have not yet received the sonship in full. We are but getting ready one day to creep from our chrysalids, and spread the great heaven-storming wings of the psyches of God. We groan, being burdened. We groan, waiting for the sonship—the redemption of the body—the uplifting of the body to be a fit house and revelation of the indwelling Spirit—like that of Christ, a fit temple and revelation of the deeper indwelling God.

The world exists for our education. It is the nursery of God's children—children, but not yet good children. Beyond its own will or knowledge, the whole creation works for the development of the children of God into the sons of God. When at last the children have arisen and gone to their Father, when they are clothed in the best robe, with a ring on their hands and shoes on their feet, shining out at length in their natural, their predestined sonship, then shall the mountains and the hills break forth before them into singing, and all the trees of the field shall clap their hands. Then shall the wolf dwell with the lamb, and the leopard lie down with the kid and the calf, and the young lion and the fatling together, and a little child shall lead them. Then shall the fables of a golden age, which faith invented, unfold their essential reality, and the tale of paradise prove itself a truth by becoming a fact. Then shall every ideal show itself a necessity, every aspiration although satisfied put forth yet longer wings, and the hunger after righteousness know itself blessed.

Then first shall we know what was in the Shepherd's mind when he said, "I am come that they may have life, and have it abundantly."[1]

The will of the Father is the root of all the child's gladness, of all his laughter and merriment. The child that loves the will of the Father is at the heart of things; his will is with the motion of the eternal wheels; the eyes of all those wheels are opened upon him, and he knows whence he came. Happy and fearless and hopeful, he knows himself the child of him from whom he came, and his peace and joy break out in light. He rises and shines. No other bliss than the will of the Father, creative and energetic, exists on earth or in heaven.[2]

Bedtime

"Come, children, put away your toys;
Roll up that kite's long line;
The day is done for girls and boys—
Look, it is almost nine!
Come, weary foot, and sleepy head,
Get up, and come along to bed."

The children, loath, must yet obey;
Up the long stair they creep;
Lie down, and something sing or say
Until they fall asleep,
To steal through caverns of the night
Into the morning's golden light.

We, elder ones, sit up more late,
And tasks unfinished ply,
But, gently busy, watch and wait—
Dear sister, you and I,
To hear the Father, with soft tread,
Coming to carry us to bed.

GOD IS MORE THAN ANYBODY KNOWS WHAT TO SAY

(A Fictional Selection from *Warlock O'Glenwarlock*)

Cosmo laughed gently. There was a tone in the laugh such as Joan seemed never to have heard before.

"How can you love God, Joan, and be afraid because one speaks of him without fear? I should no more fancy him angry with me for believing he made me for great and glad things, than my father angry with me for believing he will always do his very best for me."

"Ah, but he is your father, and that is very different!" said Joan with a sigh, of which a full interpretation, unknown to herself, may have been, that, after all, there was more difference between one father and another than between some fathers and God.

"I know it is very different," replied Cosmo; "—God is so much, much more my father than is the laird of Glenwarlock! He is eternally more to me, eternally nearer to me than my father, though my father is the best father that ever lived. God, you know, Joan—God is more than anybody knows what to say about. Sometimes, when I am lying awake at night, my heart swells and swells in me, that I hardly know how to bear it, with the thought that here I am, come out of God, and yet not *out of* him—close to the very life that said to everything *Be*, and it was!—You think it strange I should talk so?"

"Rather, I must confess! It *can't* be good to think at your age so much about religion. There is a time for everything. If you go on like this, you will die of the blues. I know it is all very proper, but such solemnity would kill me!"

Cosmo laughed again.

"Which of us is the merrier—you or me, Joan? The instant I saw you, I thought you hadn't enough of something—you weren't happy. If you knew this beautiful person we call God, and knew he was always with you, nearer than your own soul, and that you could talk to him any time, you could not keep sad for very long."

Joan gave a great sigh: her heart knew its own bitterness, and there was little joy in it for a stranger to intermeddle with. But she said to herself the boy would be a gray-haired man before he was twenty, and she must help him out of such morbid fancies.

"While we are in this world, Cosmo, we must live as creatures of this world," she said.

"As men and women of this world—yes; but you do not surely imagine that, when he put us here, he banished us from himself! He is the same—in this world and in every other, and no creature can do without him. Everything beautiful is but a bit of love frozen: the love that gives is to the gift as water is to ice. Ah, you should hear our torrent shout in the spring! The thought of God fills me so full of life, that I want to go and do something for everybody. I am never miserable. I don't believe I shall be when my father dies."

"Oh, Cosmo!—with such a father as yours! I am shocked."

But it was into her own heart that her words struck a pang, for she had compared his father and hers, and over hers she was not miserable! The poor old man lay forsaken among strangers, and she had grown strange to him also!

The sun was close upon the horizon, and its level rays shone through the hair of the boy, as, taking off his cap, he turned and looked at her.

"Lady Joan," he said slowly, and with a tremble in his voice, "I should just laugh with delight to have to die for my father. But if he were to die, I should be so proud of him I should have no room to be miserable. As God makes me glad though I cannot see him, so my father would make me glad though I could not see him. I cannot see him now, and yet I am glad because he *is*—away down there in the old castle; and when he is gone from me, I shall be glad still, for he will be *somewhere* all the same—with God, as he is now. The summer of souls will come again, and we shall run to each other."

It was an odd phrase, but Lady Joan did not laugh.[3]

A Handwritten Party Invitation Sent to Their Friends by the MacDonalds in 1885

Please come on Monday
The day after Sunday,
And mind that you start with
Something to part with;
A fire shall be ready
Glowing and steady
To receive it and burn it
And never return it.
Books that are silly,
Clothes outworn and chilly,
Hats, umbrellas or bonnets,
Dull letters, bad sonnets,
Whate'er to the furnace
By nature calls "Burn us!"
An ancient, bad temper
Will be noted no damper—
The fire will not scorn it
But glory to burn it!
Here every bad picture
Finds refuge from stricture;
Or any old grudge
That refuses to budge,
We'll make it the tomb
For all sorts of gloom,
The out-of-door path
For every man's wrath.
All lying and hinting,
All jealous squinting,
All unkind talking
And each other balking,
Let the fire's holy actions
Turn to ghostly abstractions.
All antimacassars,
All moth-egg amassers,
Old gloves and old feathers,
Old shoes and old leathers,
Greasy or tar-ry,
Bring all you can carry!
We would not deceive you:
The fire shall relieve you,
The world will feel better,
And so be your debtor.
Be welcome then—very—
And come and be merry!

GEORGE AND LOUISA MACDONALD
Bonfire at 7 P.M. Dancing at 8.
CASA CORAGGIO
Dec. 31st, 1885

25

OUR GOD IS A CONSUMING FIRE

Our God is a consuming fire.
Hebrews 12:29

Inexorable Love

God is no tame god.
Though he loves us with the tender father-heart of a child, he will not be mocked. Tears and entreaties will not work on him to the breach of one of his laws. Out of the prison of his own darkness the childlike, imperturbable God will let no one come until he has paid the uttermost farthing.

Neither is God a one-dimensional god. His love has more facets to its personality than our limited minds can fathom. Life is no series of chances with a few providences sprinkled between to keep up a justly failing belief, but is rather one providence of God. God is one. And that oneness is love, the foundational element of his being. But because we cannot grasp the inexhaustible reaches of that love, its constituent parts do not look to us as one. To our minds, the childlikeness and the consuming fire appear as division to his love. But God, I repeat, is one—the only perfect oneness in the universe.

Nothing is inexorable but love. Love is one, and love is changeless. For love loves into purity. Love has ever in view the absolute loveliness of that which it beholds. Where loveliness is incomplete and love cannot love its fill of loving, it spends itself to make more lovely, that it may love more. It strives for perfection, even that itself may be perfected—not in itself, but in the object. There is nothing eternal but that which loves and can be loved, and love is ever climbing toward the consummation when such shall be the universe, imperishable, divine.

Therefore all that is not beautiful in the beloved, all that comes between and is not of love's kind, must be destroyed.

And our God is a consuming fire.

Simple Truth Is Hard to Understand

If this be hard to understand, it is as the simple, absolute truth is hard to understand. It may be centuries of ages before a man comes to see a truth—ages of strife, of effort, of aspiration. But when once he does see it, it is so plain that he wonders he could have lived so long without seeing it. That he did not understand it sooner was simply and only that he did not see it. To see a truth, to know what it is, to understand it, and to love it, are all one. There is many a motion toward it, many a misery for want of it, many a cry of the conscience against the neglect of it, many a dim longing for it as an unknown need before at length the eyes come awake, and the darkness of the dreamful night yields to the light of the sun of truth. But once beheld, it is forever. To see one divine fact is to stand face to face with essential eternal life.

For this vision of truth God has been working for ages of ages. For this simple condition, this apex of life, upon which a man wonders like a child that he cannot make others see as he sees, the whole labor of God's science, history, and poetry has been evolving truth upon truth in lovely vision, in torturing law, never lying, never repenting. And for this will the patience of God labor while there is yet a human soul whose eyes have not been opened, whose child-heart has not yet been born in him. For this one condition of humanity, this simple beholding, has all the out-thinking of God flowed in forms innumerable and changeful from the foundation of the world. And for this, too, has the divine destruction been going forth, that his life might be our life, that in us, too, might dwell that same consuming fire which is essential love.

The Pure Consumes the Impure

Let us look at the utterance of the apostle which is crowned with this lovely terror: "Our God is a consuming fire."

Let us have grace to serve the consuming fire, our God, with divine fear—not with the fear that cringes and craves, but with the bowing down of all thoughts, all delights, all loves before him who is the life of them all, and will have them all pure. The kingdom God has given us cannot be moved, because it has nothing weak in it: it is of the eternal world, the world of being, of truth. We, therefore, must worship him with a fear pure as the kingdom is unshakable. He will shake heaven and earth, that only the unshakable may remain. He is a consuming fire, that only that which cannot be consumed may stand forth eternal. It is the nature of God, so terribly pure that it destroys all that is not pure as fire, which demands the same purity in our worship.

He will have purity. It is not that the fire will burn us if we do not worship thus; but that the fire will burn us until we worship thus; yea, will go on burning within us after all that is foreign to it has yielded to its force, no longer with pain and consuming, but as the highest consciousness of life, the presence of God.

When evil, which alone is consumable, shall have passed away in God's fire from the dwellers in the immovable kingdom, the nature of man will look the nature of God in the face, and man's fear shall then be pure. For an eternal, that is a holy, fear must spring from a knowledge of the nature, not from a sense of the power. That which cannot be consumed must be one within itself. Therefore, in such a soul the fear toward God will be one with the tenderest love. Yet, the fear of God will cause a man to flee, not from God, but from himself; not from God, but *to* him, his own Father, in terror lest he should do him wrong or his neighbor wrong. To love our brother is to worship the Consuming Fire.

Mount Sinai—A Partial Revelation

The symbol of the consuming fire would seem to have been suggested to the writer by the fire that burned on the mountain of the old law, a fire that did not consume the bush in which it burned. But the same symbol employed in the New Testament should mean more, not than it meant before, but than it was before employed to express; for it could not have been employed to express more than it was possible for them to perceive.

How could such a nation as the children of Israel, as it was in the desert, see other in that fire than terror and destruction? How should they think of purification by fire? And if they had had the thought, the notion of the suffering involved would soon have overwhelmed the notion of purification. Through the fire, God showed them what was true, though not the complete truth. It was a revelation, but a partial one—a true symbol, not a final vision.

Here was a nation at its lowest. Could it receive anything but a partial revelation, a revelation of fear? But fear is nobler than sensuality. Fear is better than no God, better than a god made with hands. In that fear at least lay deep hidden the sense of the infinite. The worship of fear is true, although very low; and though not acceptable to God in itself, for only the worship of spirit and truth is acceptable to him, yet even in his sight it is precious.

For he regards men not as they are merely, but as they shall be; not as they shall be merely, but as they are now growing, or capable of growing, toward that image after which he made them that they might grow to it. Therefore a thousand stages, each in itself all but valueless, are of inestimable worth as the necessary and connected gradations of an infinite progress. A condition which, of declension, would indicate a devil may, of growth, indicate a saint.

But we shall find that this very revelation of fire is itself, in a higher sense, true to the mind of the rejoicing saint as to the mind of the trembling sinner. For the former sees farther into the meaning of the fire and knows better what it will do to him. It is a symbol which needed not to be superseded, only unfolded. While men take part *with* their sins, while they feel as if, separated from their sins, they would be no longer themselves, how can they understand that the lightning word is a Savior—the word which pierces to the dividing between the man and the evil, which will slay the sin and give life to the sinner?

Can it be any comfort to them to be told that God loves them so that he will burn them clean? Can the cleansing of the fire appear to them anything beyond what it must always, more or less, be: a process of torture? They do not want to be clean, and they cannot bear to be tortured. Can they then do other than fear God, even with the fear of the wicked, until they learn to love him with the love of the holy?

To them Mount Sinai is crowned with the signs of vengeance. And is not God ready to do unto them even as they fear, though with another feeling and a different end from any which they are capable of supposing? He is against sin: insofar as, and while, they and sin are one, he is against them—against their desires, their aims, their fears, and their hopes. And thus he is altogether and always *for them*. That thunder and lightning and tempest, that blackness torn with the sound of the trumpet, that visible horror billowed with the voice of words was all but a faint image to the senses of the Israelite slaves of what God thinks and feels against vileness and selfishness, of the unrest of unassuageable repulsion with which he regards such conditions. God thus revealed himself in such anger so the thoughtless people, fearing somewhat to do as they would, might leave a little room for that grace to grow in them, which would at length make them see that evil, and not fire, is the fearful thing: Had they understood this, they would have needed no Mount Sinai. It was a true and, of necessity, a partial revelation—partial in order to be true.

Only the Burning of God Can Get Rid of Sin

May it not then hurt to say that God is love, all love, and nothing other than love? When we say that God is love, do we teach men that their fear of him is groundless?

No. As much as they fear will come upon them, possibly far more. But there is something beyond their fear, a divine fate, which they cannot withstand, because it works along with the human individuality, which the divine individuality has created in them.

The wrath will consume what they *call* themselves. The selves God made shall thus appear, coming out with tenfold consciousness of being, and bringing with them all that made the blessedness of the life the men tried to lead without God. They will know that now first are they fully themselves. The avaricious, weary, selfish, suspicious old man shall have passed away. The young, ever young, self will remain. That which they *thought* themselves shall have vanished. That which they *felt* themselves, though they misjudged their own feelings, shall remain—remain glorified in repentant hope. For that which cannot be shaken shall remain. That which is immortal in God shall remain in man. The death that is in them shall be consumed.[1]

Nothing but the burning love of God can rid sin out of anywhere.[2] It is the law of nature—that is, the law of God—that all that is destructible shall be destroyed. When that which is immortal buries itself in the destructible—when it receives all its messages from without, through the surrounding region of self, and none from within, from the eternal doors opening inward into God's presence—it cannot, though immortal still, know its own immortality. The destructible must be burned out of it, or begin to be burned out of it, before it can partake of eternal life. When that is all burnt away and gone, then it has eternal life. Or rather, when the fire of eternal life has possessed a man, then the destructible is gone utterly, and he is pure. Many a man's work must be burned, that by that very burning he may be saved—"so as by fire."

Terrible Doom Awaits Those Who Resist

Away in smoke go the lordships, the rabbihoods of the world, and the man who acquiesces in the burning is saved by the fire; for it has destroyed the destructible, which is the vantage point of the deathly, which would destroy both body and soul in hell. If still he cling to that which can be burned, the burning goes on deeper and deeper still into his bosom until it reaches the roots of the falsehood that enslaves him.

The one who loves God, and is not yet pure, welcomes the burning of God. Nor is it always torture. The fire shows itself sometimes only as light—but still it will be the fire of purifying. The consuming fire is just the original, active form of purity, that which makes pure, that which is indeed Love, the creative energy of God. That which is not pure is corruptible, and corruption cannot inherit incorruption.

The man whose deeds are evil fears the burning. But the burning will not come the less that he fears it or denies it. Escape is hopeless. For Love is inexorable. Our God is a consuming fire. He shall not come out until he has paid the uttermost farthing.

If the man resists the burning of God, the consuming fire of Love, a terrible doom awaits him, and its day will come. He who hates the fire of God shall be cast into the outer darkness. What sick dismay will then seize upon him! For let a man think and care ever so little about God, he does not therefore exist without God. God is here with him, upholding, warming, delighting, teaching him—making life a good thing to him. God gives him himself, though the man knows it not.

But when God withdraws from a man as far as that can be without the man's ceasing to be, when the man feels himself abandoned, hanging in a ceaseless vertigo of existence upon the verge of the gulf of his being, without support, without refuge, without aim, without end, with no inbreathing of joy, with nothing to make life good, then will he listen in agony for the faintest sound of life from the closed door. Then, if the moan of suffering humanity ever reaches the ear of the outcast of darkness, he will be ready to rush into the very heart of the Consuming Fire to know life once more, to change this terror of sick negation, of unspeakable death, for that region of painful hope.

Imagination cannot mislead us into too much horror of being without God—that living death.

The outer darkness is but the most dreadful form of the consuming fire—the fire without light, the darkness visible, the black flame. God has withdrawn himself, but not lost his hold. His face is turned away, but his hand is laid upon the man still. His heart has ceased to beat into the man's heart, but he keeps him alive by his fire. And that fire will go searching and burning on in him, as in the highest saint who is not yet pure as he is pure.[3]

Though Thou Slay Us, Yet Will We Trust in Thee

A chimney above a huge house indicates the greatness of the building below, as the volcanoes of the world tell us how much fire is necessary to keep the old earth warm. For it is not the sun itself that warms the planet. The earth is like the human heart. The great glowing fire below us is God in the heart of the earth, and the great sun is God in the sky, keeping it warm on the other side. Our gladness and pleasure, our trouble when we do wrong, our love for all about us, that is God inside us. All the beautiful things and lovable people, all the lessons we get from life, and whatever comes to us, is God on the outside.

Every life is between two great fires of the love of God, that is, so long as we do not give ourselves up right heartily to him we fear the fire will burn us. And so it does when we go against its flames and not with them, refusing to burn with the same glorious fire with which God is always burning. When we try to put it out, or get away from it, then indeed it burns.[4]

But at length, O God, will you not cast Death and Hell into the lake of fire—even into your own consuming self? Death shall then die everlastingly.

Then indeed will you be all in all. For then our poor brothers and sisters, every one—O God, we trust in you, the Consuming Fire—shall have been burnt clean and brought home. For shall a man be more merciful than God? Shall, of all his glories, his mercy alone not be infinite? Shall a brother love a brother more than a Father loves a son—more than the Brother Christ loves his brother? Would he not die yet again to save one brother more?

As for us, now we will come to thee, our Consuming Fire. And thou wilt not burn us more than we can bear. But thou wilt burn us. And although thou seem to slay us, yet will we trust in thee.[5]

PICTURING GOD THROUGH THE MISTS OF A LOW THEOLOGY

(A Fictional Selection from *Robert Falconer*)

For now arose within him, not without ultimate good, the evil phantasms of a theology which would explain all God's doings by low conceptions. In such a system, hell is invariably the deepest truth, and the love of God is not so deep as hell. Hence, as foundations must be laid in the deepest, the system is founded in hell, and the first article in the creed that Robert Falconer learned was, 'I believe in hell.' Practically, I mean, it was so; else how should it be that as often as a thought of religious duty arose in his mind, it appeared in the form of escaping hell, of fleeing from the wrath to come? For his very nature was hell, being not born *in* sin and brought forth in iniquity, but born sin and brought forth iniquity. And yet God made him. He must believe that. And he must believe, too, that God was just, awfully just, punishing with fearful pains those who did not go through a certain process of mind which it was utterly impossible they should go through without a help which he would give to some, and withhold from others, the reason of the difference not being such, to say the least of it, as to come within the reach of the persons concerned. And this God they said was love.[6]

Faith

"Earth, if aught should check thy race,
Rushing through unfended space,
Headlong, stayless, thou wilt fall
Into yonder glowing ball!"

"Beggar of the universe,
Faithless as an empty purse!
Sent abroad to cool and tame,
Think'st I fear my native flame?

"If thou never on thy track
Turn thee round and hie thee back,
Thou wilt wander evermore,
Outcast, cold—a comet hoar!

"While I sweep my ring along
In an air of joyous song,
Thou art drifting, heart awry,
From the sun of liberty!"

PUTTING OFF REPENTANCE

(A Fictional Selection from *The Elect Lady*)

H is presence cannot be *proved*; it can only be known. If he meet us, it is not necessary to the joy of his presence that we should be able to prove that he does meet us! If a man has the company of the Lord, he will care little whether another does or does not believe that he has."

"Your way is against the peace of the church! It fosters division."

"Did the Lord come to send peace on the earth? My way, as you call it, would make division, but division between those who call themselves his, and those who are his. It would bring together those that love him. Company would merge with company that they might look on the Lord together. I don't believe Jesus cares much for what is called the visible church; but he cares with his very Godhead for those that do as he tells them; they are his Father's friends; they are his elect by whom he will save the world. It is by those who obey, and by their obedience, that he will save those who do not obey, that is, will bring them to obey. It is one by one the world will pass to his side. There is no saving in the lump. If a thousand be converted at once, it is every single lonely man that is converted."

"You would make a slow process of it!"

"If slow, yet faster than any other. All God's processes are slow. How many years has the world existed, do you imagine, sir?"

"I don't know. Geologists say hundreds and hundreds of thousands."

"And how many is it since Christ came?"

"Toward two thousand."

"Then we are but in the morning of Christianity! There is plenty of time. The day is before us."

"Dangerous doctrine for the sinner!"

"Why? Time is plentiful for his misery, if he will not repent; plentiful for the mercy of God that would lead him to repentance. There is plenty of time for labour and hope; none for indifference and delay. God *will* have his creatures good. They cannot escape him."

"Then a man may put off repentance as long as he pleases!"

"Certainly he may—at least as long as he can—but it is a fearful thing to try issues with God."[7]

Appeal

If in my arms I bore my child,
  Would he cry out for fear
Because the night was dark and wild
  And no one else was near?

Shall I then treat thee, Father, as
  My fatherhood would grieve?
I will be hopeful, though, alas,
  I cannot quite believe!

I had no power, no wish to be:
  Thou madest me half blind!
The darkness comes! I cling to thee!
  Be thou my perfect mind.

26

GOD THE MERCIFUL AND JUST

Also unto thee, O Lord, belongeth mercy: for thou renderest to every man according to his work.

Psalm 62:12

What Is Justice?

The word translated *mercy* in this verse is, by some translators, made *kindness* or *goodness* or *love*. But according to many of the theories prevailing in the so-called religious world, the word would have been changed to *justice*.

Let us try to see plainly what we mean when we use the word *justice*, and whether we mean what we ought to mean when we use it—especially with reference to God. Let us attempt to come nearer to knowing what we ought to understand by justice, that is, the justice of God. For his justice is the live, active justice, giving existence to the idea of justice in our minds and hearts. Because he is just, we are capable of knowing justice. It is because he is just, that we have the idea of justice so deeply imbedded in us.

What do we most often mean by *justice?* Is it not the carrying out of the law, the infliction of penalty assigned to offense? By a just judge we mean a man who administers the law without prejudice, and where guilt is proven, punishes as much as, and no more than, the law in the case has laid down. It may not be, however, that justice has been done. The law itself may be unjust. Or perhaps the working of the law has been foiled by the parasites of law for their own gain. For even if the law be good, and thoroughly administered, it does not necessarily follow that justice is done.

Suppose my watch has been stolen from my pocket. I catch the thief. He is dragged before the judge, proven guilty, and sentenced to a just imprisonment. Will I then walk home satisfied with the result? Have I had justice done me?

The thief may have had justice done him, but where is my watch? That is gone, and I remain a man wronged. Who has done me the wrong? The thief. Who can set right the wrong? The thief, and only the thief—nobody but the man that did the wrong.

God may be able to move the man to right the wrong, but God himself cannot right it without the man.

Suppose my watch is found and restored to me; is the account settled between me and the thief? I may forgive him, but is the wrong removed? By no means. But suppose the thief repents in his heart. He has, we shall say, no longer the power to return the watch, but he comes to me and says he is sorry he stole it and begs me to accept for the time being what little he is able to bring, as a beginning of atonement. How should I then regard the matter?

Should I not feel that he had gone far to make atonement—done more to make up for the injury he had inflicted upon me, even than the mere restoration of the watch could have accomplished? Would there not lie in the thief's confession and submission and initial restoration an appeal to the divinest in me—to the eternal brotherhood? Would it not indeed amount to a sufficing atonement as between man and man? If he offered to bear what I chose to lay upon him, should I feel it necessary, for the sake of justice, to inflict some certain suffering as demanded by righteousness? I should still have a claim upon him for my watch, but would I not be likely to forget it?

He who commits the offense can make up for it—and he alone.

Can Punishment Atone for Wrong?

One thing must surely be plain—that the punishment of the wrongdoer makes no atonement for the wrong done. How could it make up to me the loss of my watch that the man was punished? The wrong would be there all the same. I am not saying the man ought not to be punished. Far from it. I am saying only that the punishment nowise makes up to the man wronged.

Suppose the man, with the watch in his pocket, were to inflict the severest beating upon himself. Would that lessen my sense of injury? Would it set anything right? Would it in any way atone? Would it give him a right to the watch? Punishment may do good to the man who does the wrong, but it is not justice.

Another thing plain is that even if the material rectification of the wrong is impossible, repentance removes the offense, which no suffering could. If the man truly repented, even were the watch gone, I at least should feel that I had no more quarrel with the man. I should even feel that the gift he had given me, that of a repentant brother, was infinitely beyond the restitution of what he had taken from me. True, he owed me both himself and the watch, but the greater more than includes the lesser.

 If it be objected: "You may forgive, but the man has sinned against God! The Lord is merciful, yes, but his justice must be satisfied," I answer: There can be no opposition, no strife whatever, between mercy and justice. Those who say justice means the punishing of sin, and mercy the not punishing of sin, and attribute both to God, would make a schism in the very idea of God.[1]

There are many who think they reverence the Most High by assuming that he can and should do anything or everything in a mere moment. In their eyes power is a grander thing than love. Though it is nowhere said in the Book that God is omnipotence, because such people are told that he is omnipotent, they call him Omnipotence. Yet when told that he is Love, they do not care to argue that he must then be loving. But his love is higher than his omnipotence.

See what it cost him to redeem the world! He did not find that easy, or to be done in a moment without pain or toil.

Yes, God is omnipotent—awfully omnipotent. For he wills, effects, and perfects the thing which, because of the bad in us, he has to carry out in suffering and sorrow. Evil is a hard thing, even for God to overcome. Yet thoroughly and altogether and triumphantly will he overcome it.

But not by crushing it underfoot—any god of man's idea could do that—but by conquest of heart over heart, of life over life, of life over death, of love over all. Nothing shall be too hard for the God who fears not pain, but will deliver and make true and blessed at his own severest cost.[2]

What Is Divine Justice?

This brings us to the question: What then truly is meant by divine justice, the sort of justice that God displays?

Human justice may be a poor distortion of justice, a mere shadow of it. But the justice of God must be perfect. If you ask any ordinary

Sunday congregation what is meant by the justice of God, would not nineteen out of twenty answer that it means God's punishing of sin? Think for a moment what degree of justice it would indicate in a man that he punished every wrong. A Roman emperor, a Turkish *cadi*, might do that, and be the most unjust both of men and judges.

But could God?

God is *one*, and the depth of foolishness is reached by that theology which talks of God as if he held different offices and differed in each.

It sets a contradiction in the very nature of God himself. It represents him, for instance, as having to do something as a judge which as a father he would not do. The love of the father makes him desire to be unjust as a judge!

Oh the folly of any mind that would explain God before obeying him, that would map out the character of God, instead of crying, "Lord, what wouldst thou have me to do?"

God is no magistrate, but if he were, it would be a position to which his fatherhood alone gave him the right. His rights as a father cover every right he can analytically be supposed to possess.

The justice of God is this, that—to use a boyish phrase—he gives every man, woman, child, and beast, everything that has being, fair play. He renders to every man according to his work. And therein lies his perfect mercy, for nothing else could be merciful to the man, and nothing but mercy could be fair to him. God does nothing of which any just man, the thing set fairly and fully before him so that he understood, would not say, "That is fair."

Who would, I repeat, say a man was a just man because he insisted on prosecuting every offender? A scoundrel might do that. How then do so many view the justice of God as merely involving his punishment of sin! A just man is one who cares, and tries, and always tries, to give fair play to everyone in everything. When we speak of the justice of God, let us see that we do mean justice! Punishment of the guilty may be involved in justice, but it does not constitute the justice of God one atom more than it would constitute the justice of man, if that is all there is to it.

Much that the Bible says about God's justice had been grossly misunderstood, and has, through the years, become a theology which is nothing but a mere tradition of men, and which wrongs God's character. The Lord of life complains of men for not judging right. To say on the authority of the Bible that God does a thing no honorable man would do is to lie against God as well as against the utter truthfulness of his Word. To uphold a lie for God's sake, because we have been taught it, rather than allow the Spirit of truth to illuminate our hearts, is to be against God, not for him.

God Must Be More *Than Man, Not Less*

God is the truth. The truth alone is on his side. While his child could not see the rightness of a thing, God would infinitely rather, even if the thing were right, have him say, "God could not do that thing," than have him believe that God could do a wrong thing. If the man were sure God did it, the thing he ought to say would be, "Then there must be something about it I do not know, which if I did know, I should see the thing quite differently."

But where an evil thing is invented to explain and account for a good thing, and a lover of God is called upon to believe the invention or be cast out, he needs not mind being cast out, for it is into the company of Jesus. Where there is no ground to believe that God does a thing, except that men who would explain God have believed and taught it, he is not a true man who accepts men against his own conscience of God. I will accept no explanation of any way of God that involves what I should scorn as false and unfair in a man.

If it is said, "It may be right of God to do something that it would not be right of man to do," I answer, "Yes, because *more* is required of the Maker, by his own act of creation, than can be required of men—not less." God can have no duty that is not both just and merciful. *More* and *higher* justice and righteousness is required of him by himself, the Truth—greater nobleness, more penetrating sympathy, and *nothing* but what, if an honest man understood it, he would say was right.

If it be a thing man cannot understand, then man can say nothing as to whether it is right or wrong. He cannot even know that God does *it*, when the *it* is unintelligible to him. What he calls *it* may be the smallest facet of a composite action. His part is silence. If it be said by any that God does a thing, and the thing seems unjust, then either we do not know what the thing is, or God does not do it. The saying cannot mean what it seems to mean, or the saying is not true. If, for instance, it be said, that God visits the sins of the fathers on the children, a man seeking to grasp the meaning behind the words, and who takes *visits upon* to mean *punishes*, and *the children* to mean *the innocent children*, ought to say, "Either I do not understand the statement, or the thing is not true, whoever says it."

God *may* do what seems to a man not right, but it must so seem to him because God works on higher, on divine, on perfect principles, too right for a selfish, unfair, or unloving man to understand. But least of all must we accept some low notion of justice in a man, and then argue that God is just in doing that same thing.

In saying these things, my work is not to attempt to destroy the false, except as it is necessary for building the true. I will enter no debate to be the champion for or against mere doctrine. I have no desire to change the opinion of man or woman. Let everyone hold to what he pleases. But I would do my utmost to disable such as think correct opinion essential to salvation, from laying any other burden on the shoulders of true men and women than the yoke of their Master. Let the Lord himself teach them. A man who has not the mind of Christ— and no man has the mind of Christ except him who makes it his business to obey him—cannot have correct opinions concerning him. Our business is not to think correctly, but to live truly. Then first will there be a possibility of our thinking correctly.

One chief cause of the amount of unbelief in the world is that those who have seen something of the glory of Christ set themselves to theorize concerning him rather than to obey him. In teaching men, they have not taught them Christ, but taught them *about* Christ. More eager after credible theory than after doing the truth, they have speculated in a condition of heart in which it was impossible they should understand. They have presumed to explain a Christ whom years and years of obedience could alone have made them able to comprehend. Their teaching of him, therefore, has gone against the common sense of many who perhaps had not half their intellect, but in whom there was no guile.

Such naturally press their theories upon others, insisting on their thinking about Christ as they think, instead of urging them to go to Christ to be taught by him whatever he chooses to teach them. From such and their false teaching I would gladly help to deliver the true-hearted.

Let the dead bury their own dead. But I would do what I may to keep them from burying the living.[3]

EVERY SIN DESERVES GOD'S WRATH AND CURSE

(A Fictional Selection from *The Maiden's Bequest*)

Every Saturday Murdoch Malison's pupils had to learn a certain number of questions from the Shorter Catechism, with their corresponding proofs from Scripture. Whoever failed in the task was condemned to imprisonment for the remainder of the day or until the task was accomplished. On one Saturday each month, moreover, the students were tested on all the questions and proofs that had been covered during the previous month.

The day in question was one of those of accumulated labor, and the only proofs Alec Forbes had succeeded in displaying was proof of his inability for the task. In consequence he was condemned to be kept in—a trial hard indeed for one whose chief delights were the open air and the active exertion of his growing body.

Seeing his downcast expression filled Annie with such concern that she lost track of the class and did not know when her turn came until suddenly the master was standing before her in silent expectation. He had approached soundlessly and then stood till the universal silence had at length aroused Annie's consciousness. Then with a smile on his thin lips, but a lowering thundercloud on his brow, he repeated the question: "What doth every sin deserve?"

Annie, bewildered and burning with shame at finding herself the core of the silence, could not recall a word of the answer given in the Catechism. So in her confusion she fell back on her common sense and experience.

"What doth every sin deserve?" repeated the tyrant.

"A lickin'," whispered Annie, her eyes filling with tears.[4]

Up and Down

The sun is gone down
    And the moon's in the sky
But the sun will come up
    And the moon be laid by.

The flower is asleep,
    But it is not dead,
When the morning shines
    It will lift its head.

When winter comes
    It will die! No, no,
It will only hide
    From the frost and snow.

Sure is the summer,
    Sure is the sun;
The night and the winter
    Away they run.

GOD DRAWS ONLY PURE LINES

(A Fictional Selection from *The Tutor's First Love*)

In the name of God he rebukes the flames of hell. And be sure that, come what may of the rest, let the flames of hell ebb or flow, that man is safe. He trusts in God so absolutely that he leaves his salvation to him. He only sets himself to do the work that God has given him to do. Let God's will be done and all is well. To him God is all in all. If it be possible to separate such things, it is the glory of God, even more than the salvation of men, that he seeks. He believes entirely that God loves, yea, is love. Therefore hell itself must be subservient to that love and must be an embodiment of it. He believes that the grand work of Justice is to make way for a Love which will give to every man that which is right, even if it should be by means of awful suffering which the love of the Father will not shun, either for himself or his children but will eagerly meet for their sakes, that he may give them all that is in his heart."

"Surely you speak your own opinions in describing the faith of the preacher."

"I do. He is accountable for nothing I say."

"How is it that so many good people consider him unorthodox and his ways suspect?"

"I do not mind that. To such well-meaning people with small natures, theology must be like a map—with plenty of lines in it. They cannot trust their house on the high tableland of this man's theology because they cannot see the outlines bounding his land. It is not small enough for them. They cannot take it in. Such people, one would think, can hardly be satisfied with creation, seeing there is no line of division anywhere in it."

"Does God draw no lines, then?"

"When he does, they are pure lines, without breadth and consequently invisible to mortal eyes, not walls of separation such as these definers would construct."

"But is it reasonable that a theory in religion be correct if it is so hard to see?"

"They are only hard to see for certain natures."

"But those people, those natures you speak of, are above

average usually. And you have granted them good intentions."

"Generally good, but very narrow perspective."

"Is it not rather hard of you then to say that they cannot understand, cannot perceive truth in the high tableland?"

"Is it hard of me? Why? They will get to heaven, which is all they want. And they will understand one day, which is more than they pray for. Till they have done being anxious about their own salvation, we must forgive them that they can contemplate with calmness the damnation of a universe, all the while believing that God is yet more indifferent than they."

"But who is to say that you are right and they are the unenlightened ones? They could bring the same charge against you, of being unable to understand them."

"Yes. And so it must remain until the Spirit of God decides the matter."[5]

In the Night

As to her child a mother calls,
　　"Come to me, child; come near!"
Calling in silent intervals,
　　The Master's voice I hear.

But does he call me verily?
　　To have me does he care?
Why should he seek my poverty,
　　My selfishness so bare?

The dear voice makes his gladness brim,
　　But not a child can know
Why that large woman cares for him,
　　Why she should love him so!

Lord, to thy call of me I bow,
　　Obey like Abraham:
Thou lov'st me because thou art thou,
　　And I am what I am!

Doubt whispers, Thou art such a blot
　　He cannot love poor thee:
If what I am he loveth not,
　　He loves what I shall be.

Nay, that which can be drawn and wooed,
　　And turned away from ill,
Is what his father made for good:
　　He loves me, I say still!

27

GOD THE DESTROYER OF SIN

*Our old man is crucified with him, that . . . sin might
be destroyed. . . .*

Romans 6:6

God Is not Obligated to Punish Sin

In the hope of giving a larger idea to the justice of God I ask, "Why is God bound to punish sin?"

If God punishes sin, it must be merciful to punish sin—for God is merciful. And if God forgives sin, it must be just to forgive sin—for God is just.

How then do we harmonize mercy, justice, and forgiveness into the oneness of God's character?

Every attribute of God must be infinite as himself. He cannot be sometimes merciful, but not always merciful. He cannot be just, but not always just. Mercy belongs to him, and needs no contrivance of theologic chicanery to justify it.

"Then do you mean it is wrong to punish sin, and therefore God does not punish sin?

By no means.

God does punish sin, but there is no opposition between punishment and forgiveness. The one may be essential to the possibility of the other. We are back to my question: *Why* does God punish sin?

"Because in itself sin deserves punishment," do you answer?

Then how can God tell us to forgive it?

"He punishes, and having punished he forgives."

That will hardly do. For if sin demands punishment, if the making right for sin is punishment, and righteous punishment is given, then the man is out from under sin's claim upon him; he is free. Why should he now be forgiven?

"He needs forgiveness, because no amount of punishment can make up for the sin that is in his nature. Nothing will fully give him all he deserves."

Then why not forgive him at once, if the punishment is not essential, if it does not adequately remedy the whole of the problem of sin? And this points out the fault in the whole idea.

Punishment is nowise an *offset* to sin. Punishment, deserved suffering, is no equipoise to sin. Suffering weighs nothing at all against sin. If sin sits on one scale, it will move it not a hairsbreadth to lay punishment and suffering on the other. They are not of the same kind, not under the same laws, any more than mind and matter. To attempt to equate them would be like placing a cubic inch of lead on the one scale, and attempting to balance it by placing a cubic yard of air on the other. The sin is unmoved. It remains where it is though an eternity of punishment and suffering be brought to bear against it.

If it were an offset to wrong, then God would be bound to punish for the sake of punishment. But he cannot be, for he forgives. Then it is not for the sake of punishment, as a thing that in itself ought to be done, but for the sake of something else, as a means to an end, that God punishes.

Primarily, God is not bound to *punish* sin; he is bound to *destroy* sin. If he were not the Maker, he might not be bound to destroy sin— I do not know. But seeing he has created creatures who have sinned, and therefore sin has, by the creating act of God, come into the world, God is, in his own righteousness, bound to destroy sin.

Destruction, not Punishment, Is Required

God is always destroying sin. In him I trust that he is destroying sin in me. He is always saving the sinner from his sin, and that is destroying sin. But vengeance on the sinner, the law of a tooth for a tooth, is not in the heart of God, neither in his hand. If the sinner and the sin in him are the concrete object of the divine wrath, then indeed there can be no mercy. Then indeed there will be an end put to sin by the destruction of the sin and the sinner together. But thus would no atonement be wrought—nothing be done to make up for the wrong God has allowed to come into being by creating man. There must be an atonement, a making-up, a bringing together—an atonement which cannot be made except by the man who has sinned.

Punishment, I repeat, is not the thing required of God, but the absolute destruction of sin. What better is the world, what better is the sinner, what better is God, what better is the truth, that the sinner should suffer—continue suffering to all eternity? Would there be less sin in the universe? Would there be any making-up for sin? Would it show God justified in doing what he knew would bring sin into the world, justified in making creatures he knew would sin? What setting-right would come of the sinner's suffering? If justice demanded it, if suffering be the equivalent for sin, then the sinner must suffer, and God is bound to exact his suffering, and not pardon; and so the making of man was a tyrannical deed, a creative cruelty. But grant that the sinner has deserved to suffer, no amount of suffering is any atonement for his sin. To suffer to all eternity could not make up for one unjust word.

An unjust word is an eternally evil thing; nothing but God in my heart can cleanse me from the evil that uttered it. But it does not follow that I saw the evil of what I did so perfectly that eternal punishment for it would be just. Sorrow and confession and self-abasing love will make up for the evil word; suffering will not. For evil in the abstract, nothing can be done. It is eternally evil. But I may be saved from it by learning to loathe it, to hate it, to shrink from it with an eternal avoidance. The only vengeance worth having on sin is to make the sinner himself its executioner.

The True Opposite of Evil

Sin and punishment are in no antagonism to each other in man, any more than pardon and punishment are in God. They can perfectly co-exist. The one naturally follows the other, punishment being born of sin, because evil exists only by the life of good and has no life of its own, being in itself death.

Sin and suffering are not natural opposites. The opposite of evil is good, not suffering. The opposition of sin is not suffering, but righteousness. The path across the gulf that divides right from wrong is not the fire, but repentance.

If my friend has wronged me, will it console me to see him punished? Will that be a rendering to me of my due? What kind of friendship would I be fit for if that were possible, even with regard to my enemy? But would not the shadow of repentant grief, the light of reviving love on his face, heal it at once, however deep the hurt had been?

Take any of those wicked people in Dante's hell, and ask wherein is justice served by their punishment. Mind, I am not saying it is not right to punish them. I am saying that justice can never be satisfied by suffering.

Human resentment, human revenge, human hate may find satisfaction in it. But there can be no destruction of evil thereby. The destruction of sin must begin where the sin originated in the first place, in the depths of a man's heart.

When a man loathes himself, he has begun to be saved. Punishment tends to this result. Not for its own sake, not as a make-up for sin, not for divine revenge, not for any satisfaction to justice. Punishment is for the sake of amendment and atonement. God is bound by his love to punish sin in order to deliver his creature. He is bound by his justice to destroy the sin in his creation.

Love is justice—is the fulfilling of the law, for God as well as for his children. This is the reason of punishment; this is why justice requires that the wicked shall not go unpunished—that they, through the eye-opening power of pain, may come to see and do justice, may be brought to desire and make all possible amends, and so become just. For Justice, that is God, is bound in himself to see justice done by his children—not in the mere outward act, but in their very being. He is bound in himself to make up for wrong done by his children, and he can do nothing to make up for wrong done but by bringing about the repentance of the wrongdoer.

Righteousness—The Beginning of Sin's End

When the man says, "I did wrong; I hate myself and the deed; I cannot endure to think that I did it!" then, I say, is atonement begun. Without that, all that the Lord did would be lost. He would have made no atonement. Repentance, restitution, confession, prayer for forgiveness, righteous dealing thereafter is the sole possible, the only true make-up for sin. For nothing less than this did Christ die. When a man acknowledges the right he denied before, when he says to the wrong, "I loathe you. I see now how you are. I could not see it before, because I refused to see it. God forgive me, make me clean, or let me die!" then Justice, that is God, has conquered sin—and not until then.

"How, then," you may say, "does the atonement of Jesus conquer sin, if all the doing must come from within the man? What atonement is there then by his shed blood?"

All the atonement that God cares for; the work of Jesus Christ on earth was the creative atonement, because it works atonement in every heart. He brings and is bringing God and man, and man and man, into perfect unity. "I in them and thou in me, that they may be made perfect in one." His death is what makes such atonement, such one-making, possible.

"That is dangerous doctrine!" some will say.

More dangerous than you think to many things—to every evil, to every lie, and among the rest to every false trust in what Christ did, instead of in Christ himself. Paul glories in the cross of Christ, but he does not trust in the cross; he trusts in the living Christ and his living Father.

Justice, then, requires that sin should be put an end to. And not only that, but that it should be atoned for. And where punishment can do anything to this end, where it can help the sinner to know what he has been guilty of, where it can soften his heart to see his pride and wrong and cruelty, justice requires that punishment shall not be spared. And the more we believe in God, the surer we shall be that he will spare nothing that suffering can do to deliver his child from death. If suffering cannot serve this end, we need look for no more hell, but for the destruction of sin by the destruction of the sinner. That, however, would, it appears to me, be for God to suffer defeat.

If God be defeated, he must destroy—that is, he must withdraw life. How can he go on sending forth his life into irreclaimable souls, to keep sin alive in them through the ages of eternity? For in such a case, no atonement would be made, and God would remain defeated, for he has created that which has sinned, and which would not repent and make up for its sin.

But those who believe that God will thus be defeated by many souls must surely be of those who do not believe he cares enough to do his very best for them. He is their Father. He had power to make them out of himself, separate from himself, and capable of being one with him. Surely he will somehow save and keep them! Not the power of sin itself can close *all* the channels between the Creator and the created.

The Saving Redemption of Suffering

The notion of suffering as an offset for sin comes first of all, I think, from the satisfaction we feel when wrong comes to grief. We hate wrong, but, not being righteous ourselves, to a degree we cannot keep from hating the wronger as well. In this way the inborn justice of our nature passes over to evil. It is no pleasure to God, as it so often is to us, to see the wicked suffer. To regard any suffering with satisfaction, unless it be sympathetically with its curative quality, comes of evil and is a thing God is incapable of. His nature is always to forgive, and just because he forgives, he punishes. Because God is so altogether alien to wrong, because it is to him a heart-pain and trouble that one of his little ones should do the evil thing, there is, I believe, no extreme of suffering to which, for the sake of destroying the evil thing in them, he would not subject them. A man might flatter, or bribe, or coax a tyrant. But there is no refuge from the love of God. That love will, for very love, insist upon the uttermost farthing.

"That hardly sounds like love," you say. "It's certainly not the sort of love I care about."

No, how should you? How should any of us care for it until we begin to know it? But the eternal love will not be moved to yield us to the selfishness that is killing us. You may sneer at such a love, but the Son of God, who took the weight of that love and bore it through the world, is content with it, and so is everyone who truly knows it.

The love of the Father is a radiant perfection. Love and not self-love is Lord of the universe. Justice demands your punishment, because it demands that your Father should do his best for you. God, being the God of justice—that is of fair play—and having made us what we are (apt to fall and capable of being raised again) is in himself bound to punish in order to deliver us.[1]

There are tenderhearted people who would never have force used nor pain suffered, who talk as if kindness could do everything. Yet were it not for suffering, millions of human beings would never develop an atom of affection. It is folly to conclude that a thing ought not to be done because it hurts. There are powers to be born, creations to be perfected, sinners to be redeemed—all through the ministry of pain—that could be born, perfected, and redeemed in no other way.[2]

The notion that the salvation of Jesus is a salvation from the consequences of our sins is a false notion. The salvation of Christ is salvation from the smallest tendency or leaning to sin. It is a deliverance into the pure air of God's ways of thinking and feeling. It is a salvation that makes the heart pure, with the will and choice of the heart to be pure.

To such a heart, sin is disgusting. It sees a thing as it is—that is, as God sees it, for God sees everything as it is. Jesus did not die to save us from punishment. He was called Jesus because he should save his people from their sins.[3]

A Prisoner

The hinges are so rusty
The door is fixed and fast;
The windows are so dusty
The sun looks in aghast:
Knock out the glass, I pray,
Or dash the door away,
Or break the house down bodily,
And let my soul go free!

WHY GOD ALLOWS EVIL

(A Fictional Selection from *The Minister's Restoration*)

S ee the loving power at the heart of things, Isy!" said James to his wife. "Out of evil God has brought good, the best good, and nothing but the good!—a good ripened through my sin and selfishness and ambition, bringing upon you as well as me disgrace and suffering. The evil in me had to come out and show itself before it could be cleared away! From some people nothing but an earthquake will rouse from them dead sleep. I was one of such! God in his mercy brought on the earthquake to wake me and save me from death.

"Ignorant people go about always asking why God permits evil. We know why! So that we might come to know—really know!—what good is like, and therefore what God himself is like. It may be that he could with a word eliminate evil altogether and cause it to cease. But what would that teach us about good? The word might make us good like oxen or harmless sheep, but would that be a worthy image of him who was made in the image of God? For a man to cease to be capable of evil, he must cease to be man! What would the goodness be that could not help being good—that had no choice in the matter, but must be such because it was so made? God chooses to be good, otherwise he would not be God: man must choose to be good, otherwise he cannot be the son of God."

"God *is* good, isn't he, James!"

"And so good to us! Just think where we each might be if he *hadn't* shown us ourselves, even in our sin. We might never have known his goodness had it not been for the evil in us."

"Oh, but that was such a hard time! To think that he was with us every step."

"That is how grand the love of the Father of men is, Isy— that he gives them a share, and that share as necessary as his own, in the making of themselves. Thus, and only thus, by willing—by choosing—the good, can they become partakers of the divine nature. All the discipline, all the pain of the world exists for the sake of this—that we may come to choose the good. God is teaching us to know good and evil in some real degree *as they are* and not as they *seem* to the incomplete. So shall we learn to choose the good and refuse the evil. He would make his children see the two things, good and evil, in some measure as they are, and then say whether they will be good children or not. If they fail, and choose the evil, he will take yet harder measures with them, salting them with continually deeper pains and cleansing of the refiner's fire.

"If at last it should prove possible for a created being to see good and evil as they are, and choose the evil, then, and only then, there would, I presume, be nothing left for God but to set his foot upon him and crush him as we might a noxious insect.

"But God is deeper in us than our own life. Yea, God's life is the very center and creative cause of that life which we call *ours*. Therefore is the Life in us stronger than the Death, inasmuch as the creating Good is stronger than the created Evil."[4]

Rejoice

"Rejoice," said the Sun; "I will make thee gay
With glory and gladness and holiday;
I am dumb, O man, and I need thy voice!"
But man would not rejoice.

"Rejoice in thyself," said he, "O Sun,
For thy daily course is a lordly one;
In thy lofty place rejoice if thou can:
For me, I am only a man."

"Rejoice," said the Wind; "I am free and strong,
And will wake in thy heart an ancient song;
Hear the roaring woods, my organ noise!"
But man would not rejoice.

"Rejoice, O Wind, in thy strength," said he,
"For thou fulfillest thy destiny;
Shake the forest, the faint flowers fan:
For me, I am only a man."

"Rejoice," said the Night, "with moon and star,
For the Sun and the Wind are gone afar;
I am here with rest and dreaming choice!"
But man would not rejoice;

For he said—"What is rest to me, I pray,
Whose labour leads to no gladsome day?
He only can dream who has hope behind:
Alas for me and my kind!"

Then a voice that came not from moon or star,
From the sun, or the wind that roved afar,
Said, "Man, I am with thee—hear my voice!"
And man said, "I rejoice."

28

*J*ESUS CHRIST IS OUR ATONEMENT

We also joy in God through our Lord Jesus Christ, by whom we have now received the atonement.

Romans 5:11

I Care Nothing for "Theology"

M any have complained throughout my lifetime about various of my views with which they take exception. If you insist upon unceremoniously casting to the winds the doctrines the church has held from time immemorial, they say, what theories do you propose to substitute in their stead?

In the name of truth, I answer, *none*. I will send out no theories of mine to rouse afresh little whirlwinds of dialogistic dust mixed with dirt and straw and holy words, hiding the Master in talk about him. If I have any such, I will not cast them on the road as I walk, but present them plainly to him to whom I may think it well to show them. For me, the character of God, made real and personal and understandable through his Son, is all. Theories and doctrines about how and why he does what he does are nothing.

Only eyes opened by the Sun of Righteousness and made single by obedience, can judge even the poor, moony pearl of formulated thought. Say if you will that I fear to show my opinion. But what faith of this kind I have, I will have to myself before God, until I see better reason for uttering it than I do now. I shun not to make public my convictions concerning the nature of the God I love and how we might grow in ever deeper knowledge of him through obedience. But with doctrines, and what men commonly call "theology," I do not care to become involved.[1]

Sadly, there are those who hold not only dry, but deadly stale, doctrines, which continue to show a kind of galvanized life from the holding of one measure of truth and the hiding of another. They are those who would have us love Christ for protecting us from God, instead of for leading us to God—the one home of safety—in whom alone is bliss, away from whom all is darkness and misery.

They have not a glimmer of the truth that eternal life is to *know* God. They imagine justice and love dwelling in eternal opposition in the bosom of eternal unity. They know next to nothing about God, and misrepresent him whenever they speak of him. If God were such as they show him, it would indeed be the worst possible misfortune to have been created, or have anything to do with God at all.[2]

Obedience Is Faith

Theory is not faith, nor anything like it. Faith is obedience; theory, I know not what. Trust in God. Obey the word—every word of the Master. That is faith; and so believing, your opinion will grow out of your true life, and be worthy of it. Peter says the Lord gives the Spirit to them that obey him—the Spirit of the Master—and that alone can guide you to any theory that it will be of use to hold. A theory arrived at any other way is not worth the time spent on it. Jesus is the creating and saving Lord of our intellects as well as of our more precious hearts. Nothing that he does not think is worth thinking. No man can think as he thinks except he be pure like him. No man can be pure like him, except he go with him, and learn from him.

To put off obeying him until we find a credible theory concerning him is to set aside the medicine we know it our duty to drink for the study of the various schools of therapy. You know what Christ requires of you is right. If you do not do what you know of the truth, I do not wonder that you seek it intellectually. But do not call anything that may be so gained, *the Truth.* How can a man, not caring himself to *be* true, judge concerning him whose life was to do, for very love, the things that man confesses his duty yet does not do? Obey the truth, I say, and let theory wait. Theory may spring from life, but never from theory.

I will not then tell you what I *think*, but I will tell any man who cares to hear it what I *believe.* Of course what I say will have enough of the character of theory that I cannot prove it; I can only endeavor to order my life by it.

I Believe in Jesus Christ

I believe in Jesus Christ, the eternal Son of God, my Elder Brother, my Lord and Master. I believe that he has a right to my absolute obedience whereinsoever I know or shall come to know his will. I believe that to obey him is to ascend the pinnacle of my being, that not to obey him would be to deny him. I believe that he died that I might die like him—die to any ruling power in me but the will of God—live ready to be nailed to the cross as he was, if God will it. I believe that he is my Savior from myself, and from all that has come of loving myself, from all that God does not love, and would not have me love—all that is not worth loving. I believe he died that the justice, the mercy of God, might have its way with me, making me just as God is just, merciful as he is merciful, perfect as my Father in heaven is perfect.

I believe and pray that he will give me what punishment I need to set me right, or keep me from going wrong. I believe that he died to deliver me from all meanness, all pretense, all falseness, all unfairness, all poverty of spirit, all cowardice, all fear, all anxiety, all forms of self-love, all trust or hope in possession, to make me merry as a child, the child of our Father in heaven, loving only what is lovely, desiring nothing I should be ashamed to let the universe of God see me desire.

I believe that God is just like Jesus, only greater yet, for Jesus said so. I believe that God is absolutely, grandly beautiful, even as the highest soul of man counts beauty, but infinitely beyond that soul's highest idea—with the beauty that creates beauty, not merely shows itself beautiful. I believe that God has always done, is always doing, his best for every man, that no man is miserable because God is forgetting him, that he is not a God to crouch before, but our Father, to whom the child-heart cries exultantly, "Do with me as thou wilt."

I believe that there is nothing good for me or for any man but God, and more and more of God, and that alone through knowing Christ can we come nigh to God.

I believe that no man is ever condemned for any sin except one—that he will not leave his sins, come out of them, and be the child of him who is his Father.

I Believe That Justice and Mercy Are One

I believe that justice and mercy are simply one and the same thing; without justice to the full there can be no mercy, and without mercy to the full there can be no justice. Such is the mercy of God that he will hold his children in the consuming fire of his distance until they pay the uttermost farthing, until they drop the purse of selfishness with all the dross that is in it, and rush home to the Father and the Son, and the brethren—rush inside the center of the life-giving Fire whose outer circles burn. I believe that no hell will be lacking which would help the just mercy of God to redeem his children.

I believe that to him who obeys, and thus opens the doors of his heart to receive the eternal gift, God gives the Spirit of his Son, the Spirit of himself, to be in him and lead him to the understanding of all truth. I believe that the true disciple shall thus always know what he ought to do, though not necessarily what another ought to do, that the Spirit of the Father and the Son enlightens by teaching righteousness. I believe that no teacher should strive to make others think as he thinks, but to lead them to the living Truth, to the Master himself, of whom alone they can learn anything, who will make them in themselves know what is true by the very seeing of it. I believe that the inspiration of the Almighty alone gives understanding. I believe that to be the disciple of Christ is the end of being, that to persuade others to be his disciples is the aim of all teaching.

I Believe in the Atonement!

"The sum of all this," I can hear my critics charge, "is that you do not believe in the atonement."

I believe in Jesus Christ. Nowhere am I requested to believe in any *thing*, or in any *statement*, but everywhere to believe in *God* and in *Jesus Christ*. In what certain men call *the atonement*, in what they mean by the word with all their endless theories about it, I do not believe. God forbid I should, for it would be to believe a lie, a lie which is to blame for much of the nonacceptance of the gospel in this and other lands.

But, as the word was used by the best English writers at the time when the translation of the Bible was made—with all my heart, and soul, and strength, and mind, I believe in the atonement (call it the *a-tone-ment*, or the *at-one-ment*, as you please). I believe that Jesus Christ *is* our atonement, that through him we are reconciled to, made *one* with, God. There is not one word in the New Testament about reconciling God to us; it is we that have to be reconciled to God.

I am not writing, neither do I desire to write, a treatise on the atonement. My business is to persuade men to be atoned to God—to be made one with him. But I will go so far to meet my questioners as to say that, even in the sense of the atonement being a making-up for the evil done by men toward God, I believe in the atonement. Did not the Lord cast himself into the eternal gulf of evil yawning between the children and the Father? Did he not bring the Father to us, and let us look upon him in the face of his true Son, that we might have that in our hearts which alone could make us love God—a true sight of him? Did Christ not insist on the one truth of the universe, the one saving truth, that God was just what he was? Did he not hold to that assertion to the last, in the face of contradiction and death? Did Jesus not thus lay down his life, persuading us to lay down ours at the feet of the Father? Has not his very life by which he died passed into those who have received him, and recreated theirs, so that now they live with the life which alone is life? Did Christ not foil and slay evil by letting all the waves and billows of its horrid sea break upon him, go over him, and die without rebound—spend their rage, fall defeated, and cease?

Jesus Christ Is Our Atonement

Verily, he made atonement! *We* sacrifice to God! No, such was a mere Old Covenant shadow. It is God who has sacrificed his own Son for us. There was no other way of getting the gift of himself into our hearts. Jesus sacrificed himself to his Father and the children to bring them together—all the love on the side of the Father and the Son, all the selfishness on the side of the children. If the joy that alone makes life worth living, the joy that God is such as Christ, be a true thing in my heart, how can I but believe in the atonement of Jesus Christ? I believe it heartily, as God means it.

Furthermore, as the power that brings about a making-up for any wrong done by man to man, I believe in the atonement. Who that believes in Jesus does not long to atone to his brother for the injury he has done him? What repentant child, feeling he has wronged his father, does not desire to make atonement? Who is the mover, the causer, the persuader, the creator of the repentance, of the passion that restores fourfold? Jesus, our propitiation, our atonement. He is the head and leader, the prince of the atonement. He could not do it without us, but he leads us up to the Father's knee: he makes us make atonement.

Learning Christ, we are not only sorry for what we have done wrong, we not only turn from it and hate it, but we become able to serve both God and man with an infinitely high and true service. We are able to offer our whole beings to God to whom by deepest right it belongs.

Have I injured anyone? With him to aid my justice, newly risen with him from the dead, shall I not make good amends? Have I failed in love to my neighbor? Shall I not now love him with an infinitely better love than was possible to me before? That I will and can make atonement, thanks be to him who is my atonement, making me at *one* with God and my fellows! He is my life, my joy, my lord, my owner, the perfecter of my being by the perfection of his own. I dare not say with Paul that I am the slave of Christ, but my highest aspiration and desire is to be the slave of Christ.[3]

The Holy Midnight

Ah, holy midnight of the soul,
    When stars alone are high;
When winds are resting at their goal,
    And sea-waves only sigh!

Ambition faints from out the will;
    Asleep sad longing lies;
All hope of good, all fear of ill,
    All need of action dies;

Because God is, and claims the life
    He kindled in thy brain;
And thou in him, rapt far from strife,
    Diest and liv'st again.

A CONVERSATION ON THE CHARACTER OF GOD

(A Fictional Selection from *The Highlander's Last Song*)

When Ian ceased, a silence deep as the darkness fell upon them. To Ian, the silence seemed the very voice of God, clear in the darkness. Raised on the doctrines of his parents, he had in recent years taken it upon himself to read the New Testament from a deeper perspective and with more open eyes. The faith he now possessed was indeed a greater and more personal one than he had known in his youth, though his mother did not have eyes to see the true state of his heart. To her the silence and the darkness about them signified a great gulf between her and her boy.

"Are you sure it was the voice of God, Ian?" she said.

"No, Mother," answered Ian, "but I hope it was."

"Hopes, my dear boy, are not to be trusted."

"That is true, Mother, and yet we are saved by hope."

"We are saved by *faith*."

"Indeed, and I know faith."

"You rejoice my heart. But faith in what?"

"Faith in God, Mother."

"That will not save you."

"No, but God will."

"The devils believe in God and tremble."

"I believe in the Father of Jesus Christ, and do not tremble."

"You ought to tremble before an unreconciled God!"

"Like the devils, Mother?"

"Like a sinful child of Adam. Whatever your fancies, Ian, God will not hear you unless you pray to him in the name of his Son."

"Mother, would you take God from me?"

"What a frightful thing to lay to my charge!"

"Mother, I would gladly perish forever to save God from being the kind of God you would have me believe him. I love God. But I have learned to love him not through your teaching me about him, but by *knowing* him—through the world he made and through the character of Jesus. And I will not think of him other than good. Rather than believe he does not hear every creature that cries to him, whether he knows Jesus Christ or not, I would believe there was no God at all."

"That is not the doctrine of the gospel."

"It is, Mother. Jesus himself says, 'Every one that hath heard and learned of the Father cometh to me.' "

"Why, then, do you not come to him, Ian?"

"I do come to him. I come to him every day. I believe in nobody but him. Only God makes the universe worth being, or life worth living. But my believing does not look like what believing has always meant to you."

"Ian, I cannot understand you. If you believe like that about him—"

"I don't believe *about* him, Mother! I believe *in* him."

"We will not dispute about words! The question is, do you place your faith for salvation in the sufferings of Christ for you?"

"I do not, Mother. My faith is in Jesus himself, not in his sufferings."

"Then the anger of God is not turned away from you."

"Mother, I say again—I love God, and will not believe such things of him as you say."

"Then you do not accept the Bible as your guide."

"I do, Mother, for it tells me of Jesus Christ. There is no such teaching as you say in the Bible."

"How little you know your New Testament!"

"It is one of the few books I *do* know! For the last several years, since I have been trying to understand who God is rather than what people say about him, I have read it constantly. Now I could not live without it. No, I do not mean that. I *could* do without my Testament. Jesus would *be* all the same!"

"Oh, Ian! And yet you will not give Christ the glory of satisfying divine justice by his suffering for your sins!"

"Mother, to say that the justice of God is satisfied with suffering is a piece of the darkness of hell. God is willing to suffer, and ready to inflict the suffering to save from sin, but no suffering is satisfaction to him or his justice."

"What do you mean by his justice, then?"

"That he gives you and me and everybody fair play."

The ordinary sound of the phrase offended the moral ear of the mother.

"How can you speak so lightly of him? You will be speaking against him next!"

"No, Mother. He speaks against God who says he does things that are not good. It does not make a thing good to call it good. I speak *for* him when I say he cannot but give fair play. He knows man is sure to sin; he will not condemn us because we sin; he lets us do that for ourselves. He will condemn us only if we do not turn away from sin, for he has made us able to turn from it."

"He will forgive sin only for Christ's sake."

"He forgives us for his own name's sake, his own love's sake. There is no such word as *for Christ's sake* in the New Testament—except where Paul prays us for Christ's sake to be reconciled to God. It is in the English New Testament, but not in the Greek."

"Then you do not believe that the justice of God demands the satisfaction of the sinner's endless punishment?"

"I do not. Nothing can satisfy the justice of God but absolute fair play. The justice of God is the love of what is right, and the doing of what is right. Eternal misery in the name of justice could satisfy none but a demon whose bad laws had been broken."

"But it is the Holy One who suffers for our sins."

"Oh, Mother! Can justice do wrong to satisfy itself? Did Jesus *deserve* punishment? If not, then to punish him was to wrong him."

"But he was willing; he consented."

"He yielded to injustice—but the injustice was man's, not God's. If justice insisted on punishment, it would at least insist on the guilty being punished, not the innocent. Mind, I say *being punished*, not *suffering*: that is another thing altogether. It satisfied *love* to suffer for another, but it does not satisfy *justice* that the innocent should be punished for the guilty. The whole idea of the atonement in that light is the merest figment of the paltry human intellect to reconcile difficulties of its own invention. The sacrifices of the innocent in the Old Testament were the most shadowy type of the true meaning of Christ's death. He is indeed the Lamb that takes away the sins of the world. But not through an old-covenant sacrifice of the innocent for the guilty. No, the true atonement of Christ is on an altogether higher and deeper plane. And that is the mystery of the gospel. To interpret the mission of Jesus through the eyes of the Old Testament is to ignore his very words. He came bringing freedom from the old, bringing light, bringing good news, bringing the fulfillment of the types! He said, 'Behold, I make all things *new!*' Don't you see, Mother? Jesus is not an Old Testament sacrifice; he is God! He *loves* us! Once, when Alister had done something wrong, Father said, 'He must be punished—unless someone will be punished for him.' I offered to take his place, partly because it seemed expected of me, partly that I was moved by vanity, and partly because I saw what was likely to come next."

"And what did come next?"

"He scarcely touched me, Mother," answered Ian. "The thing taught me something very different from what he had meant to teach by it. That he failed to carry out his idea of justice helped me afterward to see that God could not have done it either, for that was not justice. And if my father could not punish me in my innocence, how much more could God not punish his own in his far purer innocence."

"Your father believed that he did."

"He accepted it, saturated with the tradition of the elders before he could think for himself. He does not believe it now."

"But why, then, should Christ have suffered?"

"It is the one fact that explains everything else," said Ian. "But I see no reason to talk about that now. So long as your theory satisfies you, Mother, why should I show you mine? When it no longer satisfies you, when it troubles you as it has troubled me, and as I pray God it may trouble you, then I will share my very soul with you."

"I do not see what other meaning you can put upon the statement that he was a sacrifice for our sins."

"Had we not sinned he would never have died; and he died to deliver us from our sins. He against whom was the sin became the sacrifice for it; the Father suffered in the Son, for they are one. But if I could see no other explanation than yours, I would not, could not accept it—for God's sake I would not."

"How can you say you believe in Christ when you do not believe in the atonement!"

"It is not so, Mother. I do not believe what you mean by the atonement. What God means by it, I do believe. But we are never told to believe in the atonement; we are told to believe in Jesus Christ—and, Mother, in God's name, I do believe in him."

"What do you call believing in him, then?"

"Obeying him, Mother—to say it as briefly as I can. I try to obey him in the smallest things he says—only nothing he says is small—and so does Alister. I strive to be what he would have me. A man may trust in Christ's atonement to his absolute assurance, but if he does not do the things he tells him—he does not yet believe in him. He may be a good man, but if he does not obey—well, you know what Jesus said would become of those who called him, Lord, Lord, but did not do what he said."[4]

From:
A Hidden Life

But is my will alive, awake?
   The one God will not heed
If in my lips or hands I take
   A half-word or half-deed.

Hour after hour I sit and dream,
   Amazed in outwardness;
The powers of things that only seem
   The things that are oppress;

Till in my soul some discord sounds,
   Till sinks some yawning lack;
Then turn I from life's rippling rounds,
   And unto thee come back.

Thou seest how poor a thing am I,
   Yet hear, whate'er I be;
Despairing of my will, I cry,
   Be God enough to me.

My spirit, low, irresolute,
   I cast before thy feet;
And wait, while even prayer is mute,
   For what thou judgest meet.

29

GOD THE ALMIGHTY, POWERLESS AGAINST MAN'S WILL

*Unto him that blasphemeth against the Holy Ghost it shall
not be forgiven.*

Luke 12:10

Unforgiveness—Shutting God Out

There are two sins, not of individual deed, but of spiritual condition, which cannot be forgiven. That is, they cannot be excused, passed by, made little of by the tenderness even of God, in whom are all *deeds*, no matter how vile, forgiven the instant we turn our hearts toward him. But these conditions of which I speak cannot be forgiven inasmuch as they will allow no forgiveness to come into the soul. They will permit no good influence to go on working alongside of them. They shut God out altogether.

Therefore the man guilty of these can never receive into himself the holy, renewing, saving influences of God's forgiveness. God is outside of him in every sense, except that which springs from God's creating relation to him, by which, thanks be to God, he yet keeps hold of him, although against the will of the man who will not be forgiven. Against that will, even almighty God is powerless.

The one of these sins is against man; the other against God himself.

The first is unforgiveness to our neighbor, the closing of the door of our heart to him. It may be a lesser evil to murder a man than to refuse to forgive him. Only God knows such things. The former may be the act of a moment of passion: the latter is the heart's choice. It is *spiritual* murder to hate, to brood over the feeling that excludes; it is the idea of the hatred. We listen to the voice of our own hurt pride or hurt affection. Insofar as we can, we quench the relations of life between us; we close up the passages of possible return.

This is to shut out God, the Life, the One. For how are we to receive the forgiving presence while we shut out our brother from our portion of the universal forgiveness, the final restoration? If God appeared to us, how could he say, "I forgive you," while we remained unforgiving to our neighbor? Suppose it were possible that he should say so, his forgiveness would be no good to us while we were yet uncured of our unforgiveness. It would not touch us. It would not come near us. It would hurt us, for we should think ourselves safe and well, while the horrible disease was eating the heart out of us.

Tenfold the forgiveness lies in the words, "If ye forgive not men their trespasses, neither will your heavenly Father forgive your trespasses." Those words are kindness indeed. For when we forgive our neighbor, in flows the consciousness of God's forgiveness to us. For God to withhold his forgiveness from the man who will not forgive his neighbor is love as well as necessity. If God said, "I forgive you" to a man who hated his brother, how would the man interpret it? Would it not mean to him, "You may go on hating. I do not mind it. You have had great provocation and are justified in your hate"? No doubt God takes what wrong there is, and what provocation there is, into the account; but the more provocation, the more excuse that can be urged for the hate, the more reason, if possible, that the hater should be delivered from the hell of his hate, that God's child should be made the loving child he was meant to be.

For God to forgive an unforgiving man would cause the man to think, not that God loved the sinner, but that he forgave the sin, which God never does. *Every* sin meets with its due fate—inexorable expulsion from the paradise of God's humanity. He loves the sinner so much that he cannot forgive him in any other way than by banishing from his bosom the demon that possesses him, by lifting him out of that mire of his iniquity.

No one, however, supposes for a moment that a man who has once refused to forgive his brother, shall therefore be condemned to endless unforgiveness on the part of God. What is meant is, that while a man continues in such a mood, God cannot be with him as his friend. Not that he will not be his friend, but that the friendship—being all on one side, that of God—must take forms such as the man will not be able to recognize as friendship. Forgiveness is not love merely, but love *conveyed as love* to the erring, so establishing peace toward God and forgiveness toward our neighbor. The unforgiveness, therefore, lasts only so long as the spirit of unforgiveness exists in the man's heart. In the act of his repentance his own heart is opened to receive the forgiveness God would shower upon him.

When Forgiveness Does Not Lie Open to Man

The second condition of man's heart which blocks out God's forgiveness from reaching it has to do with our relationship with God rather than man. Let us look at *"the* unpardonable sin," as this mystery is commonly called, and see what we can find to understand about it.

All sin is unpardonable. There is no compromise to be made with it. We shall not come out except clean, having paid the uttermost farthing.

But the special unpardonableness of those sins we are here considering lies in their shutting out God from being able to influence the man. Possibly in the case of the former sin, I may have said this too strongly. Perhaps the love of God may have some part even in the man who will not forgive his brother, although if he continues unforgiving, that part must gradually decrease and die away. Possibly resentment against our brother might yet for a time leave room for some divine influences by its side, although either the one or the other must speedily yield.

But the man who denies truth, who consciously resists duty, who says there is no truth, or that the truth he sees is not true, who says that which is good is of Satan, or that which is bad is of God, who denies the Spirit—such a man willfully shuts out the Spirit and, therefore, cannot be forgiven. For without the Spirit no forgiveness can enter the man to cast out Satan. Without the Spirit to witness with his spirit, no man could know himself forgiven, even if God appeared to him and said so. The full forgiveness is, as I have said, when a man feels that God is forgiving him; and this cannot be while he opposes himself to the very essence of God's will. Forgiveness simply does not lie open to such a man. It is not that God *refuses* to forgive him. It is that God *cannot* forgive him while he remains in that state of denying the truth of God's Spirit. The only mechanism whereby forgiveness is able to operate—namely, the union of God's Spirit with the man's spirit—is in this case nonexistent, by the man's *choice*, not God's refusal.

As far as we can see, the men of whom this was spoken in the scripture in the eleventh chapter of Luke were men who resisted the truth with some amount of perception that it was the truth—men, from selfishness and love of influence, so set against one whom they saw to be a good man, that they denied the goodness of what they knew to be good. Was not this, their *condition*, unpardonable? How, through all this mass of falsehood, could the pardon of God reach the essential humanity within it? These men had almost separated their humanity from themselves, had taken their part with the powers of darkness. While they were such, forgiveness was an impossibility. Out of that they must come, else there was no word of God for them. But the very word that told them of the unpardonable state they were in was just the one form the voice of mercy could take in calling on them to repent. They must hear and be afraid.

I think they refused the truth, knowing it was true—not carried away by passion nor blinded by their prejudice nor condemning one form of truth by the love they bore for another form of it, but by cold self-love, envy, avarice, and ambition. They did not merely do wrong knowingly, but set their whole natures knowingly against the light. Of this nature must the sin against the Holy Spirit surely be. "This is the condemnation," (not the sins that men have committed, but the condition of mind in which they choose to remain) "that light is come into the world, and men loved darkness rather than light, because their deeds were evil." In this sin against the Holy Spirit, I see no single act of sin, but a willful condition of mind.

What Can God Do With the Closed Man?

Once a man falls into such a condition of spiritual closedness, is God able to do anything more with him? Is it a fixed, final condition? How is the man ever to get out of the state? If the Spirit of God is shut out from his heart, how is he to become better?

In answer, let me pose another question: may there not be other powers and means of the Spirit preparatory to its highest office with man, its witnessing with our spirit to the truth? God who has made us can never be far from any man who draws the breath of life—nay, must be in him, not necessarily in his heart, as we say, but still in him. May not, then, one day some terrible convulsion from the center of his being, some fearful earthquake from the hidden gulfs of his nature, shake such a man so that through all the deafness of his death, the voice of the Spirit may be faintly heard, the still small voice that comes after the tempest and the earthquake? May there not be a fire that even such can feel? Who shall set the bounds to the consuming of the fire of our God and the purifying that dwells therein?

My friends, I offer this only as a contribution toward the understanding of our Lord's words. But if we ask him, he will lead us into all truth—not necessarily into the intellectual and analytical understanding of all things spiritual, but into the truth he desires us to manifest in our life with him. And let us not be afraid to think, for he will not take it ill.

No amount of discovery in his words can tell us more than *we* have discovered, more than we have seen and known to be true. For all the help the best of his disciples can give us is only to discover, to see for ourselves.

And beyond all our discoveries in his words and being, there lie depths within depths of truth that we cannot understand. Yea, even now sometimes we seem to have dim glimpses into regions from which we receive no word to bring away.

The fact that some things have become to us so much more simple than they were, and that great truths have come out of what once looked common, is ground enough for hope that such will go on to be our experience through the ages to come. Our advance from our former ignorance can measure but a small portion of the distance that lies, and must ever lie, between our childishness and his manhood, between our love and his love, between our dimness and his mighty vision.[1]

Tomorrow

My tomorrow is but a flitting
  Fancy of the brain;
God's tomorrow an angel sitting,
  Ready for joy or pain.

My tomorrow has no soul,
  Dead as yesterday;
God's—a brimming silver bowl
  Of life that gleams and plays.

My tomorrow, I mock you away!
  Shadowless nothing, thou!
God's tomorrow, come, dear day,
  For God is in thee now.

OBEDIENCE BRINGS US OUT OF THE DARKNESS

(A Fictional Selection from *The Baron's Apprenticeship*)

What if we are not yet able to understand nature's secret, therefore not able to see it although it lies open to us? What if the difficulty lies in us? What if nature is doing her best to reveal? What if God is working to make us know—if we would but let him—as fast as he can?

One idea will not be pictured, cannot be made present to the mind by any effort of the imagination—one idea requires the purest faith: a man's own ignorance and incapacity. When a man knows, then first he gets a glimpse of his ignorance as it vanishes. Ignorance cannot be the object of knowledge. We must *believe* ourselves ignorant. And for that we must be humble of heart. For God is infinite, and we are his little ones, and his truth is eternally better than the best shape in which we see it.

Jesus is perfect, but our idea of him cannot be perfect. Only obedient faith in him and in his Father is changeless truth in us. Even that has to grow, but its growth is not change. We glimpse a greater life than we can feel; but no man will arrive at the peace of it by struggling with the roots of his nature to understand them, for those roots go down and out, out and down infinitely into the infinite. By acting upon what he sees and knows, hearkening to every whisper, obeying every hint of the good, following whatever seems light, man will at length arrive. Thus obedient, instead of burying himself in the darkness about its roots, he climbs to the treetop of his being; there, looking out on the eternal world, he understands at least enough to give him rest.

In his climbing, the man will somewhere in his upward progress of obedience awaken to know that the same Spirit is in him that is in the things he beholds. God is in the world, the atmosphere, the element, the substance, the essence of his life. In him he lives and moves and has his being. Now he lives indeed; for his Origin is his, and this rounds his being to eternity. God himself is his, as nothing else *could* be his.[2]

Come Unto Me

Come unto me, the Master says:—
    But how? I am not good;
No thankful song my heart will raise,
    Nor even wish it could.

I am not sorry for the past,
    Nor able not to sin;
The weary strife would ever last
    If once I should begin!

Hast thou no burden then to bear?
    No action to repent?
Is all around so very fair?
    Is thy heart quite content?

Hast thou no sickness in thy soul?
    No labour to endure?
Then go in peace, for thou art whole;
    Thou needest not his cure.

Ah, mock me not! I often sigh;
    I have a nameless grief,
A faint sad pain—but such that I
    Can look for no relief.

Come, come to him who made thy heart:
    Come weary and oppressed;
To come to Jesus is thy part,
    His part to give thee rest.

New grief, new hope he will bestow,
    Thy grief and pain to quell;
Into thy heart himself will go,
    And that will make thee well.

THE ONLY TRUE THEOLOGY

(A Fictional Selection from *A Daughter's Devotion*)

I don't love God," he said.

"I dare say not," replied Mary. "How should you, when you don't know him?"

"Then what's to be done? I can't very well show myself where I hate the master of the house!"

"If you knew him, you would love him."

"You are judging me by yourself. But there is as much difference between you and me as between light and darkness."

"Not quite that much," replied Mary with a smile. "If you knew Jesus Christ, you could not help loving him, and to love him is to love God."

"*Know Jesus Christ!* How am I to go back two thousand years?"

"What he was then he is now," answered Mary. "And you may even know him better than they did at the time. For it was not until they understood him better, by his being taken from them, that they wrote down his life."

"I suppose you mean I must read the New Testament?" said Mr. Redmain.

"What I would have you do is read the life and death of the Son of Man, the master of men."

"I can't read. I should only make myself twice as ill."

"I will read it to you, if you will let me."

"How did you come to be such a theologian?"

"I am no theologian. This is one of those cases where those who call themselves his followers do not always believe the very thing the Master said. He said God hid these things from the wise and prudent and revealed them to babes. I had a father who was child enough to know them, and I was child enough to believe him, and so grew able to understand them for myself. The whole secret is to do the thing the Master tells you: then you will understand what he tells you. The opinion of the wisest man, if he does not do the things he reads, is not worth a straw. He may be partly right but you have no reason to trust him."

"Well, you shall be my chaplain. Tomorrow, if I'm able to

listen, you shall see what you can make of the old sinner."

"*I* shall be able to make nothing of you. It is *He* who does all the making."

"Ah, yes! Tut, tut! Of course! You know what I mean in any case."

Mary did not waste words. What would have been the use of correcting the poor spiritual dullard with every lumbering step, at any word inconsistent with the holy manners of the high countries? Once get him to court, and the power of the presence would subdue him, and make him over again from the beginning, without which absolute renewal the best observance of religious etiquette is worse than worthless. Many good people are such sticklers for the proprieties! For myself, I take joyous refuge with the grand, simple, everyday humanity of the man I find in the story—the man with the heart like that of my father and my mother and my brothers and sisters. If I may but see and help to show him a little as he lived to show himself, and not as church talk and church ways and church ceremonies and church theories and church plans of salvation and church worldliness generally have obscured him for hundreds of years, and will yet obscure him for hundreds more, until he comes himself to remove the scales from the eyes of his own church-bound son and daughters![3]

Summer Song

"Murmuring, 'twixt a murmur and moan,
Many a tune in a single tone,
For every ear with a secret true—
The seashell wants to whisper to you."

"Yes—I hear it—far and faint,
Like thin-drawn prayer of drowsy saint;
Like the muffled sounds of a summer rain;
Like the wash of dreams in a weary brain."

"By smiling lip and fixed eye,
You are hearing a song within the sigh:
The murmurer has many a lovely phrase—
Tell me, darling, the words it says."

"I hear a wind on a boatless main
Sigh like the last of a vanishing pain;
On the dreaming waters dreams the moon—
But I hear no words in the doubtful tune."

"If it tell thee not that I love thee well,
'Tis a senseless, wrinkled, ill-curved shell:
If it be not of love, why sigh or sing?
'Tis a common, mechanical, stupid thing!"

"It murmurs, it whispers, with prophet voice
Of a peace that comes, of a sealed choice;
It says not a word of your love to me,
But it tells me I love you eternally."

30

GOD THE UNYIELDING JUDGE

Verily I say unto thee, Thou shalt by no means come out thence, till thou
hast paid the uttermost farthing.

Matthew 5:26

There Is No Escape

There is great common sense in the words of the Lord regarding the settling of matters with an adversary before he drags you into court. Arrange what claim lies against you; compulsion waits behind it. Do at once what you must do one day. As there is no escape from payment, escape at least from the prison that will enforce it.

Do not drive Justice to extremities. Duty is imperative; it must be done. It is useless to think to escape the eternal law of things. Yield of yourself rather than compelling God to compel you.

To the honest man who wants to be honest, the word is of right gracious import. To the untrue, it is a terrible threat. He who is of God's mind in things rejoices to hear the word of the changeless Truth. The voice of Right fills the heavens and the earth and makes his soul glad; it is his salvation. But it is a dread sound in the ears of those whose life is a falsehood.

There has been much cherishing of the evil fancy that there is some way of getting out of the region of strict justice, some mode of managing to escape *all* that is required of us. But there is no such escape. A way to avoid any demand of righteousness would be an infinitely worse way than the road to the everlasting fire, for its end would be eternal death. No, there is no escape.

There is no heaven with a little of hell in it—no plan to retain this or that of the Devil in our hearts or our pockets. Our Satan must go, every hair and feather!

Neither shall you think to be delivered from the necessity of *being* good by being made good. God is the God of the animals in a far lovelier way, I suspect, than many of us dare to think, but he will not be the God of a man by making a good beast of him. You must be good; neither death nor any admittance into good company will make you good; though, doubtless, if you are willing and try, these and all other best helps will be given you.

There is no clothing in a robe of *imputed righteousness*, that poorest of legal cobwebs spun by spiritual spiders. It is apparently an old "doctrine," for St. John seems to point directly at it where he says, "Little children, let no man lead you astray; he that doeth righteousness *is* righteous, even as he is righteous."

We Must Choose to Be Righteous

Christ is our righteousness, not that we should escape punishment, still less escape *being* righteous, but as the live potent Creator of righteousness in us, so that we, with our wills receiving his Spirit, shall like him resist unto blood, striving against sin. He *is* our righteousness, and that righteousness is no fiction, no pretense, no imputation.

What is righteousness but fairness—from God to man, from man to God and to man? It is giving everyone his due—his large mighty due. Any system which tends to persuade men that there is any salvation but that of becoming righteous as Jesus is righteous, without a man's own willed share in the making, that a man is saved by having his sins hidden under a robe of imputed righteousness—that system, so far as this tendency, is not of God.

I read in this parable of the unforgiving servant that a man had better make up his mind to be righteous, to be fair, to do what he can to pay what he owes, in any and all the relations of life—all the matters wherein one man may demand of another, or complain that he has not received fair play. Settle your matters with those who have anything against you, while you are yet together and things have not gone too far to be settled. You will have to do it one day, and then it could be under less easy circumstances than now. Putting off is of no use. You must. The thing has to be done; there are means of compelling you.

"In this particular affair, however," I can hear you complain, "I am in the right."

In answer I say that I have reason to doubt whether you are capable of judging righteously in your own cause. But right or wrong is hardly to the point. This is not fundamentally a question of things; it is a question of condition, of spiritual relation and action toward your neighbor. If in yourself you were all right toward him, you could do him no wrong. And it need hardly concern you whether he does you wrong. Even if he should take advantage of you, that is only so much the worse for him, but does you no harm. It is a very small matter to you whether another man does *you* right; it is life or death to you whether you do *him* right. Whether he pay you what you count his debt or not, you will be compelled to pay him all you owe him. If you owe him a pound and he owes you a million, you must pay him the pound whether he pay you the million or not. There is no business parallel here. If, owing you love, he gives you hate, you, owing him love, have yet to pay it. A love unpaid you, a justice undone you, a praise withheld from you, a judgment passed on you, will not absolve you of the debt of loving, giving justice, praising, and judging fairly. These uttermost farthings you must pay him, whether he pay you or not. We have a good while given us to pay, but a crisis will come—always sooner than those who are not ready for it expect—a crisis when the demand unyielded will be followed by prison.

The same holds with every demand of God: by refusing to pay, the man makes an adversary who will compel him—and that for the man's own sake. If you say, "I will not," then God will see to it. There is a prison, and the one thing we know about that prison is that its doors do not open until entire satisfaction is rendered, the last farthing paid.

The main debts whose payment God demands are those that lie at the root of all right, those we owe in mind, and soul, and being. Whatever in us can be or make an adversary, whatever could prevent us from doing the will of God, or from agreeing with our fellow—all must be yielded. Our every relation, both to God and our fellow, must be acknowledged heartily and met as readily.

If the man accepts the will of God, he is the child of the Father, and the whole power and wealth of the Father is for him, and the uttermost farthing, it will easily be paid. If the man denies the debt, or, acknowledging it, does nothing toward paying it, then—at last—the prison!

Repentance—The Only Way Out of Darkness

God in the dark can make a man thirst for the light who never in the light sought anything but the dark. The cells of the prison may differ in degrees of darkness; but they are all alike in this, that not a door opens but to payment. There is no day but the will of God, and he who is of the night cannot be forever allowed to roam the day. Unfelt, unappreciated, unprized, the light must be taken from him, that he may know what the darkness is.

How will a man come out of that darkness? Can there be any way out of the misery? Only by repentance, by making the payment he so long refused to make. And what if it were the man he had most wronged, most hated, most despised who now came near him to help him find his way out of the darkness? Perhaps the man he had most injured, and was most ashamed to meet, would become a refuge from himself—oh, how welcome!

It will take a thousand, perhaps ten thousand little steps to come up from the darkness, each a little less dark, a little nearer the light— but, ah, the weary way! He cannot come out until he has paid the uttermost farthing!

Once begun, however, repentance may grow more and more rapid! If God once gets a strong hold, if with but one finger he touches the man's self, swift as possible will he draw him from the darkness into the light. For even the forlorn, self-ruined wretch was made to be a child of God, a partaker of the divine nature, an heir of God and joint heir with Christ. Out of the abyss into which he cast himself, refusing to be the heir of God, he must rise and be raised. To the heart of God, the one and only goal of the human race—the refuge and home of all and each, he must set out and go, or the last glimmer of humanity will die from him.

Whoever will live must cease to be a slave and become a child of God. There is no halfway house of rest, where ungodliness may be dallied with, and not prove quite fatal. Be they few or many cast into such prison of darkness, there can be no deliverance for a human soul, whether in that prison or out of it, but in paying the last farthing, in becoming lowly, penitent, self-refusing—so receiving the sonship, and learning to cry, "Father!"[1]

HIS LOVE WILL COMPEL US

(A Fictional Selection from *Donal Grant*)

Y ou go too far for me," said his lordship, looking a little uncomfortable, as if there might be something in what the fellow said, "but I think it is almost time for me to try and break
myself a little of the habit. By degrees one night—you know—
eh?"

"I have little faith in doing things by degrees, my lord—
except such indeed as by their very nature cannot be done at
once. It is true a bad habit can only be contracted by degrees,
and I will not say, because I do not know, whether anyone has
ever cured himself of one by degrees, but it cannot be the best
way. What is bad ought to be got rid of at once."

"Ah, but you know that it might cost you your life!"

"What of that, my lord? Life, the life you mean, is not the
first thing."

"Not the first thing! Why, the Bible says, 'All that a man hath
will he give for his life!' "

"Yes; that is in the Bible; but who said it?"

"What does it matter who said it?"

"Much always; everything sometimes."

"Who said it then?"

"The Devil."

"The Devil he did! And who ought to know better, I should
like to ask!"

"Every man ought to know better. And besides, it is not what
a man will or will not do, but what a man ought or ought not
to do!"

"Ah, there you have me, I suppose! But there are some things
so damned difficult, that a man must be very sure of the danger
he is in before he can bring himself to do them!"

"That may be, my lord; and in the present case your lordship
must know that it is not the health alone these drugs undermine,
but the moral nature as well!"

"I know it; and that therefore I cannot be counted guilty of
many things I have done, seeing they were done under the
influence of these hellish concoctions. It was not I, but these

things working on my brain, and making me see things for the time in altogether false light. This will be considered when I come to be judged—if there be in truth a day of judgment."

"One thing I am sure of," said Donal, "that your lordship, as well as every man, will have fair play. But there is this to be considered; at first, if you did not know what you were about, you might not be much to blame, though it is impossible to say when there may not be a glimmer of light left; but afterwards, when you knew that you were putting yourself in danger of doing what you knew not, you must have been as much to blame as if you had made a Frankenstein-demon, and turned him loose on the earth, knowing you would not be in the least able to control him."

"And is not that what the God you believe in does every day?"

"My lord, the God I believe in has *not* lost his control over either of us."

"Then let him set the thing right! Why should we have to toil to draw his plough with but one horse where there ought to be four?"

"He will see to it, my lord; do not fear—though it will probably be in a way your lordship will hardly like. He is compelled to do terrible things sometimes."

"What should compel him?"

"The love that is in him, the love that he is, toward us who would have our own way to the ruin of everything he cares for!"[2]

Unyielding Witness of Truth

(A Fictional Selection from *The Fisherman's Lady*)

M r. Graham walked gently up to the bedside.

"Sit down, sir," said the marquis courteously, pleased with the calm and unobtrusive bearing of the man. "They tell me I'm dying, Mr. Graham."

"I'm sorry it seems to trouble you, my lord."

"What! Wouldn't it trouble you then?"

"I don't think so, my lord."

"Ah! You're one of the elect, no doubt?"

"That's a thing I never did think about, my lord."

"What do you think about then?"

"About God."

"And when you die you'll go straight to heaven, of course."

"I don't know, my lord. That's another thing I never trouble my head about."

"Ah, you're like me then. I don't care much about going to heaven. What do you care about?"

"The will of God. I hope your lordship will say the same."

"No, I won't. I want my own will."

"Well, that is to be had, my lord."

"How?"

"By taking his will for yours as the better of the two, which it must be in every way."

"That's all moonshine!"

"It is light, my lord."

"Well, I don't mind confessing, if I am to die, I should prefer heaven to the other place, but I trust I have no chance of either. Do you now honestly believe there are two such places?"

"I don't know, my lord."

"You don't know! And you come here to comfort a dying man?"

"Your lordship must first tell me what you mean by 'two such places.' And as to comfort, going by my notions, I cannot tell which you would be more or less comfortable in: and that, I presume, would be the main point with your lordship."

"And what, pray sir, would be the main point with you?"

"To get nearer to God."

"Well, I can't say I want to get nearer to God. It's little he's ever done for me."

"It's a good deal he has tried to do for you, my lord."

"Who interfered? What stood in his way, then?"

"Yourself, my lord."

"Were I anywhere else—You are a blasted coward to speak so to a man who cannot even turn on his side to curse you. You would not dare it but that you know I cannot defend myself."

"You are right, my lord; your conduct is indefensible."

"By heaven! If I could but get this cursed leg under me, I would throw you out of the window!"

"I shall go out by the door, my lord. While you hold by your sins, your sins will hold by you. If you should want me again, I shall be at your lordship's command."

He rose and left the room, but had not reached his cottage before Malcolm overtook him with a second message from his master. He turned around at once.

"Mr. Graham," said the marquis a few moments later, "you must have patience with me. I was very rude to you, but I was in horrible pain."

"Don't mention it, my lord."

"Then you really and positively believe in the place they call heaven?"

"My lord, I believe that those who open their hearts to the truth shall see the light on their friends' faces again, and be able to set right what was wrong between them."

"It's a week too late to talk of setting right."

"It's never too late. Go and tell her you are sorry, my lord. That will be enough for her."

"Ah! But there's more than her concerned."

"You are right, my lord. There is another—one who cannot be satisfied that one of his children should be treated as you treated women."

"But the deity you talk of—"

"I beg your pardon, my lord: I spoke of no deity. I talked of a living Love that gave us birth and calls us his children. Your deity I know nothing of."

"Call him what you please. He won't be put off so easily."

"He won't be put off at all. Not one jot or tittle. He will forgive you anything, but he will pass nothing."

"Do you really suppose God cares whether a man comes to good or ill?"

"If he did not, he could not be good himself."

"Then you don't think a good God would want to punish poor wretches like us?"

"Your lordship has not been in the habit of regarding himself as a poor wretch. And remember, you can't call a child a poor wretch without insulting the father of it."

"That's quite another thing."

"But on the wrong side for your argument, seeing the relation between God and the poorest creature is infinitely closer than that between any father and his child."

"Then he can't be so hard on us as the parsons say, even in the afterlife?"

"He will give absolute justice, which is the only good thing. He will spare nothing to bring his children back to himself, their sole well-being, whether he achieve it here—or there."

It was Mr. Graham who broke the silence that followed.

"Are you satisfied with yourself, my lord?"

"No, by George!"

"You would like to be better?"

"I would."

"Then you are of the same mind with God."

"Yes, but I'm not a fool. It won't do to say I should like to be. I must be, and that's not so easy. It's too hard to be good. I would have to fight for it, but there's no time. How is a poor devil to get out of such an infernal scrape?"

"Keep the Commandments."

"That's it, of course. But there's not time, I tell you—no time! At least that's what those cursed doctors will keep telling me."

"If there were but time to draw another breath, there would be time to begin."

"How am I to begin? Which am I to begin with?"

"There is one commandment that includes all the rest."

"Which is that?"

"To believe in the Lord Jesus Christ."

"That's cant!"

"After thirty years' trial of it, it is to me the essence of wisdom. It has given me a peace which makes life or death all but indifferent to me."

"What am I to believe about him, then?"

"You are to believe *in* him, not *about* him."

"I don't understand."

"He is our Lord and Master, Elder Brother, King, Savior, the Divine Man, the human God. To believe in him is to give ourselves up to him in obedience—to search out his will and do it."

"But there's no time, I tell you!" the marquis almost shrieked.

"And I tell you there is all eternity to do it in. Take him for your Master, and he will demand nothing of you which you are not able to perform. This is the open door to bliss. With your last breath you can cry to him, and he will hear you as he heard the thief on the cross. It makes my heart swell to think about it. No cross-questioning of the poor fellow, no preaching to him. He just took him with him where he was going to make a man of him."

"Well, you know something of my history: what would you have me do now, at once I mean. What would the Person you are speaking of have me do?"

"That is not for me to say, my lord."

"You could give me a hint."

"No. God himself is telling you. For me to presume to tell you would be to interfere with him. What he would have a man do he lets him know in his mind."

"But what if I had not made up my mind before the last came?"

"Then I fear he would say to you, 'Depart from me, you worker of iniquity.' "

"That would be hard when another minute might have done it."

"If another minute would have done it, you would have had it."

A paroxysm of pain followed, during which Mr. Graham silently left him.[3]

Dejection

O Father, I am in the dark,
 My soul is heavy-bowed:
I send my prayer up like a lark,
 Up through my vapory shroud,
  To find thee,
  And remind thee
I am thy child, and thou my father,
Though round me death itself should gather.

Lay thy loved hand upon my head,
 Let thy heart beat in mine;
One thought from thee, when all seems dead,
 Will make the darkness shine
  About me
  And throughout me!
And should again the dull night gather,
I'll cry again, Thou art my Father.

31

GOD OUR FORGIVING FATHER

If you forgive men their trespasses, your heavenly Father will also forgive you.

Matthew 6:14

Love Goes in Front of Forgiveness

God's divine forgiveness creates our forgiveness, and therefore can do so much more. It can take up all our wrongs, small and great, with their righteous attendance of griefs and sorrows, and carry them away from between our God and us.

Christ is God's forgiveness.

Before we approach a little nearer to this great sight, let us consider the human forgiveness in a more definite embodiment—as between a father and a son. For although God is so much more to us, and comes so much nearer to us than a father can be or come, yet fatherhood is the last height of the human stair whence our understanding can see him afar off, and where our hearts can first know that he is nigh.

There are various kinds and degrees of wrongdoing, which need varying kinds and degrees of forgiveness. An outburst of anger in a child, for instance, scarcely wants forgiveness. The wrong in it may be so small, that the parent has only to influence the child for self-restraint, and the rousing of the will against the wrong. The father will not feel that such a fault has built up any wall between him and his child.

But suppose that he discovered in him a habit of sly cruelty toward his younger brothers or sisters, or the animals of the house. How differently would he feel! Would not the different evil require a different *form* of forgiveness? I mean, would not the forgiveness have to take the form of that kind of punishment fittest for restraining, in the hope of finally rooting out the wickedness? Could there be true love in any other kind of forgiveness than this? A passing-by of the offense might spring from a poor human kindness, but never from divine love. It would not be *remission*. Forgiveness can never be indifference. Forgiveness is love toward the unlovely.

God is forgiving us every day—sending from between him and us our sins and their fogs and darkness. Witness the shining of his sun and the falling of his rain, the filling of their hearts with food and gladness, that he loves them that love him not. When some sin that we have committed has clouded all our horizon and hidden him from our eyes, he sweeps away a path for his forgiveness to reach our hearts, that it may, by causing our repentance, destroy the wrong and make us able even to forgive ourselves. For some are too proud to forgive themselves, until the forgiveness of God has had its way with them, has drowned their pride in the tears of repentance and made their heart come again like the heart of a little child.

Looking at forgiveness, then, as the perfecting of a work ever going on, as the contact of God's heart and ours, we may say that God's love is ever in front of his forgiveness. God's love is the prime mover, ever seeking to perfect his forgiveness. The love is perfect, working out the forgiveness. God loves where he cannot yet forgive—where forgiveness, in the full sense, is as yet simply impossible, because no contact of hearts is possible, because that which lies between has not even begun to yield to the broom of his holy destruction.

Some things, then, between the Father and his children, as between a father and his child, may comparatively, and in a sense, be made light of, (I do not mean made light of in themselves; away they must go) inasmuch as, sins though they be, they yet leave room for the dwelling of God's Spirit in the heart, forgiving and cleansing away the evil. When a man's evil is thus fading out of him, and he is growing better and better, God's forgiveness is coming into him more and more.[1]

Eternally Loving Fatherhood

Think, brothers, think, sisters, we walk in the air of an eternal and loving and forgiving fatherhood. Every uplifting of the heart is a looking up to the Father. Graciousness and truth are around, above, beneath, yes, *in* us. When we are least worthy, most tempted, hardest, unkindest, let us even then commend our spirits into his hands. Where else would we dare send them?

How the earthly father would love a child who would creep into his room with angry, troubled face, and sit down at his feet, saying when asked what he wanted: "I feel so naughty, papa, and I want to get good." Would he say to his child: "How dare you! Go away, and be good, and then come to me"?

Shall we dare to think God would send us away if we came thus? Would we not let all the tenderness of our nature flow forth upon such a child? And shall we dare to think that if we, being evil, know how to give good gifts to our children, God will not give us his own Spirit when we come to ask him? Will not some heavenly dew descend cool upon the hot anger? Some genial raindrop on the dry selfishness? Some glance of sunlight on the cloudy hopelessness? Bread, at least, will be given, and not a stone; water, at least, will be sure, and not vinegar mingled with gall.[2]

For the Spirit of God lies all about the spirit of man like a mighty sea, ready to rush in at the smallest chink in the walls that shut him out from his own—walls which even the tone of a violin afloat on the wind of that Spirit is sometimes enough to rend from battlement to base, as the blast of the rams' horns rent the walls of Jericho.[3] He only awaits the turning of our face toward him.

Nor is there anything we can ask for ourselves that we may not ask for another. We may commend any brother, any sister, to the common fatherhood. And there will be moments when, filled with that Spirit which is the Lord, nothing will ease our hearts of their love but the commending of all men, all our brothers and all our sisters, to the one Father. Nor shall we ever know full repose in the Father's hands, never shall we be able to rest in the bosom of the Father, till the fatherhood is fully revealed to us in the love of the brothers. For God cannot be our Father except as he is their Father; and if they do not see him and feel him as their Father, we cannot know him as ours. Never shall we know him aright until we rejoice and exult for our race that he is *the* Father.[4]

TWO RESPONSES TO GOD'S VOICE

(A Fictional Selection from *The Gentlewoman's Choice*)

The night began differently with the two watchers. The major was troubled in his mind at what seemed the hardheartedness of the mother, for he loved her with a true brotherly affection. He brooded long over the matter, but by degrees forgot her and fell to thinking about his own mother.

As the major sat thinking, the story came back to him which she had told him and his brothers, all now gone but himself, as they sat around her one Sunday evening in their room. The story was about the boy who was tired of being at home, and asked his father for money to go away. His father gave it to him, thinking it better he should go than grumble at the best he could give him. The boy had grown naughty and spent his money in buying things that were not worth having, and in eating and drinking with greedy, coarse people until at last he had nothing left to buy food with and had to feed swine to earn something. Then finally he had begun to think about going home.

It all came back to the major's mind just as his mother used to tell it—how the poor prodigal, ragged and dirty and hungry, had set out for home, and how his father had seen him coming a great way off and knew him at once, and ran out to meet him, welcoming him with a kiss. True, the prodigal came home repentant, but the father did not wait to know that—he ran to welcome him without condition.

As the major thus reflected, he kept coming nearer and nearer to the Individual lurking at the keyhole of every story. Only he had to go home; otherwise, how was his father to receive him?

I wonder, he mused, *if when a man dies, that is counted as going home. I hardly think so, for that is something no man can help. I would find myself no better off than this young rascal when he goes home because he can't help it!*

The result of this thinking was that the major, there in the middle of the night, got down on his knees and tried, as he had not done in years, to say the prayers his mother had taught him—speaking from his heart as if one was listening, one who, in the dead of the night, did not sleep, but kept wide awake in case one of his children should cry.

In his wife's room, Gerald Raymount sat on into the dead of the night. After a long while, as his wife continued to sleep soundly, he thought he would go down to his study and find something to turn his thoughts from his misery. None such had come to him as to his friend. He had been much more of a religious man than the major, but it was the *idea* of religion, and the thousand ideas it broods, more than the practice of it daily, that was his delight. He philosophized and philosophized well of the relations between man and his Maker, of the necessity to human nature of a belief in God, of the disastrous consequences of having none, and such like things. But having an interest in God is a very different thing from living in such a close relationship with the Father that the thought of him is an immediate and ever-returning joy and strength. He was so busy understanding with his intellect that he missed the better understanding of heart and imagination. He was always so pleased with the thought of a thing that he missed the thing itself—whose *possession*, not its thought, is essential. Thus when the trial came, it found him no true parent, because the resentment he bore the youth for having sinned against *his* family was stronger than the longing for his son's repentance. Love is at the heart of every right way, and essential forgiveness at the heart of every true treatment of the sinner.

He rose, and treading softly, went to his study. The fire was not yet out; he stirred it and made it blaze, lighted his candles, took a book from the shelf, sat down, and tried to read. But it was no use; his troubled thoughts could hold no company with other thoughts. The world of his kind was shut out; he was a man alone because he was unforgiving and unforgiven. His soul slid into the old groove of misery, and so the night slipped away.[5]

Evening Hymn

O God, whose daylight leadeth down
    Into the sunless way,
Who with restoring sleep dost crown
    The labour of the day!

What I have done, Lord, make it clean
    With thy forgiveness dear;
That so today what might have been,
    Tomorrow may appear.

And when my thought is all astray,
    Yet think thou on in me;
That with the newborn innocent day
    My soul rise fresh and free.

Nor let me wander all in vain
    Through dreams that mock and flee;
But even in visions of the brain,
    Go wandering toward thee.

Bethany House Publishers and Sunrise Books Publishers— *Committed to Preserving the Works of George MacDonald for New Generations.*

BETHANY HOUSE PUBLISHERS
Minneapolis, Minnesota 55438

The Novels of George MacDonald Edited for Today's Reader

EDITED TITLE	ORIGINAL TITLE
The Fisherman's Lady	Malcolm
The Marquis' Secret	The Marquis of Lossie
The Baronet's Song	Sir Gibbie
The Shepherd's Castle	Donal Grant
The Tutor's First Love	David Elginbrod
The Musician's Quest	Robert Falconer
The Maiden's Bequest	Alex Forbes
The Curate's Awakening	Thomas Wingfold
The Lady's Confession	Paul Faber
The Baron's Apprenticeship	There and Back
The Highlander's Last Song	What's Mine's Mine
The Gentlewoman's Choice	Weighed and Wanting
The Laird's Inheritance	Warlock O'Glenwarlock
The Minister's Restoration	Salted with Fire
A Daughter's Devotion	Mary Marston
The Peasant Girl's Dream	Heather and Snow
The Landlady's Master	The Elect Lady

George MacDonald: Scotland's Beloved Storyteller
by Michael Phillips

SUNRISE BOOKS, PUBLISHERS
Eureka, California 95501

The Sunrise Centenary Editions of the Original Works of George MacDonald in Leatherbound Collector's Editions

NOVELS

Alec Forbes of Howglen
Sir Gibbie
Thomas Wingfold, Curate
Malcolm
Salted with Fire
The Elect Lady

SERMONS

Unspoken Sermons, Series One
Unspoken Sermons, Series Two
The Hope of the Gospel

POEMS

A Hidden Life and Other Poems
The Disciple and Other Poems

THE MASTERLINE SERIES OF STUDIES AND ESSAYS ABOUT GEORGE MacDONALD

From a Northern Window: A Personal Remembrance of George MacDonald by his son Ronald MacDonald

The Harmony Within: The Spiritual Vision of George MacDonald by Rolland Hein

George MacDonald's Fiction: A Twentieth-Century View by Richard Reis

God's Fiction: Symbolism and Allegory in the Works of George MacDonald by David Robb

NOTES

Chapter One

1. *The Baron's Apprenticeship*, pp. 82, 151–152.
2. *Unspoken Sermons*, Second Series, "Life."
3. *The Curate's Awakening*, pp. 16–17.

Chapter Two

1. *Unspoken Sermons*, Third Series, "The Creation in Christ."
2. *The Minister's Restoration*, p. 117.
3. *The Lady's Confession*, p. 227.
4. *Warlock O'Glenwarlock*, chapter 24.
5. From a letter written by George MacDonald to Professor George Rolleston of Oxford, June, 1881.
6. *Unspoken Sermons*, First Series, "The Child in the Midst."
7. *The Laird's Inheritance*, pp. 31–34.

Chapter Three

1. *Hope of the Gospel*, "Salvation from Sin."
2. *The Curate's Awakening*, pp. 112, 201, 137, 159–160.
3. *The Hope of the Gospel*, "Salvation from Sin."
4. *The Curate's Awakening*, p. 200.
5. *The Hope of the Gospel*, "Salvation from Sin."
6. *The Musician's Quest*, pp. 199–200.

Chapter Four

1. *Unspoken Sermons*, Third Series, "Kingship."
2. *The Curate's Awakening*, pp. 94–95.

Chapter Five

1. *The Lady's Confession*, p. 122.
2. *Unspoken Sermons*, Third Series, "The Truth."
3. *The Laird's Inheritance*, p. 282.

Chapter Six

1. *Donal Grant*, chapter 5.
2. *Unspoken Sermons*, Third Series, "The Truth."
3. *The Seaboard Parish*, chapter 19.

Chapter Seven

1. *Unspoken Sermons*, First Series, "The Higher Faith."
2. *The Musician's Quest*, pp. 61–62.
3. *Robert Falconer*, chapter 12.
4. *The Musician's Quest*, pp. 62–66.

Chapter Eight

1. *Unspoken Sermons*, Second Series, "Life."
2. *A Daughter's Devotion*, p. 123.
3. *The Baron's Apprenticeship*, pp. 175–176.
4. *Unspoken Sermons*, Second Series, "Life."
5. *Unspoken Sermons*, Third Series, "The Creation in Christ."
6. *The Peasant Girl's Dream*, pp. 194–195.

Chapter Nine

1. *The Hope of the Gospel*, "Jesus in the World."
2. *Warlock O'Glenwarlock*, chapter 51.
3. *The Hope of the Gospel*, "Jesus in the World."
4. *The Seaboard Parish*, chapter 13.
5. *The Hope of the Gospel*, "Jesus in the World."
6. *The Curate's Awakening*, pp. 104–105.
7. *The Laird's Inheritance*, p. 153.

Chapter Ten

1. *The Miracles of Our Lord*, "Introduction."
2. *The Miracles of Our Lord*, "The Government of Nature."
3. *Sir Gibbie*, chapter 12.
4. *The Baronet's Song*, pp. 112–113.
5. *Sir Gibbie*, chapter 32.

Chapter Eleven

1. *A Daughter's Devotion*, p. 122.
2. *Unspoken Sermons*, Second Series, "The Voice of Job."
3. *The Highlander's Last Song*, pp. 182, 155.

4. From a letter written by George MacDonald to his fiance, May 12, 1849.
5. *Annals of a Quiet Neighborhood*, chapter 11.
6. *The Musician's Quest*, pp. 95–96.

Chapter Twelve

1. *Orts/A Dish of Orts*, "True Christian Ministering."
2. *The Gentlewoman's Choice*, p. 24.
3. *Orts/A Dish of Orts*, "True Christian Ministering."
4. *The Lady's Confession*, pp. 33–36.
5. *The Curate's Awakening*, pp. 141–143.

Chapter Thirteen

1. *The Hope of the Gospel*, "The Yoke of Jesus."
2. *The Curate's Awakening*, pp. 111–115.

Chapter Fourteen

1. *Unspoken Sermons*, First Series, "The Child in the Midst."
2. *Weighed and Wanting*, chapter 56.
3. *The Tutor's First Love*, p. 23.
4. *The Minister's Restoration*, pp. 113–114.

Chapter Fifteen

1. *Unspoken Sermons*, Third Series, "The Light."
2. *David Elginbrod*, chapter 58.
3. *The Gentlewoman's Choice*, pp. 53–54.
4. *Unspoken Sermons*, Third Series, "The Light."
5. *The Baron's Apprenticeship*, pp. 174–175.

Chapter Sixteen

1. *What's Mine's Mine*, chapter 11.
2. *Unspoken Sermons*, Second Series, "The Fear of God."
3. *The Highlander's Last Song*, p. 174.

Chapter Seventeen

1. *Unspoken Sermons*, Third Series, "Righteousness."
2. *A Daughter's Devotion*, pp. 128–129.
3. *Unspoken Sermons*, Third Series, "Righteousness."
4. *Wilfrid Cumbermede*, chapter 59.
5. *The Marquis' Secret*, p. 102.

Chapter Eighteen

1. *Unspoken Sermons*, Third Series, "The Creation in Christ."
2. *A Daughter's Devotion*, pp. 122–123.
3. *Unspoken Sermons*, Third Series, "The Creation in Christ."
4. *The Curate's Awakening*, pp. 54–55.

Chapter Nineteen

1. *Unspoken Sermons*, Second Series, "The Voice of Job."
2. *The Curate's Awakening*, p. 115.
3. From a letter of George MacDonald to his wife, July 14, 1855.
4. *Unspoken Sermons*, Second Series, "The Voice of Job."
5. *The Musician's Quest*, pp. 66–67.

Chapter Twenty

1. *Unspoken Sermons*, Second Series, "The Last Farthing."
2. *The Curate's Awakening*, p. 107.
3. *The Shepherd's Castle*, pp. 96–97.

Chapter Twenty-One

1. *Unspoken Sermons*, Second Series, "The Voice of Job."
2. *Donal Grant*, chapter 42.
3. *The Elect Lady*, chapter 32.

Chapter Twenty-Two

1. *Unspoken Sermons*, Second Series, "The Voice of Job."
2. *Weighed and Wanting*, chapter 31.
3. *Unspoken Sermons*, Second Series, "The Voice of Job."
4. *Sir Gibbie*, chapter 38.

Chapter Twenty-Three

1. *Unspoken Sermons*, Second Series, "The Voice of Job."
2. *Thomas Wingfold, Curate*, chapter 40.
3. *Robert Falconer*, chapter 55.
4. *Unspoken Sermons*, Second Series, "The Voice of Job."
5. *Donal Grant*, chapter 37.

Chapter Twenty-Four

1. *Unspoken Sermons*, Second Series, "Abba, Father!"
2. *The Baron's Apprenticeship*, pp. 236–37.
3. *Warlock O'Glenwarlock*, chapter 22.

Chapter Twenty-Five

1. *Unspoken Sermons*, First Series, "The Consuming Fire."
2. *The Curate's Awakening*, p. 184.
3. *Unspoken Sermons*, First Series, "The Consuming Fire."
4. *Donal Grant*, chapter 20.
5. *Unspoken Sermons*, First Series, "The Consuming Fire."
6. *Robert Falconer*, chapter 12.
7. *The Elect Lady*, chapter 11.

Chapter Twenty-Six

1. *Unspoken Sermons,* Third Series, "Justice."
2. *The Gentlewoman's Choice,* p. 81.
3. *Unspoken Sermons,* Third Series, "Justice."
4. *The Maiden's Bequest,* p. 47.
5. *The Tutor's First Love,* pp. 192–193.

Chapter Twenty-Seven

1. *Unspoken Sermons,* Third Series, "Justice."
2. *The Highlander's Last Song,* p. 61.
3. *Unspoken Sermons,* Third Series, "Justice."
4. *The Minister's Restoration,* pp. 206–207.

Chapter Twenty-Eight

1. *Unspoken Sermons,* Third Series, "Justice."
2. *Donal Grant,* chapter 1.
3. *Unspoken Sermons,* Third Series, "Justice."
4. *The Highlander's Last Song,* pp. 83–86.

Chapter Twenty-Nine

1. *Unspoken Sermons,* First Series, "It Shall Not Be Forgiven."
2. *The Baron's Apprenticeship,* p. 155.
3. *A Daughter's Devotion,* pp. 284–285.

Chapter Thirty

1. *Unpoken Sermons,* Second Series, "The Last Farthing."
2. *Donal Grant,* chapter 30.
3. *The Fisherman's Lady,* pp. 259–262.

Chapter Thirty-One

1. *Unspoken Sermons,* First Series, "It Shall Not Be Forgiven."
2. *Unspoken Sermons,* First Series, "The Hands of the Father."
3. *Robert Falconer,* chapter 28.
4. *Unspoken Sermons,* First Series, "It Shall Not Be Forgiven."
5. *The Gentlewoman's Choice,* pp. 185–86.

Thank you for selecting a book from
BETHANY HOUSE PUBLISHERS

Bethany House Publishers is a ministry of Bethany Fellowship
International, an interdenominational, nonprofit organization
committed to spreading the Good News of Jesus Christ around
the world through evangelism, church planting, literature
distribution, and care for those in need. Missionary training is
offered through Bethany College of Missions.

Bethany Fellowship International is a member of the National
Association of Evangelicals and subscribes to its statement of
faith. If you would like further information, please contact:

Bethany Fellowship International
6820 Auto Club Road
Bloomington, MN 55438 USA